Advance Praise for *Wikibrands*

"These are uncertain times for many companies. New competitors can emerge in the blink of an eye, riding a wave of Web-powered popularity, and brand value can also rise and fall in an instant, thanks to social media tools that didn't even exist five years ago. Businesses of all kinds are trying to find their way through this wilderness, and those that prosper will be the ones who learn how to take advantage of these new tools to connect and engage with their customers and client communities. *Wikibrands* is required reading for anyone who wants to thrive in this new landscape. It is both a comprehensive overview of the principles that govern the new digital world and a practical set of guidelines for how to approach and make use of them. Highly recommended."

—*Mathew Ingram, senior writer, Giga OM*

"In an age when everything is interactive, don't let your business fall behind—read *Wikibrands*. The top-down model is in decline, and brands—at least the ones poised to be successful—are moving to the new individually focused, bottom-up model of customer involvement. With specific advice and examples, this book will show you the new landscape of business in the twenty-first century, where customers want to participate, not just buy. *Wikibrands* is your guide to the future of business, a must-read for marketing professionals, entrepreneurs, and anyone looking to understand the new landscape of brands today."

—*Jean Twenge, author of* Generation Me *and* The Narcissism Epidemic

"*Wikibrands* provides the deep insight and clear guidance that businesses need to succeed in a world where mass collaboration and open innovation are turning old marketing models upside down. Authors Sean Moffitt and Mike Dover bring a wealth of experience, expertise, practical knowledge, and good humor to unravel the complexities and debunk the hype. Any organization looking to tap into the enthusiasm and creativity of Young World consumers needs to read this book."

—*Rob Salkowitz, author of* Young World Rising

WIKI BRANDS

REINVENTING YOUR
COMPANY IN A
CUSTOMER-DRIVEN
MARKETPLACE

SEAN MOFFITT AND MIKE DOVER

New York   Chicago   San Francisco   Lisbon   London   Madrid   Mexico City
Milan   New Delhi   San Juan   Seoul   Singapore   Sydney   Toronto

The *McGraw·Hill* Companies

1 2 3 4 5 6 7 8 9 10 11 12 13 14 15 16   QFR/QFR   1 9 8 7 6 5 4 3 2 1 0

ISBN   978-0-07-174927-5
MHID   0-07-174927-6

This publication is designed to provide accurate and authoritative information in regard to the subject matter covered. It is sold with the understanding that neither the author nor the publisher is engaged in rendering legal, accounting, securities trading, or other professional services. If legal advice or other expert assistance is required, the services of a competent professional person should be sought.
    —*From a Declaration of Principles Jointly Adopted by a Committee of the American Bar Association and a Committee of Publishers and Associations*

Library of Congress Cataloging-in-Publication Data

Moffitt, Sean.
    Wikibrands : reinventing your company in a customer-driven marketplace /
by Sean Moffitt, Mike Dover.
        p.   cm.
    ISBN 978-0-07-174927-5 (alk. paper)
    1. Branding (Marketing).   2. Product management.   3. Internet
marketing.   4. Wikis (Computer science).   I. Dover, Mike.   II. Title.

    HD69.B7M653   2011
    658.8'27—dc22   2010029785

Interior design by Think Book Works

This book is printed on acid-free paper.

To Colleen, Kiera, Regan, and Siobhan
—Sean

To Jennifer and Kate
—Mike

Contents

Foreword
Reinvention of the Brand

BY DON TAPSCOTT

This is an important, perhaps a seminal, book. It was inspired by a multimillion-dollar research program I initiated in 2005 called Marketing 2.0. Mike Dover and Sean Moffitt were two of our outstanding thought leaders and produced some profound new thinking about the brand. I encouraged them to write a book to develop their findings, and the result is a substantive and stimulating work with far-reaching implications for anyone who cares about marketing and the future of business.

For fifteen years, my colleagues and I have argued that it was only a matter of time before the Web revolutionized marketing.[1] Today, as new communications media become ever-more pervasive, conventional wisdom about advertising, promotion, publicity, public relations, and the brand itself is finally being shattered. Traditional ideas are rooted in the assumption that unidirectional, one-size-fits-all, print and broadcast media would always be used to communicate messages to faceless, powerless, inert customers.

Historically, the brand has been seen as a promise, an image, a badge, or (as many popular books described it) "a word in the mind."[2] It was not viewed as something that exists in the minds and actions of customers, but an asset to be owned and controlled by companies. Brands were established primarily through mass communications, by inundating consumers with the same image and message over and over through various media.

Today, the brand is becoming a more complex construct. In fact, the brand has an architecture of sorts that includes various critical elements requiring constant attention and strategy. The foundation of this brand architecture is a firm's integrity—honesty, reliability, consideration, and candor. Integrity is important because of the growing demand for transparency. Consumers can evaluate the value of products and services like never before. Employees share formerly secret information about corporate strategy, management, and challenges. To collaborate effectively,

companies and their business partners have no choice but to share intimate knowledge with one another. Finally, in a world of instant communications, Wikileakers, inquisitive media, and Googling citizens, people
everywhere can routinely put firms under the microscope.

Companies are being stripped naked, and corporate fitness is no longer
optional. The precondition for customer trust in a brand is integrity. If the
financial meltdown of the past few years tells us anything, it's that firms
need to be buff, providing good value and exhibiting integrity as part of
their corporate DNA.[3]

Perhaps more important, because of the new social Web, the brand has
evolved from being an image to becoming a relationship. This transformation is driven by a lot more than social networking. Sure, the half-billion
people on Facebook love to talk about products, services, and companies,
as do the 150 million or so on Twitter. But countless other communities
and vehicles are turning the old brand on its head, providing an opportunity for companies to build deep relationships with consumers.

Consider this factoid. Between the beginning of recorded history and
the year 2003, there were five exobytes (equal to one quintillion bytes) of
information recorded. To put this in perspective, there were five exobytes
of information generated and recorded over the last two days—most of it
by the public. In fact most information and content today are being generated by individuals and consumers, not by companies.

When you add in the norms of the most important emerging marketplace—a new generation that has "grown up digital"—you've got a formula
for radical change in marketing. Given the propensity of these young people to ignore advertisements in traditional media, their growing ability to
scrutinize companies, and their surging power in the marketplace, they
are driving the change in thinking discussed in this book. A new form
of marketing is emerging in which brand managers and sharp executives
emphasize customer engagement, brand collaboration, and in some cases,
even shared brand ownership.

Smart companies are eschewing less effective, command and control
marketing and communication methods. As the Net Generation comes of
age, hundreds of millions of passionate users and consumers are taking
an active role in determining, shaping, and redefining brands independent of company involvement. Winning companies and brands are learning to engage and co-create with these customers rather than shouting
over or ignoring the noise of the marketplace. To bridge the marketing
divide, the concept of controlling the brand is now giving way to collabo-

rating with a stakeholder group with whom most companies are unfamiliar: their customers.

The advertising industry has been slow to understand and adapt to these changes. The industry began early in the twentieth century in the United States, when regional newspapers seeking advertisements found an agent to link them up with suppliers who wanted to reach the paper's audience. Nascent agencies solicited ads from manufacturers and other companies and offered to create the advertisements for the papers in exchange for a 15 percent commission of advertising revenues. The agencies provided the link between the producer and the newspaper. Today, the 15 percent rule has pretty much collapsed, and agencies have had to reinvent themselves and their function to create new value. But their instincts are still to use traditional media and traditional thinking about the brand, to "promote" their clients' products rather than engaging consumers in building much more appropriate and powerful relationships.

In fact, it makes sense for companies to view their customers as part of their businesses rather than as external entities. Customers want to be engaged. They have power through access to near-perfect information about products and corporate behavior. They interact through multidirectional, one-to-one, and highly tailored communications media. They, not companies, control the marketing mix. They choose the medium and the message. Rather than receiving broadcast images, they do the casting.

So just as Wikipedia views its contributors as part of its network, companies can use the thinking of wikibrands to bring their customers into the fold. Rather than "focusing" on customers as conventional wisdom proclaims, marketers can engage them. Co-innovation and new value exchanges can replace old-style "customer centricity" and market segmentation. And customers, rather than being passive recipients of goods, services, and messages can participate actively and directly with corporations.

The result of all this is that you can create better value and better customer loyalty through participation and engagement. Remember (not so long ago) all the predictions that the Web pioneers such as Amazon, eBay, Google, and more recently, Facebook were doomed to disaster because their competition was only a click away? What the doomsayers didn't understand was the power of relationships. When firms use the Web to truly engage customers, the relationships can be strong and lasting. I'm tempted to describe this as a new form of wealth, such as "relationship capital," that firms need to develop and manage like other forms of capital.

If you read and act on this book, you'll retire the old Four Ps of marketing (product, place, price, and promotion). You'll chuck out old concepts of the brand as an image that you own and control. And you'll set a course to engage your customers and benefit from a new paradigm in marketing appropriate for the digital age.

Enjoy and prosper!

DON TAPSCOTT is the co-author of thirteen books about technology in business and society, most recently *Macrowikinomics: Rebooting Business and the World* (with Anthony D. Williams). His *Grown Up Digital: How the Net Generation Is Changing Your World* discussed how the Net Generation is revolutionizing marketing, and *Wikinomics* (also with Williams) was the best-selling management book in the United States in 2007. He is chairman of the think tank nGenera Insight and vice chairman of Spencer Trask Collaborative Technologies.

Acknowledgments

We were fortunate to be part of several multimillion-dollar syndicated research programs with our colleagues Don Tapscott and Dr. Joan Bigham. The genesis of this project would not be possible without the support of forward-thinking companies and government organizations, including IBM, Cisco, Hewlett-Packard, Kimberley-Clark, Citibank, Herman Miller, Service Canada, SAP, MetLife, Disney, Roche, Federal Express, General Motors, Best Buy, Procter & Gamble, Canada Post, Canadian Tire, TD Bank, DaimlerChrysler, Sobeys, Accenture, PwC, OglivyOne, Manpower, Drake International, British Telecom, the U.S. Department of Defense, ScotiaBank, and Nokia.

Many smart people generously shared their time and insight with us before and during the writing of this book. We know this list of heroes and intellectuals will expand in the future, but for now we would like to recognize Sami Viitamäki, Richard Binhammer, Ferg Devins, Julie Roehm, Sean O'Driscoll, Rod Brooks, James Cherkoff, Brian Fetherstonhaugh, Euan Semple, Jake McKee, Jackie Huba, Kira Wampler, Bev Tudhope, Janet Kestin, Chip Wilson, Niraj Dawar, Leigh Himel, Jim Hedger, Frank Graves, Kirk Robinson, Sylvano Carrasco, Rob Quintana, David Eaves, David Bercovitch, Dave Carroll, Larry Evans, Constance Steinkuehler, Simon Pulsifer, Asa Dotzler, David Bradfield, Mary Graham, Molly Schonthal, Ann Handley, Glen K. Amo, William Azaroff, Alan Moore, Gary Koehling, Diane Hessan, Robbie Vitrano, David Deal, Bob Lord, Olivier Blanchard, Scott Monty, Adam Garone, Matthew Wadley, Suzanne Siemens, Madeleine Shaw, Peter van Stolk, Chris Matthews, Victor Samra, LaSandra Brill, B. J. Emerson, Owen Mack, Michael O'Connell, Adam Wallace, Bryan Person, Rohit Bhargava, Trish Mumby, Rob Kozinets, Simon Sinek, Mike McDerment, Don Mitchell, Tracy Benson, Krista Thomas, Scott Wilder, Christine Morrison, Marilynn Pratt, Steve Molis, Matt Brown, Kasi Bruno, Claire Jenkins, Dan Pink, Amber Naslund, Jennifer Evans, Will Novosedlik, Marcel Lebrun, Stephen J. Morrison, Edward Terpening, Dan Schawbel, Jay Baer, Lois Kelly, Barry Judge, John Phoenix, Connie Bensen, Emanuel Rosen, Mario Sundar, Mack Collier, Holly Potter, Jim Deitzel, Sarah Molinari, Fran Kershaw, Chuck Martin, Pete Blackshaw, William Bakker, Alex Blum, Piers Fawkes,

Peter van Stolk, Joe Cothrel, Daniel Debow, Andy Sernovitz, Susan Wassel, Nigel Dessan, Merritt Colaizzi, Valeria Maltoni, Ross Kimbarovsky, Beth Kanter, Chris Bruzzo, Jeff Hayzlett, Jamie Pappas, Brian Magierski, Brian Wilhite, Vaughan Merlyn, Abhishek Daga, Mukand Mohan, Jason Falls, Katie Payne, Eric Karjaluoto, Stephen Bailey, Frank Feather, Sascha Carlin, Jeremiah Owyang, Adrian Salamunovic, Nestor Portillo, Mark Earls, Emmanuel Vivier, Polly Pearson, Kevin Urie, Bob Lord, Jenn McClure, Idris Mootee, Tormod Askildsen, and Lisa Rodwell. Follow the full list of interviewees and team of wikibrand all-stars and ambassadors on **wiki-brands .com**.

We would like to thank the team at McGraw-Hill, including our editor, Mary Glenn; editorial support, Susan Moore and Tania Loghmani; cover designer, Ty Nowicki; and publicity, marketing, and sales gurus Julia Baxter, Gaya Vinay, Staci Shands, Claudia Hawkins, Sally Ashworth, Sarah Cassie, and Doug Blair; as well as our agent, Rick Broadhead. On the *Wikibrands* team, we were fortunate to have the editorial expertise of Jennifer Durley, Daniel Williamson, and Erin Lemon, as well as great content support from Alex Marshall, Kevin Morris, Roma Chopra, Erin Bonokoski, and Brittani Jarvis and community managers Punit Sthankiya, Tiffany Assman, and Ash Molaei.

As a participant across a number of industries and networks, Sean has had the privilege to connect with a vast network of supporters, mavens, mentors, champions, and experts too numerous to mention here. Here are some who have made a lasting impression: Jim McCutcheon, Bob Wlodarchuk, Robert Lato, Halton Doyle, Herb Mackenzie, Jim Letwin, Ed Burghard, Peri Ann Luprypa, Dan Rajczak, Jill Schoolenberg, Mary McPherson, Mary Beth Williamson, James Thompson, Yves Ameline, Tim Penner, Mike Bradica, Steve Doyle, Michael Downey, Eric Blais, Lynn Mepham, Steve Pulver, Louis Gagnon, Lou Clements, Richard Bailey, Jill King, Josh Cobden, Dave Thorpe, Mirabel Palmer-Elliott, Bryan Uba, Ted Graham, Kate Trgovac, Chris Hobson, Eric Buchegger, Kim Scott, Karim Jalbout, Nadia Rushdi, Kathy Hnatiuk, David Jones, Max Valiquette, Shane Skillen, Andrew Cherwenka, Jon Mamela, Candace Faktor, Rick Shaver, Malcolm Gladwell, Everett Rogers, Seth Godin, and Tom Peters. A network of truly kick-ass executives and managers exists at theleague.ca and special commendations for people with influence can be found on my corporate blog at agentwildfire.com. Special thanks to my parents, Harry and Eileen, and siblings, Bryan and Karen, for providing the role models and encouragement.

Working at a think tank for twelve years provided Mike with the opportunity to work with many impressive people. The entire roster of our new wikibrands research faculty can be found at **wiki-brands.com**, but we'd like to specifically recognize Abby Wilner, Alan Majer, Alex Lowy, Alexandra Samuel, Ameet Wadhwani, Amy Cortese, Anastasia Goodstein, Andrea Wood, Andy De, Ann Cavoukian, Anthony Williams, Anya Kamenetz, Audrey Wubbenhorst, Bart Goodwin, Bill Gillies, Bob Morison, Brendan Peat, Brian Gillooly, Bruce Rogow, Bruce Sellery, Bruce Stewart, Charlie Fine, Chris Ling, Chris Lynch, Chris O'Leary, Chuck Martin, Colby Thames, Corinne Gibas, Dan Herman, Daniela Kortan, Darcelle Hall, Darren Meister, Dave Cosgrave, Dave Singleton, David Agnew, David Cameron, David Kruzner, David Ticoll, David Wilcox, Denis Hancock, Denis O'Leary, Derek Pokora, Derrek Lennox, Ed McDonnell, Eli Singer, Frank Capek, Fred Carter, Grant Buckler, Haydn Shaughnessy, Heather Shaw, Hubert Saint-Onge, Ian Da Silva, Ian Ketcheson, Jason Papadimos, Jean Twenge, Jeff DeChambeau, Jeff Kaplan, Jennifer Deal, Jim Cortada, Jody Fisher, Jody Stevens, Joe Pine, Joe Sauer, Joe Sexsmith, John Geraci, John Yip, Jude Fiorillo, Katie King, Kevin Young, Krista Napier, Laura Carrillo, Lenni Jabour, Lisa Chen, Margaret Schweer, Maryantonett Flumian, Mathew Ingram, Max Stevens-Guille, Mike Glavich, Ming Kwan, Natalie Klym, Naumi Haque, Neil Howe, Neil Pasricha, Nick Bontis, Nick Vitalari, Nicole Morin, Patrick Harnett, Paul Artiuch, Paul Barter, Peter Haine, Phil Dwyer, Phil Hood, Pierre-Luc Bisaillon, Priscilla Li, Rachel Bryan, Rena Granovsky, Rich Lauf, Rich Wilson, Rob Leblanc, Rob Salkowitz, Roberta Smith, Ryan Thompson, Sarah Laughlin, Scott Robinson, Sean Hutchison, Shaherose Charania, Stan Kutcher, Stanley Rodos, Steve Elmore, Steve Guengerich, Steve Papermaster, Steve Ressler, Susie Buehler, Tammy Erickson, Thusenth Dhavaloganathan, Tim Bevins, Tim Warner, Tony Gifford, and Willem Galle. Also, thanks for support from my parents, Bill and Ruth Dover.

PART 1

THE WIKIBRANDS STORY

CHAPTER 1

THE BIRTH OF WIKIBRANDS

From Ownership, Trust, Want, Preference, Love, and Now Participation— a 150-Year Fascination

wikibrand(s): noun

A progressive set of organizations, products, services, ideas, and causes that tap the powers of customer participation, social influence, and collaboration to drive business value.

Derived from the Hawaiian word *wiki*, traditionally meaning "quick" but more currently meaning "tribal knowledge" and "a collaborative website," and the Middle English word *torch*, whose current business meaning is "a distinctive name identifying a product or a manufacturer."

"Individual commitment to a group effort—that is what makes a team work, a company work, a society work, a civilization work."

—**VINCE LOMBARDI**, *legendary football coach*

Wikibrands represent the future of business—a future that calls for a fundamental shift in long-held business management tenets on how we approach customers. We have entered a new generation of brand building. The litmus test for a thriving business in this marketplace is "Does your brand deliver genuine participation?" This issue does not touch marketing alone nor is it solely a public relations concern. Neither is it single-mindedly a technology or social media manifesto. However, if you are in the business of driving company direction and delivering winning performance in today's customer-controlled marketplace, wikibranding is a wake-up call, strategy guide, and execution road map, as relevant for the C-suite as it is for front-line managers.

Let us take a step back. Since 1875, and likely even before, when Bass Ale registered the first branded trademark, brands have become a controlling force in the marketplace, representing something customers look for alternatively to buy, trust, want, prefer, or love. In many companies, the brand has become their single most important operating and financial asset.

For more than a century, businesses have effectively cultivated customer loyalty, competitive advantage, and positive benefit perceptions for their owners through the tools of brand management. Traditional mass marketing efforts have acted as long-term value generators, allowing brands to command significant price premiums over commodity and price-based adversaries. Coca-Cola, IBM, BMW, McDonald's, and Heineken have epitomized the strength of a well-positioned brand marketed to a mass consumer audience through traditional media channels. In fact, Coca-Cola corporate lore claims that if the company suddenly lost all of its physical assets, it could get funding to rebuild the entire enterprise using only the power of the brand as collateral.

Although there are many more recent headlines like "Can the Wrong Fame Smear Your Brand," "Attack of the Blogs," "Brands Under Attack," and "The Decline of Brands," we assert that brands are still very relevant to the evolution of postindustrial business strategy and the building of business value. Face it: brands still belong, even in the marketplace of the future.

Business founders and managers can depart or retire. Organizations can be "right-sized." Media can be overhauled. Production can be completely outsourced. Logos can change. Whether you like it or not, what remains is still a mystifying belief in brands. Don't take our word for it. Think about what might tempt you. If Apple launched a refrigerator, wouldn't you be the slightest bit interested? If Google opened a restaurant, wouldn't a good chunk of you line up around the corner? If BMW launched a personal computer, wouldn't you give it a test drive? If World of Warcraft launched a real-life amusement park, a large percentage of its eleven million players would probably make the pilgrimage.

Before we appear too defensive on the side of the brand flag and conventional mass marketing theory, be assured that we believe a significantly new practice needs to exist. The status quo is not an option. We're not entirely throwing the "brand baby out with the bathwater," but we see all too clearly a call to change, particularly in *how* business goes about building itself up in a customer-controlled marketplace. We must guard our-selves against laziness, against allowing our vision to blur what is going on in the world outside the corporate walls. Too often it is easy to become comfortable and stop experimenting. Even entrepreneurs and start-ups can be guilty of blindly imitating outdated best practices and consultants' advice that worked in a bygone era. As John Lennon summarized, "Life is what is happening to you while you're busy making other plans." Perhaps the famous Beatle was a wikibrand advocate ahead of his time.

Wikibranding provides a manifesto that allows progressive-minded souls—and even some establishment types—to implement the change required in their organizations. In *Groundswell: Winning in a World Trans-formed by Social Technologies*, Charlene Li and Josh Bernoff make the math pretty simple: engaged brands are growing their value by 18 percent; those that don't engage are declining by 6 percent.[1] This is a chicken-or-egg argu-ment, but the choice is pretty obvious: engage.

For a long time, companies created products and services and then pushed them out to customers using the tools of the period. The Four Ps of marketing—product, place, promotion, and price—were sacrosanct (we will present two alternative versions of this model). When strategies were formed, the role of the customer was in the business of planning and push-ing out these messages through media intermediaries. The message was controlled; the role of consumers was to listen and buy. Now faced with a dramatic shift in how technology-enabled collaboration changes rela-tionships, an Internet-savvy generation will bring about huge changes in business and culture. How businesses create value through brands will be transformed by the relationships and experiences these businesses have with customers. Brands will no longer be an abstract concept in the mind but will require a new, more sophisticated architecture that involves two-way conversation and integrity.

What caused the shift? Consumers found that, through peer-to-peer connection and social media, they had a voice in the brand conversation. It has been suggested by both traditionalists and some early Web adopters that five years into the mainstreaming of social media, people will become tired of these tools. In exchange for the return of their privacy and leisure time, they will gladly placate themselves with the passive consumption of entertaining messages via big media funded by organizations, albeit in dif-ferent formats. For those people seeking relief from this social media pollu-tion, we're sorry to say the genie is out of the bottle for good.

Collaborative technologies and social media that connect family, friends, colleagues, and interest groups are not just a fad; they are the currency that runs the future marketplace. The growth and reach of new media and new technology is mind-boggling and undeniable. Compared to even a decade ago, the pace of change is staggering. As recently as 2000, could we have conceived of a world in which five hundred million people from around the world spend an average of forty-two minutes a day chatting with, liking, checking in with, and playing with each other in a digital playground called Facebook?

The early twenty-first century is distinguished by the pace and intensity of change in the marketing and media landscape. Trends such as the emergence of more than one hundred million citizen bloggers,[2] more than two billion Internet users,[3] and more than four billion mobile phone users[4] (which is more than have regular access to running water) only begin to tell the story.

Could we have predicted, even optimistically, that Internet use would vault ahead of the incumbent media heavyweight TV? Well, it has. With a reach of more than two billion and one-hundred-fold growth since 1995, the Internet has knocked off marketers' mainstay, and it isn't looking back. Although some user fatigue has occurred in the blogosphere and on social networking sites, people are collectively spending 82 percent more time on social networks in 2010 than in the previous year.[5]

We admit this is a real paradox. Brands have never been more important to companies than they are today, even in an atmosphere in which customers have taken control. The tools to build these globally known stalwarts or hungry underdogs are far less predictable than they've ever been. Stasis is not an option, but that is what a lot of companies exhibit. Marketing organizations figure prominently among the casualties of this new age. Two-thirds of organizations have rebranded themselves in the last three years.[6] A majority of senior marketers are feeling dissonance within their organizations and distance from their external customer base.[7] The average tenure of a chief marketing officer is hovering at around twenty-eight months, a full two years less than the next most tenuous executive position: CIOs.[8]

In the first decade of the millennium, spurred on by the global economic correction, the proverbial pin dropped on the marketing function. Forward-thinking marketers have begun to recognize the gap. Only 6 percent of executive marketers rate their digital operations as excellent; the biggest need identified in new plans is to construct a digital marketing makeover in their platforms, programs, and people.[9] Senior marketers have begun to realize that if they want to avoid having their corporate stars eclipsed, they need to switch their attention from what they do (advertising, communications, public relations, and sales) to how they do it (customer connection, brand engagement, and online community participation).

If marketers have recognized their loss of influence inside their organizations, they almost certainly know of their current diminishing status outside of it too. The environment can be downright hostile. Small groups of well-organized customers have publicly exposed market titans such as Dell, Wal-Mart, and Sony for employing less than ethical or substandard company practices. Not only has this ripple effect of well-connected customer dissatisfaction disrupted the way companies operate, but it also points to a power shift in the emerging brand landscape—a shift toward customers.

Why? Quite simply, the levers of brand development have changed dramatically over the last twenty years. Since the height of mass marketing's efficiency peaked in the early eighties, a number of trends relating to media (such as fragmentation), marketing (such as customization), marketplace activity (such as abbreviated product life cycles), and broader cultural behavior (such as heterogeneous consumers) have collectively diminished the effectiveness of traditional branding efforts.

Winning companies and brands are succeeding by learning to engage and co-create branding efforts *with* their most loyal and engaged customers:

▷ Traditional packaged goods marketers such as Procter & Gamble are creating powerful new customer connections through frequent and experimental use of Facebook; word-of-mouth relationship forums such as Vocalpoint, Tremor, Being Girl, and Home Made Simple; and traditional/social mashup [10] hits like the Old Spice Guy video campaign.

▷ Fashion upstart lululemon is harnessing the evangelical passion of its employees and ambassador networks.

▷ Software company Intuit is opening itself to a steady stream of innovation and applications, as well as customer support, based on online community involvement.

▷ Open source companies, like Mozilla, are tapping brand enthusiasm via comprehensive, community-based marketing efforts.

▷ Retail icons, such as Starbucks, are making marketing and customer orientation central to their brand by mastering customer experience.

▷ Maverick start-up company Naked Pizza is revolutionizing customers' relationship with fast food through a preachy, healthy brand image that interacts with its clients via Twitter (to the uninitiated, a microblogging platform that allows users to text messages known as *tweets* of up to 140 characters).

Rather than lobbing promises and messages ceaselessly over the chaos of today's tone-deaf marketplace, these smart companies are thinking about how active customer participation can get their brands noticed, talked about, and endorsed through their customer grapevine. Instead of controlling the brand, marketers are opening it up to exciting new possibilities. In short, these brands are going "wiki." The wikibranding movement is reshaping the way in which companies build brand value. Traditional notions of stage-managing brands are shifting in favor of an open and authentically shared ownership among marketer, employees, and customers.

The Evolution of Brands

Perhaps the march to a wikibrand world is Darwinism at play. A historical perspective suggests that we could have predicted the next wave of brand building. For a long period of time, a brand was simply a logo indicating ownership, as shown in Table 1.1. As mass production emerged in the nineteenth century, early packaged goods companies used branding to establish familiarity and trust in markets that were more accustomed to local products.

TABLE 1.1 GENERATIONS OF BRAND BUILDING

BRAND GENERATION	BRAND PURPOSE	BRAND-CUSTOMER FUNCTION
Trademark (until 1860)	Mark of brand ownership (e.g., cattle)	Something you buy
Brand mark (1860–1920s)	Mark of brand quality (e.g., Ivory soap)	Something you trust
Mass market brand (1920s–early 1980s)	Mark of positive associations (e.g., Marlboro)	Something you want
Post–mass market brand (1980s–late 1990s)	Mark of superior brand attributes (e.g., Tylenol)	Something you prefer
Love mark (early 2000s)	Mark of inspirational brand values/stories/design (e.g., Apple)	Something you love
Wikibrand (the future)	Mark of brand interaction (e.g., Facebook)	Something you participate in

The sophistication of branding increased in the early twentieth century as brands began to convey attributes and associations that implied ambition. The rising standard of living in the West increased discretionary income, while the emergence of new media, like radio and TV, enabled companies to market their products in an engaging fashion to broader audiences. Brands became less about satisfying basic needs and more about satisfying desires and communicating social status through ownership.

By the eighties, as markets became increasingly saturated with imported products, line extensions, and generic competition, brand positioning and brand equity management became essential tools for marketers seeking to highlight key product attributes and establish preference over their competitors.

More recently, the narrowing of product performance differences, record levels of customer cynicism, and the increasing depth of media volume have had brand owners striving to establish emotional connections with customers based on kindred values, likable brand stories, and enhanced design aesthetics. Kevin Roberts, CEO of Saatchi & Saatchi, anointed these popularly as "lovemarks." Today, the "plan-and-push-and-love-us" approach to branding is increasingly impotent, and brand owners are being forced to consider new options. Customer trust and satisfaction in brands is declining precipitously, while the customer's ability to find pertinent information, inform others, and self-organize has never been stronger.[11]

Positive and negative brand experiences and content now spread rapidly across social circles as barriers have virtually been erased by evolving Web software, multimedia, mobile, electronic, and file storage technologies. Today's successful brand strategies rely less on "managing perceptions," "spinning information," and "controlling the message"—the hallmarks of an earlier time.

If we can learn anything from this recent history of brands, it is the following:

▷ Fundamental changes in brand management coincide with big shifts in media, communications, and marketplace conditions. We have that now.

▷ Branding shifts have all been a reaction to some kind of scarcity. At one time, these were constraints on capital, distribution channels, markets, media availability, and shelf space; now the scarcity is consumer attention, time, and trust.

▷ Every era of change has brand winners and losers; the winners adapt to change before it's too late. We're seeing this play out firsthand in the meteoric rise and fall of companies.

▷ While most changes are evolutionary, the windows of opportunity between changes are getting smaller, as society adapts to new paradigms more quickly. In today's business climate, cultural adoption of change has never been more agile.

▷ Each brand epoch has been marked by a distinct generational tribe with common cultural hallmarks that hold sway over the culture for a time: the flappers and Gatsbys of the Roaring Twenties, the liberal and free-loving baby boomers, the innovative and anticorporate Generation X, and now the connected and collaborative Net Generation (also called Generation Y, or Millennials).[12]

The Marketing Divide: The Customer Is in Control

The branding power of traditional media (TV, print, and radio) has been seriously eroded by new consumer technologies such as personal video recorders (PVRs), satellite radio (such as Sirius), online social networks (including Facebook, Bebo, Orkut, and MySpace), and user-generated sharing sites like YouTube. Simultaneously, there's been an explosion of product choice, competition, and variety, which will only increase as rising giants China and India spawn a growing number of truly global competitors across different industries.

At the intersection of all this technology and choice stands a customer who is faced with the challenge of keeping up with this fast-moving world. Digitally adept people are arguably the best-positioned market segment to deal with this glut of activity, and they have become amazingly good at multitasking, filtering out marketing messages, and arriving at purchase decisions based on information from their peers. The net effect: the customer is in control (Figure 1.1).

The Media: The Noise Grows Louder

Network TV viewership is at its lowest point in history. Music radio is in steep decline. Newspaper circulation has been slipping since 1987. Magazine, book, and box office sales are stagnant, while physical CD and DVD sales are declining. Increasingly, these traditional media formats are

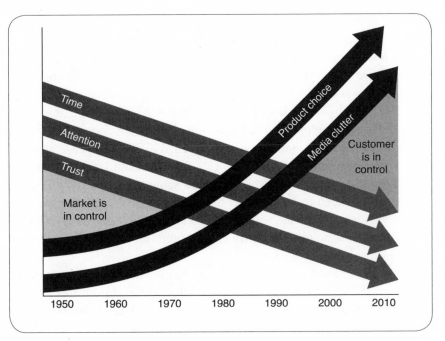

FIGURE 1.1 THE MARKETING DIVIDE   Source: Agent Wildfire Inc.

being augmented and even replaced by a cacophony of Web-based media and other alternatives, such as ringtones, game consoles, digital signage, branded entertainment, and sponsorship avenues.

Paradoxically, the diminishing returns on traditional media have sparked a vicious media spiral. In an effort to bolster waning audience attention and lessening impact, traditional media have hiked advertising volume. The average duration of commercial time has risen to eighteen minutes for every hour of programming on some TV stations. Every year, TV clutter increases 1–3 percent.[13] This tidal wave of noise serves to increase consumer dissatisfaction and "tune-out."[14] Even more ironically, this spawns even higher investments in traditional media advertising. The result is that marketers are paying substantially more to reach diminishing audiences of disinterested and dissatisfied consumers.[15]

At the same time, cross-media usage is on the rise. Today's "eyeballs" do not have the same value as their predecessors did a century ago, when undivided attention was the norm. For example, 70 percent of current media users claim to be consuming multiple media concurrently on a regular basis.[16] Members of the Net Generation are notorious multitask jugglers and voracious media consumers, enjoying an average of twenty hours' worth of media within a seven-hour period; it's a safe bet that today's eye-balls are strained from plenty of darting around.[17]

As the din of media intensifies, the opportunity to create a "shared moment" with the customer slips further away. Adding to the confusion is the sheer assortment of media options. Three U.S. TV channels gave rise to twenty, which in turn became five hundred, which led to a glut of thou-sands of competing options. Not only are there more choices of *what* to watch, there are more choices of *how* to watch. A PVR provides a simple way to record shows (recall the scene in *City Slickers* about the machinations of VCR programming: "The cows can tape something by now!"). Popular shows are uploaded to the Internet moments after the original broadcast ends. DVD sets of complete seasons are popular stocking stuffers. What do these three viewing methods have in common? They allow the consumer to bypass commercials easily.

A handful of local radio stations have transformed into Internet music providers tailored to individual tastes. Meanwhile, instantaneous Web access to news from everywhere means that today's local daily print news-paper now competes directly with an infinite number of paid and citizen-generated media options from around the world.

As the noise grows louder and more desperate by the minute, the ques-tion must be asked: "Does anyone listen?"

The Marketplace: The Battle Wages On

Workers are bypassing vacation and working longer hours because the market demands it. Something that was once a desirable innovation (e.g., the basic cell phone) soon becomes an industry norm, and before long, a newer model replaces it (e.g., feature-rich smartphones). Eventually prod-ucts with more appealing features become the milestones of progress that consumers crave and provide significant justification for working longer and harder.

Consumers want better, faster, and cheaper products made exactly the way they like them. In spite of living in an age of abundance, relaxation seems to elude most people. The reason is simple: in spite of already having a great many possessions, consumers are still insatiable.

This is not surprising given the explosion of choice that surrounds them. Seven times as many items can be found in a typical grocery store today, compared to stores from a generation ago.[18] eBay's ninety million active members participate in auctions for more than $15 billion of merchandise per quarter.[19] For those who like music, eleven million songs await on the iTunes Store.[20] Readers can peruse Amazon.com's twenty-eight million book titles (of course, Jeff Bezos would remind you that the site now sells much more than books).[21]

As documented in Chris Anderson's *The Long Tail: Why the Future of Business Is Selling Less for More*, customers are increasingly flocking to microniches in retail, entertainment, technology, food, and fashion, as new forms of production and retailing aid and abet the subdivision.

Each successive generation of brand building has been marked by some gap or desire in the culture at large and a different marketing driver of value. In the golden age of branding, brands became the messengers and outward badges of surrogate identity ("I drive a Cadillac; look at me!"). Now the decline of traditional "social capital"—the real-world trust and goodwill held for institutions like government, family, police, and religion—and the deterioration of local community ties have made brands focal points for social participation and shared group values ("I'm an Apple fanatic. Are you one too?").

Evidence? Consider that, at the time of this writing, Starbucks has more than 1 million Twitter followers, is "liked" by more than 15 million on Facebook, and has attracted 100,000 user-generated contributions to its MyStarbucksIdea.com site. And this isn't a case of selecting the front-runner to overstate a point. Many other companies have similar-sized or larger networks; for example, Whole Foods has more than 1.8 million followers on Twitter.[22]

In *Bowling Alone*, Robert Putnam points to the collapse of the American community and the void of social capital that now exists:[23]

- ▷ The average person lives in fourteen homes during his or her lifetime. We do not put down roots in our neighborhood/city.
- ▷ We spend a third less time on family dinners. We have become disconnected from family rituals.
- ▷ The average person will have ten to fourteen jobs before the age of thirty-eight. We have become less defined by our occupation.
- ▷ We spend 45 percent less time having friends over to our homes. We have lost touch with our close social circles.

In the absence of this social capital, enlightened brands are providing forums for participation and engagement that tap into people's shared interests and socialization needs. Brand engagement has become the holy grail for marketers, and embracing brand communities are a promising means of achieving it.

The shift from broadcast-based messaging and media to community-based collaboration and conversation requires fundamental changes to marketing practices. Customers have seized control, and CEOs know it. In a Microsoft roundtable survey, CEOs ranked customer service and customer experience as their second and third priorities, just behind business strategy.[24] Contrast that with the fixation marketers have on advertising (ranked twelfth by CEOs) and promotions (ranked fourteenth), and you see how marketers have drifted away not only from what actually drives company value, but also from what their executives believe drives value.

In today's economy, building brand value has become more a function of what you actually do rather than what you say you do; how you live the brand rather than how you manage the brand; and who is involved in your network rather than who is being targeted by your communication. Wikibrands enable this new view of marketing and are achieving business impact—often with less investment.

The business world has woken up to the fact that there really isn't a choice. The distance between organization and customer has to be bridged. The last couple of decades have been marked by extracting as much efficiency and cost containment as possible out of organizations. Companies have almost reached the limits of outsourcing, downsizing, right-sizing, and reorganizing for delivering bottom-line performance. Cisco's CEO John Chambers has made the following bet: "The second phase of productivity growth is going to be about collaboration and network-enabled technologies. This is candidly being driven by our customers. They've said we need to understand better what you're going to do, where you're going to interoperate, where you're going to compete."[25]

A ray of light exists. Five years into the mainstreaming of social media, smart companies are finally figuring out how active customer participation can drive their business forward. For example, Frito-Lay has run successful contests in many countries where consumers created commercials that aired during the Super Bowl or developed new products with impressive creative and payout performance.

In a connected world and cluttered marketplace, brands are tapping into the instinctual human need for genuine participation, peer-to-peer dialogue, and shared media to survive and thrive. Word of mouth. User-generated content. Social media. Microblogging. Prosumerism. Online communities. Crowdsourcing. Customer-driven experience. Customer rating systems and forums. It's all so powerful, exciting, and new. But what's a brand to do?

We looked at the question of how business operates in these spheres through the worlds of brand development, customer collaboration, and the social Web to challenge key assumptions, debunk myths, and get to the heart of the matter. Wikibrands provide hard-won lessons on how to use the powers of customer collaboration, not just for Web start-ups and personal brands, but also for large companies and their brands.

Drawing from multimillion-dollar research projects, studies of hundreds of brand-customer collaborations, and direct interviews with hundreds of leading executives, marketing leaders, digital and online community architects, we have identified how and why successful brands compete in the twenty-first century, their core motivations for venturing into customer collaboration, and the nine elements essential for successfully building and managing a wikibrand. We also uncover implications for anyone who wants to conduct business successfully in today's landscape.

As this book's subtitle states, it is about reinvention. It is a tough road to "turn and pivot" department functions or entire companies. By looking at top companies that are practicing wikibrands, we provide the arguments and ability to make the case for change in all companies and industries.

We have provided a balanced viewpoint from a wide variety of resources on what businesses need to do succeed with wikibrands. A higher-order challenge exists within companies today. It's not "Should we do engagement anymore?" It's more "What do we do?" and "How do we do it?" in order to lead opinion and stakeholder groups to rally behind the brand.

Who is this book for? When we set off on this venture of distilling the insights from the world's top organizations, we believed businesspeople, entrepreneurs, and executives were our core audience. This book is about winning and thriving in a muddied and quickly changing marketplace. Of course, given our backgrounds and the stories provided, we believe marketing and communications people who are empowered to lead this charge would naturally find this book helpful in managing the sea of change. On the flip side, we believe this text can also find a place in the world of digital experts and social media enthusiasts and establish some discipline and rigor for how these powerful social tools can work effectively and realistically within corporate environments. Finally, we think anybody who has an intellectual curiosity about how some of the world's most engaged businesses wake up every morning and engage their audiences will find it interesting.

This book is supplemented by a regularly updated website that features links to all the videos and key websites mentioned; Hall of Fame, a videoblog of our research journey; site membership; and a practical online wikibrand guidebook. In addition, awards for the best wikibrands will be announced. We too have seen the social Web and want to create an ecosystem of content, community, and interest well beyond the confines of the printed page. In each chapter of this book, our experts and colleagues provide role models, success stories, best practices, and reference tools to bring our conclusions to life. We would like to hear your stories—visit our website at **wiki-brands.com**.

Business-customer collaboration can be one of the biggest gifts to land in a marketer's lap since the advent of TV and a prized jewel for digital firms to monetize their wares. It's a unique chance to get Silicon Valley, Madison Avenue, Wall Street, and Main Street (and their international equivalents) to work together. The choice is simple for brands, their owners, and key stakeholders—open up to your audience and become much more engaged with customers, or risk being rendered irrelevant outside and inside your company. The big question is whether you will take advantage of this opportunity. **Heed the call—and let's get wiki!**

CHAPTER 2

THE WIKIBRAND RALLYING CRY

The New "Mad Men"

The AMC show "Mad Men" has been a favorite of TV critics and resonates with those of us who passionately follow brand culture. Even without a big studio budget, the show dazzles viewers with its obsessive attention to detail, from authentic promotional material to the proper covers for the secretaries' typewriters. Would the junior people in your office look puzzled at the very mention of "typewriter covers"? They would certainly be surprised by the office culture that includes (by our standards) outrageously sexist behavior, fistfights in the bullpen, and ubiquitous afternoon cocktails.

What could the real world of today and the JFK-era world depicted in "Mad Men" possibly have in common? Perhaps more than meets the eye. Similar to the constellation of flawed characters from the fictional Sterling Cooper Draper Pryce ad agency, we all struggle with our convenient illusions and vices to explain the chaos around us. The Cold War has left, but the war on terror is here now. In the sixties, the broadcast-driven consumer age had become the mainstream. There was a sea change of industrial expansion and media

> "Advertising is based on one thing, happiness. And you know what happiness is? Happiness is the smell of a new car. It's freedom from fear. It's a billboard on the side of the road that screams reassurance that whatever you are doing is okay. You are okay."
>
> —DON DRAPER,
> *creative director,*
> *Sterling Cooper Draper Pryce,*
> *on the television show "Mad Men"*

upheaval. By 1963, newspapers had finally been supplanted by TV as the key source of information. And Don and his agency of "mad men" were helping clients master this exciting, sexy, new medium. This is not altogether dissimilar to the massive changes confronting today's business, with digital, mobile, and the Web leaping out of TV's shadow and a whole new set of mad men (and women) now trying to figure it out for themselves and their clients.

Don Draper, the handsome and seemingly self-assured creative director and pitchman played by Jon Hamm, in a moment of clairvoyance about why people buy, states, "You are the product. You feeling something. That's what sells." So it is with our current use of Facebook, LinkedIn, and Twitter. We want to project a face to the world that is positive, fresh, appealing, and human. We realize all too well on a personal and corporate level that in today's environment we are the product we're selling.

As much as we voyeuristically look at the characters on "Mad Men" and their blind, in-the-moment response to the immense political, business, and social change going on in their era, many of us are oblivious to the massive changes going on around us right now. The show is cathartic; we can laugh or revel in how different times were just forty to fifty years ago with twenty-twenty hindsight. But is our time really any different? Years from now, when they chronicle the early part of this century, will people laugh at the same things we swooned over and found captivating? The "Mad Men" characters' fascination with the TV medium is equivalent to our addiction to Facebook and social networks. Their need for continuing wealth is our drive for seeking purpose. Their need to understand the collective psyche of their customers and play it back to those customers in broadcast media is our current need to embrace and engage customers on a more intimate and personal level and syndicate the fruits of the exchange through digital media. *Plus ça change, plus c'est la même chose.* [1]

So forget social media. Forget social networks. Forget even social influence marketing (the term we happen to like best) for a moment. They have all made their way into our digital vernacular. All their laurels, and some darts, put them in the time vault of interesting, early 2000s, people-driven phenomena. They will be the buzzwords of the early twenty-first century. In fact, Brian Wallace, vice president of digital marketing and media for Research in Motion, declared that compartmentalizing social media as an ongoing concern is nonsense: "Two years from now, if I still have a director of social media, I should be fired!" [2]

The blogosphere army provides great examples of the democratization of the media; simple economics ensure that proofreading and fact-checking departments cannot match resources with thousands of people who have wide-ranging expertise and are perched at their computers all day long. One such example is when, during the 2004 presidential election campaign, CBS reported that it had obtained memos critical of George W. Bush's military record, ostensibly authored by his commanding officer, Lt. Colonel Jerry B. Killian. The blogosphere immediately called the veracity of the documents into question, asking how modern word processing features such as proportional printing and superscript fonts could have been present on Vietnam-era military typewriters.[3] Many people credit the impact of the bloggers (on "The Daily Show," Jon Stewart called them font experts, or "Helveticologists") as a factor in accelerating Dan Rather's retirement.[4]

Wikipedia is probably the best-known example: a Web-based, collaboratively created encyclopedia with more than fifteen million entries in 262 languages (24 of the language versions have more than a hundred thousand articles).[5] It is the most frequently accessed reference source on the Internet and has forced traditional encyclopedias to transform their business models. The related site Wikitravel has more than fifty thousand entries and won a Webby award for best travel website. Wikileaks publishes anonymous submissions and leaks of sensitive documents from governments and other organizations, while preserving the anonymity of their sources. In June 2010, an army intelligence officer was arrested for providing the site with classified U.S. combat video and hundreds of thousands of classified State Department records.[6]

Wikibranding is about something larger than social media or new marketing, it's really about "social business"—a business imperative. The demands placed on corporations and the modes by which they influence customer relationships are shifting irrevocably. Wikibranding is an attempt to get true brand engagement, customer experience, and social collaboration into the very nucleus of an organization and not leave them hanging out on the periphery. Wikibranding gets the customer-facing agenda back on the executive table and C-suite. It is not small change; it's a big, cultural driving force. Wikibranding is not what a dreamlike world of customer bliss should be; it's a pragmatic road map for winning in the current marketplace. So strap on your seat belt; this could be a fun, rewarding, and bumpy ride.

Building on *Wikinomics*

In 2006, Don Tapscott and Anthony Williams wrote a best-selling book, *Wikinomics: How Mass Collaboration Changes Everything*, from which we take a good deal of our seed inspiration for this book. At the time, the authors challenged deeply rooted assumptions about business and consolidated a number of prescient topics into new and interesting arguments. They pointed out that enterprises that embraced technology and collective genius and capability were establishing successful new business models and ripping open inefficient and slow-moving industries by tapping four key principles:

1. **Being open:** Allowing customers, peers, and others more access to the company's intellectual capital in order to collaborate and create something new.
2. **Peering:** Recognizing that people form their own communities to create value, such as open source, and prefer these communities to traditional hierarchies that concentrate on control.
3. **Sharing:** Overturning the economics of scarcity in favor of wide distribution and tailoring. In this regard, value comes not from distribution but from application of the company's products and services.
4. **Acting globally:** Making collaboration possible over long distances, tapping into a bigger pool of human physical resources by breaking down geographical boundaries, minimizing redundancies, and developing a global information technology (IT) platform.

These principles and the seven types of new business models identified in *Wikinomics* have weathered both criticism and the march of time. We recognize that our text builds on Don and Anthony's principles, but the crushing pace of change over the last four years necessitates an update. We also thought there were vital elements specific to wikibrands that could build on their pioneering work:

▷ **Role of brand:** An often-ignored topic of the collaboration discussion. How are the external-facing functions of marketing, communications, sales, public relations, and customer service and experience affected and changed by fundamentally new engagement, collaboration, and media practices?

▷ **New evidence:** What has been learned about business from the sweeping transformation of the social Web and a significant history of companies practicing in collaborative spaces?

▷ **Methods:** There have been many books written about why organizations should change, but we prefer to dive deeper under the hood of business. We believe that identifying the how and what—strategies, tactics, tools, and technologies from the world's leading companies— can better help companies reinvent themselves.

Why Now? The Seven Divides: Compelling Reasons to Change

David Bradfield, senior vice president and global digital chair for Fleishman-Hillard, intimates that other than cultural anthropologists, nobody has been trained sufficiently to cope with the depth of change in this space. Exceptional cultural awareness, dialogue, and listening skills were never the top considerations in hiring or promoting executives before, but they are requirements now. According to Bradfield,

> Big paradoxes exist here—we're being told to respect yet command our customer base. We need to stop pushing the conversation and instead *join* the conversation, but we're left with the legacy of paid media, owned media, earned media, and now this new thing, shared media. . . It's thrown the doors wide open and broken down silos in companies. Yet some companies have had turf wars on who owns these new areas. Ironically, the landscape is shifting so quickly, function heads oftentimes don't know what turf they're fighting about. The external pressures are pressing— they're visible, threatening, and largely uncontrollable. A macro realignment is required that's based on a broader, holistic view of branding and communications and how business needs to be managed.[7]

This type of change is wholesale and difficult. For some, it might (self-ishly) be easier to tread water for the next couple of years and wait for the next regime to unglue some very sticky practices. Is it worth the effort? Do you really need to change now? Why?

Let's make the case. Most change happens when you identify a current state of affairs that contrasts so markedly with a future state that there is more risk in staying put than in moving forward—change becomes the only logical answer. In the 2010 "Buzz Report," we surveyed the top rank-

TABLE 2.1 TOP FACTORS IN THE CHANGING IMPORTANCE OF SOCIAL MEDIA, WORD OF MOUTH, AND COMMUNITY BUILDING

	TOP 3 VOTE	RANK
Customer Experience Factors		
Need for authenticity and transparency in customer experience	41%	#1
Decline in consumers' discretionary time	11%	#12
Effect of Web 2.0 and the prosumer	9%	#14
Media Factors		
Rise of social networks	39%	#2
Consumers' waning attention to media/messages	24%	#4
Media fragmentation/clutter	22%	#5
Technology Factors		
Increasing role of wireless/mobile communications	33%	#3
Rise in online technology/media	20%	#6
Marketing Factors		
Changes in mass marketing effectiveness	20%	#7
Better measurability of new marketing/media formats	19%	#8
Vanishing mainstream customers	11%	#13
Loss of product differentiation	7%	#16
Business Model Factors		
Loss of consumer trust/credibility in corporations	17%	#9
Evidence of user-generated content affecting enterprises	12%	#11
Shortening of product life cycles/business models	7%	#15
Mass customization of product/business models	7%	#17
Generational Factors		
Influence of the Net Generation (anyone under 30)	16%	#10
Economic Factors		
Proliferation of brands/product choices	6%	#19
Enhanced global competition	5%	#20
Sales distribution changes (online to offline, concentration of retail)	3%	#21

ing factors driving executives' need to consider this type of change and embrace customer-centric practices. Table 2.1 displays the top twenty-one factors, ranked by the percentage in respondents' top three claimed drivers in consideration. We have grouped these factors into seven different categories of concern, drilled deeper, and found evidence as to why these seven factors were not only the main influences that profoundly impact business but also key divides between traditional methods and our wikibrands.

The Customer Experience Divide

Your CEO really wants to lead a wikibrand; he or she just doesn't know it yet. Very few CEOs immerse themselves in the world of social media—or marketing, for that matter. If you're in the function that is empowered to lead the wealth of wikibrand activity (marketing), they really don't care a lot about your current day-to-day. What they do care about is the customer. Improving customer service and optimizing the customer experience are big priorities for CEOs and, not coincidentally, at the heart of wikibrands. Eighty-seven percent of managers and executives believe managing the customer/brand experience is the key battleground for business. James Carville's rallying cry for Bill Clinton's election—"It's the economy, stupid!"—could be repurposed for the modern chief marketing officer (CMO) and social Web use: "It's the customer, stupid!"

For customers, providing great product quality and satisfaction are now the price of admission for brands. Evidenced by our survey, what the pursuit of "quality" meant to companies in the eighties and nineties is what "authenticity" means to companies now. People and customers are taking a much more activist role and want to see integrity in the companies they're doing business with. We love former Nike and Starbucks marketing executive Scott Bedbury's quip: "Consumers are looking for the real deal; the days of the corporate comb-over are numbered."[8]

Perhaps this maxim has always been true, but now customers have the power and voice to assert more control over brands and are exacting heavy costs on those businesses that do not provide the higher-order benefits of authenticity, entertainment, innovation, and responsiveness before, during, and after purchase. In a nutshell, this generation of customers has high standards; they want to be involved; and when products and services don't meet their specifications, they are more than willing to demand their pound of flesh.

TABLE 2.2 EIGHT CUSTOMER EXPERIENCE NORMS

DESIRED NORM	EVIDENCE TO SUPPORT	IMPACT ON BUSINESS DEVELOPMENT
Freedom: Choice is like oxygen.	"I like having many choices on what/where to buy." (74% strongly/ somewhat agree)	Businesses need to provide an expanded view of who they are and deliver a larger set of market choices.
Customization: Customers get what they want, when they want, and are able to change it.	"I often change or modify things I own to make them fit who I am." (54% strongly/somewhat agree)	Businesses require more flexible approaches for offering products and marketing, allowing users to "tailor" offerings and messages.
Scrutiny: Access to and transparency of information is a given.	"I take time to investigate information about products before buying." (74% strongly/somewhat agree)	Businesses need to stop "spinning the media" and "producing hype," and start providing genuine product facts and stories that are easily searchable.
Authenticity: Corporate integrity and openness are at a premium.	"I'll tell my friends not to purchase from companies that make untrue promises." (73% strongly/ somewhat agree)	Businesses need to encourage and embrace authenticity and transparency about their motives, operations, products, and marketing.
Collaboration: Customers are hard-wired for group work and co-creation.	• Only 10% wouldn't be willing to collaborate on products they're interested in. • 66% would be willing to participate in research. • 61% would be willing to help design products. • 37% would be willing to join a brand discussion group.	Businesses need to facilitate two-way dialogue and tap into the passions of their customer base through community building, customer advisory boards, ambassador programs, and employee empowerment.
Entertainment: Customers want entertainment and play in every aspect of their lives.	"Having fun while using a product is just as important as the product doing what it is supposed to do." (67% strongly/somewhat agree)	Businesses need to provide not merely functional products but overlay emotion and sensory-laden brand experiences.
Speed: "Faster and instantaneous" is the customer's and employee's mantra.	"I am someone who wants the latest and greatest version of everything." (48% strongly/ somewhat agree)	Businesses need to encourage real-time information flow, faster transactions, and just-in-time management.
Innovation: Disruption, adaptation, and improvement are the name of the game.	"I take advantage of opportunities companies give me to help make their products and services better." (60% strongly/somewhat agree)	Businesses need to foster active consumer participation before products are developed and consider innovation less of an event and more of an ongoing pursuit.

Source: nGenera Insight, "N-Gen Global Research Study," 2007

A study of more than eight thousand members of the Net Generation[9] identified eight cardinal lifestyle and cultural norms—freedom, customization, scrutiny, integrity, collaboration, entertainment, speed, and innovation—that companies need to take into account when developing products and marketing plans; the results are shown in Table 2.2.

Joe Pine, co-author of *The Experience Economy: Work Is Theatre & Every Business a Stage*, says, "If you charge for tangible things, you are in the goods business. If you charge for the activities your employees perform, you are in the service business. If, and only if, you charge for the time your customers spend with you, are you in the experience business."[10] Wikibranding is about creating great experiences *with*—not *at*—your customers.

The Media Divide

Traditional media is experiencing a dramatic change. In 2009, digital media and entertainment spending grew by 10 percent versus a drop in nondigital spending of 6 percent. In contrast to the doom and gloom surrounding traditional media, the rise of social networks has been the second largest factor influencing executives to consider changing company practices.[11] A lot of this growth is never fully reflected in media dollars because this segment requires as much time and manpower as it does media activation dollars. Whether it's because executives have personally joined these social networks and seen the potential for themselves or their employees have influenced them, 84 percent of executives believe they will spend more time, money, and staff in these spaces by 2011.[12]

It is not like people woke up one morning and fell out of love with media; they are still happily consuming 3,532 hours per year.[13] That's close to ten hours per day and a 24 percent increase over 1975.[14] A good chunk of this consumption is via TV, radio, and print. The change is that today's eyeballs are not so valuable. In an attention and attraction economy, where the din of media and cross-media usage continues to rise, marketers are paying substantially more to reach diminishing, dissatisfied, and distracted consumers.

The content game has changed. Upward of half the news and information consumed by younger audiences is being driven by people- not media-generated sources, and people's willingness to pay for content is also being challenged.[15] Traditional media no longer have a stranglehold over the attention of media planners and brand owners. Although the smaller percentage of media spend now (digital is estimated at 17 percent of total media spends), 62 percent of executives and managers believe social media, word of mouth, and peer-to-peer influence will overtake traditional media influence within our generation.[16] Getting into these peer-to-peer networks and staying relevant will be businesses' most important customer development job in the years to come. The challenge? A majority of marketers claim they don't know the tools any better than their customers do.

The Technology Divide

With mobile, social media, and file-sharing/storage tools and technologies becoming pervasive, the barriers to participation are coming down, the number of connections is increasing, and people are relying more frequently on "people they know" rather than traditional authorities. The Internet is effectively linking people and providing a virtual bullhorn to the masses.

In a pre-Internet world, word of mouth meant telling people two or three at a time about wonderful new discoveries. Buzz was slow to build. Now the average person belongs to two social networks, and if those two networks happen to be Facebook and Twitter, that represents the potential for a 280-person-strong domino effect that can lead to exponential connections with others.

The likelihood of peer-to-peer communication becoming even more pervasive through better technology is high. User behavior is already adapting: half of Facebook users visit the site every day; 25 percent of users answer text messages in the bathroom and slightly more do so during meals. We won't go into what percentage of people admitted to having texted during more intimate moments.[17]

Eighty-three percent of us believe radically new social media and word-of-mouth technologies and tools will be developed over the next few years.[18] New uses of technology are going to impact us profoundly. Wireless-enabled mobile marketing, location-specific/GPS/wi-fi–enabled marketing, and social networks are the top three bets for media that will experience the biggest growth in the next few years, syncing consumers up with more of those around them, more often, and at more touchpoints. Wikibrands will be rewarded for being omniscient and omnipresent in these technologies.

The Marketing Divide

Formidable hurdles face traditional branding and broadcast efforts to reach the modern activist customer. Companies using these methods have experienced a much steeper drop in the trust, loyalty, and perceived differentiation held for their brands. Brands are losing on four key parameters: [19]

▷ Brand differentiation has declined in forty out of forty-six categories, and only 7 percent of prime-time commercials were found to have a differentiating message.

▷ Consumer loyalty has dropped—with only one in ten consumers being committed to a single brand, a drop from four in ten over a six-year period.

▷ Brand trust is eroding. Even though Edelman's Trust Barometer points to "transparent and honest practices" and "a company I can trust" as the two biggest factors affecting corporate reputation, only 8 percent of people trust what companies say about themselves, and only 17 percent believe companies take what they say seriously. (Ironically, in the same study, people who actively engaged in social media were twice as likely to believe that companies were interested in them.)

▷ Time spent watching advertising is eroding. Sixty-nine percent of people are interested in mechanisms that skip or block advertising completely.

Over the last century, brands have been challenged alternately by scarcities in scalable production, distribution channels, media, and shelf space, which caused shifts in the power structure. With many of these obstacles now gone, the new scarcities are customer time, attention, and trust.

The Business Model Divide

Start-ups that have embraced collaboration using a mix of open source, partnerships, and superior technology to deliver products and services are reinventing industries. Can you think of a new business whose success has spread like wildfire over the last ten years that hasn't had Web collaboration, customer engagement, or technological innovation as one of its key pillars? There are very few cases.

Challenging inefficient, corporate, and monopolistic practices and building non-geographic-bound and community-based networks and media is the new formula. These business models have fewer start-up costs, are less resource intensive, and pose less overall financial risk. You can understand why venture capitalists and innovative companies have jumped in with both feet.

Consider the time and wealth reallocation in the entertainment landscape: iTunes with music, YouTube and Hulu with video entertainment, leading blogs and social bookmarking sites with news media, and Amazon's continuing impact on publishing. Client-server models of business governance will change; such change will frequently come from the edges and work its way to the middle of markets. The first signs of it are evident in banking, where alternate social banking models like Prosper, Zopa, Lending Club, and Community Lend threaten entrenched banking models.

The 2009 adage of "too big to fail" will soon become "no such thing as too big not to be reinvented." More than 60 percent of top CEOs believe the market environment will become increasingly more volatile, more uncertain, and more complex, leading to a restructuring of their industries; only 50 percent feel prepared to handle it.[20]

Consider two of the largest sacred cow industries:

▷ **Health care:** Given the ballooning costs and a U.S. economic strategy based on better services and lower costs, a smart prognosticator would safely bet on the wikification of health care services over the next decade.

▷ **Education:** In an era of lower standards of living and strained government budgets, families' ability to send their kids to Ivy League or even state schools will be put under pressure. The online experiments of pioneering institutions like the University of Phoenix will become de rigueur practices in higher learning.

Think your industry is immune to peer-to-peer interaction, customer collaboration, and deeply embedded stakeholder engagement? Think again. No industry, business, or brand can insulate itself for long from the need to adopt wikibrand practices. If you can see the prospect of extracting better value and experiences out of an industry or a way of doing business, a smarter business model will find that vacuum and establish itself.

The Generational Divide

Demographics play an important role in the future of wikibrands. The Net Generation in particular shares a strong disdain for interruptive advertising. Younger people turn to technology to save time and filter through the detritus of consumer messages and media. Spam filters, PVRs, RSS, pop-up ad blockers, and peer recommendation sites are all part of the Net Generation's defensive arsenal.

This collective experience has changed the group's basic expectations for the delivery of business and brand value. It offers a lot of individualized benefits but demands consumers' participation along the way. Based on their sheer numbers, current and projected economic clout, and increasing organizational influence, they are no longer a target demographic of curious but inconsequential study. Their hunger for involvement needs to be satiated by brands.

As their demographic ages, their values and influence will become those of the entire population, as did those of their baby boomer parents and grandparents before them. The Net Generation is flexing its muscles. As N-Geners scale the workforce ladder and spend more money in the marketplace, their unique consumer needs, behaviors, and relationships to brands will carry more decisive weight.

By the sheer size of their numbers (eighty million North Americans) and their hardwired orientation, they are amplifying wikibrand effects and demanding a shared exchange with the companies that sell to them. Lest you lose faith in the future of brands, there is a way forward. Although brand owners may feel taken for granted, 90 percent of global N-Geners will collaborate with and even evangelize companies that make the effort to establish a meaningful two-way relationship.[21]

In a Net Generation world, the value of a brand "Influencer" (an opinion leader who has pronounced connections, credibility, passion, and persuasion powers versus an average person) also rises substantially. According to The Keller Fay Group, word-of-mouth Influencers average 149 conversations each and every week about brands and products.[22] When they are Web-enabled, these brand conversations can leapfrog across social groups and travel exponentially faster and farther. N-Geners have twice as large a circle of word-of-mouth influence than the rest of the population due to their higher degree of Internet and mobile connectedness.[23]

The Net Generation's penchant for creation and participation is also swiftly transforming the economy. N-Geners have much higher levels of contribution to social networks, tapping their urge to share, create, mash up,[24] and produce ideas, content, and applications. Wikibrands are now adopting their playbook.

The Economic Divide

Among leading CEOs, macroeconomic factors have risen to the third most influential external factor (behind markets and technology) affecting business growth. That's up from number five just two years ago. The consolation for this heightened angst is that smart business leaders capitalize on times of complexity to grow. Remember that General Electric started in the recession of 1873, Disney began during the struggles of the 1920s, Microsoft debuted in the downturn of 1975, and Amazon consolidated gains in the postbubble world of the early 2000s.

Given the meltdown of the global economy of 2008 and 2009 and continuing consumer confidence issues, marketing departments are being asked to do more with less: 93 percent of CMOs have seen budget cuts.[25] They also expect to see more results from their social media budgets, seeking to establish a connection between social media and bottom-line business goals. One study points to social media metrics tied to tracking revenue as the number-one measurement CMOs need to address.[26] Because of the crisis, values have shifted, allowing companies to consider wikibranding as a viable avenue to pursue. By themselves, traditional businesses could put up a good defense; as a perfect storm of elements comes together at the same time, swift, responsive change is the only option. If the march to progress in how business engages customers had a twelve-step program, the first step would be that admitting change is required. The next one? What needs to change?

The Wake-Up Call

Revolutionaries and quick-moving companies are taking your business and your customers. In traditional companies, executives and managers have become enslaved by the way things have always been done and brand rules. They are relying on a newly available wealth of data but mistaking the scoreboard for the game.

Lois Kelly, author of *Beyond Buzz: The Next Generation of Word-of-Mouth Marketing* and a partner in Beeline Labs, states it simply:

> The best CEOs and CMOs I know are waking up, wading through the B.S., and asking one critical question—how am I going to be relevant and interesting to our customers and employees? The best ones have an intellectual curiosity but with a handle on the politics to get things done. They are thoughtful and open to the possibilities but have a disciplined handle on data to take calculated risks. Every brand has the potential to be talkable. The best executives are making it happen, gearing up for today's economy and standing for something, becoming more human, and taking it to their customers. The poorest ones don't understand this new world, so they dismiss it.[27]

Top executives are getting it. John Chambers, CEO at Cisco, says, "Everything we do at Cisco, the customers come first. It took us about six years to grasp the power of social networking, but once we saw how it could change how we can interact with customers, we moved."[28] Mark Parker, CEO at Nike, adds "The power has shifted to consumers. The ability we have to connect with consumers is the single most important competitive advantage in business today. 'The Consumer Decides' is one of Nike's maxims that really defines who we are and how we compete as a company."[29] Doug Ulman, CEO at Livestrong, goes even further: "Social media will change health care forever. At the end of the day, it is people coming together and interacting that will change the paradigm."[30]

Sean O'Driscoll, owner of Seattle-based Ant's Eye View and former general manager for Microsoft's communities, suggests there is a problem with the litany of advice that exists in the new media space about how to make social work with business: "The suggestion that a firm needs to merely participate in the conversation is a little naive. My response to a consultant who suggested that was, 'Microsoft was mentioned 2.5 million times in the blogosphere the previous year, and we have more than eighty-nine thousand employees. How can you realistically be expected to operationalize a response to all of them?'"[31] *Wikibrands* is our attempt to institutionalize a plan.

Do Brands Even Belong on My Social Couch?

Face it, as much as marketing people may laud the inventiveness of viral successes like Burger King's "Subservient Chicken," appreciate the simplicity and beauty of Dove's "Campaign for Real Beauty," or praise the altruistic cause marketing of Pepsi's "Refresh Everything," corporate success in social spaces is rare.[32] Very rare.

Consumers' personal relationships and how they spend time interacting has been transformed by social networks and social media. And the industry canaries in the social coal mine—namely the entertainment and content industries of music, movies, publishing, and broadcast and print media—have been turned over, if not toppled, by the onset of new media and technology.

Despite some inherent advantages of geographic scale, size of company opportunity, scope of potential customer contribution, and global impact, the successes that corporate entities have had in social media have been spotty. Their generally token Web efforts have been overshadowed by the runaway popularity or personal brand visionaries like Gary Vaynerchuck, Chris Brogan, and Arianna Huffington or the Web platforms of global giants like Twitter, Facebook, and Foursquare.

Tellingly, only seven of the top one hundred follower Twitter accounts are what we would call conventional brands. Which leads to the question: do people even want business and brands in their new social media spaces?

We say, yes. The inability of organizations to realize breakthroughs in these environments is not as much an indictment of brands and corporate entities as it is of the inability of businesses to adopt the engagement culture, dialogue-driven practices, and resource-driven needs of the digital marketplace. Wikibrands are an exception to the rule.

A myth has been propagated by a hard-core Internet crowd that brands don't belong in their sphere. It conflicts with popular sentiment. Eighty-five percent of people want a stronger connection with brands in social media, and 56 percent feel a stronger connection to companies they interact with in this way.[33] The new and fastest-growing darling of the social networks, Twitter, has members who engage with brands three times more pervasively than does the average population.[34]

The upshot is that the peer-to-peer media world has reached a tipping point where savvy marketers and advertisers can no longer avoid online, social, and participatory forms of marketing and media as a key channel for branding. In our corporate days, we recognized that one of the most compelling calls to action was our competition doing something we weren't. Guess what? They're already there. At least 79 percent of Fortune 100 companies are using Twitter, Facebook, YouTube, or blogs; 20 percent are using them all.[35]

No, the failure isn't that consumers don't want intimacy with businesses and brands in their social environments, it's that they don't want marketers—or at least traditional marketers. The mandate of businesses that operate in this new world is participation; authenticity; rich, two-way dialogue; and transparency.

The Culture Gap: Being Social Versus Doing Social

James Cherkoff, director at Collaborate Marketing, works with leading CMOs and describes the executive quandary in adopting new socialized approaches:

Senior executives and marketers struggle with the application of social media and collaboration programs. They react with, "We know the bike is broken, but it's the only bike we've got. I can't take my multimillion-dollar budget out of TV and dump the whole lot into this new space because there's no business model there." I think one conversation I've had many times in the last number of years is with CMOs who sometimes feel that they have to take sides between old media and new media—that it's one or the other. I find this to be a very strange mind-set, because they seem to think that either they have to be in this new space or they have to be in their old space.[36]

The reality is that businesses don't have to choose sides. They do need to choose the intelligent and balanced application of culture, strategy, content, tools, and technology. Wikibrands attempt to sift through the hype to find the essence of how top-performing businesses have shifted their practices and perspectives to accommodate a very different customer universe.

Businesses must embrace a real, genuine, heartfelt way of doing things. They need to embrace a culture shift. Jay Baer, one of the leading experts in how businesses tap into the new customer grapevine, makes the distinction: "There is a big difference between 'doing social' and 'being social.'"[37] In too many circumstances, the traditional business engine attempts to use the same tools and tactics that have worked over the last half-century in a new media. A tweak here, a new flavor there, but principally the same art of vaulting "brand stuff" over the media fence and seeing what works. It's like the industry has gone away for a weekend retreat but hasn't really changed its underlying faith. That's "doing social."

The prerogative of postmodern businesses is to make prudent bets on and experiments for the future. Becoming a wikibrand has to work, because companies are running out of options. They have tapped efficiency to its upper limits, cluttered the airwaves to the point of tune-out, and outsourced business and brand operations to the farthest outposts. One of the last battlegrounds is the customer experience. Unfortunately, given the humanness of interaction, businesses are struggling with a task that is more artistry than science.

Being social requires a shift in mind-set at the executive, organizational, and marketing levels in order to align branding with the new "conversation economy." Baer says, "Activating your fans requires passion and interest; just don't treat them like baseball cards. Don't post a Facebook page and check the box called 'social media' as an indicator of success. Social media is merely an ingredient; we're talking the need for a full entrée."[38] In interviewing hundreds of companies and the experts who help them, we found that many of the last decade's fastest-growing and more socially active companies have made significant changes. They've opened up their organizations to customer involvement as a basis for organizational structure design—a driver of company and marketing practices, and media choices—and as a way to measure performance.

The Wikibrand Culture Gap

Faith. It takes a lot to change someone's core beliefs. It would appear that the same level of obstinacy exists among our corporate audience. Sometimes there's a cathartic moment when executives change their stripes out of crisis, courage, or frivolity, but it is tough to unlearn long-standing habits.

Ross Kimbarovsky, founder of crowdSPRING, mentions that there are a lot of pretenders in social media: "What we need to get to is profiling the wonderful set of companies that are doing great things in social spaces. We have a total underappreciation of these brands and a tremendous amplification of large companies who are doing the bare minimum and being celebrated."[39]

By the way, have you ever noticed that most of the traditional ways of doing business have been established using the efficiency model of military operations? We marvel at the language of the traditional corporate world: you must *conquer* your competitors, *dominate* market share, *combat* perceptions, go on the *offensive*, use *guerrilla* tactics. Sound familiar?

As much as corporate mission statements attempt to show appreciation for customers, you need to make a gut check. Are you really in the trenches with your customers, or are you an aloof battlefield commander leading from the rear? Instead of military terms, let's use the metaphors of church, school, and party to demonstrate the difference.

Consider the traditional organization as a church. In most churches, there are authorities and the congregation. The church's leaders manage and host all the proceedings with selective and only occasional moments when the population can participate. In most churches, there are dogmas and standard practices that have existed, in some cases, for thousands of years. Direction and responses to contentious issues are not to be questioned in open forums but are decided on behind closed doors by an influential few (and sometimes by divine intervention).

Switch the priests or pastors to CEOs and the congregation to customers, and this is not dissimilar to the behavior of corporation barons of the 1920s, the postwar boom industries of the 1950s, the "mad men" of the 1960s, or the merged and acquired global companies of the 1980s. The problem? Consumers' respect for authority, receipt of one-way interaction, and tolerance of limited opportunity for influence and involvement have diminished.

Now consider the modern brand. Customer satisfaction is seen as important and is given a place as one of the company's top five to ten missions. It has an entrenched spot on the company project grids, and executives point to a number of new media projects in testing that could prove valuable. Consider these businesses the "schools of customer engagement."

Schools are engaged institutions. Their teachers live among the population. They customize their activities to each student's learning style. A school's mission is to develop the students, and most of them are committed to serving their students zealously. Teachers have pure motives; many of the best ones even spend extra time after school coaching teams or providing additional mentoring. Teacher-student ratios are ideally small. There is a good connection—students feel they know their teachers, and teachers feel they know their students.

But here's the rub. In most schools, there still exists an authority-subordinate relationship. Teachers have their schedules and a curriculum they need to cover, so things can get regimented. Students need to line up to come in from recess.

The postmodern organization's ability to engage its customer base is much better compared to the role of a party organizer/host. People look forward to and love parties, particularly when the ambience is just right. Parties succeed when the venue is the right size, the food and drinks are an epicurean delight, there are some formal games and activities, conversation is brisk, the people are interesting, and someone makes sure the fun doesn't get too far out of hand. The host may make a few announcements but never tries to control the conversation. Even better, the party organizer follows up a day later and asks guests how they enjoyed the gathering and perhaps invites them over dinner. People will go out of their way for this type of person and perhaps become lifelong friends.

Notice the difference between the organization as a church, an educator, and a host. That's the difference we're talking about between companies resisting, going through the motions, and genuinely embracing their inner wikibrand.

Why You Are the Right Person to Manage This Change

If you are asking yourself why you should manage your company's change, then you're likely the right person to start a wikibrand. Wikibrands tend to start in three ways in companies: executive leadership sets up the environment to make it work out of either crisis (such as Dell) or reinvention (such as Cisco); a group of colleagues rise up inside a company and starts experimenting (as with Lego); or it is buried in your company's DNA from the start. Recognize that, as a new corporate reality, this is going to require a lot of extra work and sweat. Are you really committed to becoming a wikibrand and seeing it through to the end, or is it just the flavor of the week?

Imagination and prudence are not mutually exclusive. You need to ask yourself some important questions before building a wikibrand. A full fifty-question assessment appears in Chapter 17, but here is a sampling:

▷ Why are you starting this effort?
▷ Is your CEO comfortable with opening your brand up to its customers, fans, and stakeholders?
▷ Is there an executive champion who will support this effort?
▷ Does/could your firm have the passion for this? Why?
▷ Do your customers want this?
▷ Do you want to truly listen and capitalize on your community's/customers' input?
▷ Do/could you have the manpower and resources to support the effort?
▷ Does your organization provide a consistent effort throughout the customer experience?
▷ Can you make a large enough commitment to see the returns?
▷ From what areas of community input could you most benefit?

The wikibrand rallying cry is clear. We are transforming between the industrial age mantra of competition and the information age credo of cooperation. Seven key forces are at work, creating a significantly different culture and marketplace that we will scarcely recognize years from now. Brands do belong in the social Web; the best ones will learn the rules of the participation age and extract the many benefits of engagement and collaboration (see Chapter 4 for benefits). Becoming a wikibrand doesn't mean choosing sides between all the things you're doing now and all the new things you'll do in the future. It does mean embracing a culture shift. We'll call on Dwight D. Eisenhower to make our final argument: "Neither a wise nor a brave man lies down on the tracks of history to wait for the train of the future to run over him."

CHAPTER 3

A WIKIBRAND ROAD MAP

Taking the High Road and Avoiding the Potholes of a Collaborative Brand Path

Many people have found social media religion and have rushed to publish. This book has been more than a decade in the making. Sean's journey began back in 1997 as a brand manager on Tide detergent. As much as he had come to respect the Procter & Gamble (P&G) algorithmic, "search-and-reapply" way of doing business, he started to recognize patterns in the outside world that were out of sync with P&G's traditional values and practices.

People did not watch commercials anywhere near as much as research suggested. The overprotective moms with a dirty laundry problem-resolution scenario portrayed in TV ads bored his immediate social circles and family to tears. The company was too internally focused and blind to the fast-changing world around it.

And why did the initial product innovation brainstorms and "blue sky idea" focus groups that created so much enthusiasm produce only fairly mundane, validated ideas from P&G's research "black box"? Well-differentiated product ideas that seemed attractive and exciting turned into "me-too"

"A story should be remembered for its soul, and not for its bell and whistles."[1]

—**BERNAJEAN PORTER,**
digital storyteller

brand extension ideas like mountain spring– or lemon-scented detergents. The organization was overly reliant on efficiency and predictability; it wasn't very effective at dealing with a marketplace that wanted "awesome" and was quickly tuning P&G out when it delivered merely "average."

Particularly incongruent was the notion of marketing the flagship brand Tide to essentially one homogenous target audience, even though it inhabited the hearts, minds, and washing machines of millions of varied households. This seemed incompatible to smartly growing a business. Procter & Gamble was lacking soul as a company; there was little humanness in how it engaged its audiences.

In looking at the logs of customer comments that percolated into P&G's customer service hotlines about Tide (then transferred to thick paper printouts), employees couldn't believe the time, effort, enthusiasm, and lengths that some people went to in providing new product ideas, uses, constructive criticism, and industry intelligence. Who were these people who would contribute freely with no expectation of recompense? Why wasn't the company doing anything with this valuable information? And why were the customer service people who managed these interactions given so little clout? P&G had put its most important asset—customers—at the bottom of the value chain.

In short, Sean started to doubt the traditional marketing method of delivering business value. That started him on a quest to see things from the edge. He read all forms of new-age thought leadership books. He became a brand heretic. First there were the peer influence books: *Permission Marketing: Turning Strategies into Friends and Friends into Customers* by Seth Godin (1999), *The Tipping Point: How Little Things Can Make a Big Difference* by Malcolm Gladwell (2000), and *Anatomy of Buzz: How to Create Word-of-Mouth Marketing* by Emanuel Rosen (2002). Then there were the personal brand books: *The Brand You 50* by Tom Peters (1999) and *Free Agent Nation: The Future of Working for Yourself* by Daniel Pink (2001). Finally, he read material that tried to reconcile the fast-moving dot.com world with the era of brands: *A New Brand World* by Scott Bedbury (2003), *The Fall of Advertising and the Rise of PR* by Al and Laura Ries (2004), and *Lovemarks* by Kevin Roberts and A. G. Lafley (2005). All of these books were foundational works that influenced the paradigm through which we see wikibrands.

The magazines were great (and much thicker than they are now). *Fast Company*, *Wired*, and *Business 2.0*—we loved them all and collected them with the enthusiasm of kids collecting baseball and hockey cards, storing away their prescient insights for future application. Along the way, we scanned the Web; read e-newsletters voraciously; and joined as many trade associations as we could to learn (hopefully months, if not years, before our colleagues) what new technologies, media, business concepts, and cultural trends were about to hit us.

After successfully applying what he had learned from all this newfound knowledge of customer experiences and engagement as head of marketing for Guinness (and helping build the top-performing global business in the black-pinted world), Sean started up Agent Wildfire, touted as Canada's "word-of-mouth company." This was pre-Facebook, before Twitter, ahead of the social media revolution. He was a martyr in a strange corporate landscape that couldn't understand what was happening to itself.

Fast forward to today, and we must admit to a bit of a shock that so little change has happened in the core of how companies build effective customer-driven business and effective brands. Why are businesses and marketers still surprised by the growth and impact of Web 2.0, social media, word of mouth, online community, peer-to-peer influence, or whatever catchphrase accompanies this instinctive need for prospects, customers, and people to connect and socialize when given the tools to do so? We all knew this was coming. It was predictable. We talked about it then, and we talk about it even more now. We just chose to disregard the tea leaves.

Well, like it or not, businesses now have to come to grips with three reconcilable thoughts:

▷ **Brands are fundamentally important.** They are likely the second or third most important asset of financial value to most companies; in many well-known examples, they represent more than 50 percent of a company's financial value. They are not merely logos or a roll call of features; they are a point of view on how products and businesses project to the world. Although the tactics may have changed, customers still place extraordinary value on them, pay more for them, and want to participate in them.

▷ **Peering, sharing, openness, and acting globally are all still on the rise.** Although our initial, unbridled enthusiasm may have waned a bit, these forces are accelerating change in the political landscape (President Obama massively outperformed Senator McCain in the social media battle), the media landscape, and increasingly in the corporate landscape. Hopefully, the seven divides outlined in Chapter 2 successfully argued that this no longer a fad or an early adopter fetish but a mainstream phenomenon.

▷ **These two concepts need to intersect.** There is a codependence here that needs to shake the core of how both businesses and collaborative platforms operate. This is not a Facebook page or a branded Twitter profile; there is something larger that businesses need to understand and adopt. Monetization, authenticity, customer experience, and resourcing all play a role in promoting the idea of wikibrands.

In writing this book, we recognized the plethora of effective publications that have come before and demonstrated quite evocatively the reason why marketers and businesses should care about customer engagement, the importance of crowd intelligence, the influence of word of mouth, and the rising tide of social media. We are standing on the shoulders of literary and blogging giants.[2]

The crushing pace of what's happening in the consumer world has also abetted our cause. We now have five times as many Internet and mobile users than we did at the start of the millennium. Although business acknowledgment of what's happening out in the social world is just beginning in many places, the early adopters have embraced it, accepted it, and in some cases even moved past it. Think about what social, people-based concepts, products, and buzzwords have taken off and mainstreamed themselves in the first decade of this century alone:

▷ **2000:** buzz marketing; Napster; books such as *The Cluetrain Manifesto* (markets getting smarter and faster), *The Tipping Point* (small things creating big differences)
▷ **2001:** viral marketing, customer experience, iPods
▷ **2002:** Influencer marketing
▷ **2003:** iTunes, participatory media
▷ **2004:** word of mouth, wiki, blogs, customer-made, crowdsourcing
▷ **2005:** Web 2.0. brand communities, MySpace, podcasts, social media, peer production, corporate blogs
▷ **2006:** user-generated content; YouTube; video blogs (vlogs); prosumption; virtual worlds such as Second Life; microcredit; knowledge networks; books such as *The Long Tail*, *The Wisdom of Crowds*, and *Wikinomics*
▷ **2007:** Facebook, iPhones, social networks, blogger outreach
▷ **2008:** mashups, apps, Facebook connect, Software as a Service (SaaS), Obama as a social media phenomenon, widgets, social banking, the social graph, community management

▷ **2009:** cloud computing, Twitter, microblogging, Hulu, privacy issues, OpenID
▷ **2010:** mobile apps and payments, Foursquare, geotagging, location-based networking, iPads and tablets, augmented reality, real-time search, Internet TV

With *Wikibrands*, instead of beating the social drum and being cheer-leaders for why you need to change, we strove to build a credible piece of work that explained more what the very best hundred companies are doing and how they are approaching the same challenges you are facing to create a winning culture, business strategies, processes, and tactics. We believe these stories need to be told with some important differences from work we've already seen on the subject:

▷ **Rigorous discipline:** We set out to write not a personal opinion book but rather a substantive publishing initiative developed by investigating hundreds of brand experiences and conducting interviews with the architects behind these efforts. The results are distilled through the authors' lenses of forty combined years of progressive experience across strategy, marketing, digital, and communications practices.
▷ **A balanced viewpoint:** We have no axe to grind nor embedded functional bias. Although there was a temptation to strip down what exists in traditional businesses, we would be equally wrong to blindly adopt the bleeding edge philosophy that moves faster than business. We operate across these different worlds and have accessed people who we believe are the best resources and who understand the need for balance.
▷ **Practical ways brand practitioners succeed:** Many business owners don't need to be convinced of the need for change; that was last decade's challenge. The current challenge is how to do it sensibly and move not only individuals but the large stakeholder groups to rally behind these efforts. We believe we can help by thoroughly investigating organizations to find out what has made their experiments successful.
▷ **Evidence-based practices on why people need to change:** Too often, authors and pundits don't substantiate their opinions. We have primary research and survey information not broadly revealed to the general public that back up our general conclusions.
▷ **Basics of *Wikinomics* research:** We worked with the best-selling author Don Tapscott on the research underlying several of his books.

Don encouraged us to build on his work and write a book on how those principles can be used to improve marketing.

▷ **Outside the Echo Chamber:** We have not been overexposed ourselves to the larger community and thought leaders who tend to see the world through a partisan lens. We believe we have blended the best of Silicon Valley, Madison Avenue, Main Street, and international influences.

We wanted to create a work that would be helpful for businesses and organizations that are trying to humanize themselves. What better way to provide credibility to that argument than by showing businesses across a wide spectrum that were succeeding. We studied more than one hundred communities and conducted hundreds of primary interviews with practitioners, industry thought leaders, and Influencers.

The *Wikibrands* story was developed through two highly acclaimed studies[3] as part of research programs[4] operated under the leadership of Don Tapscott, Joan Bigham, Mike Dover, and Jody Stevens at New Paradigm, a Toronto-based think tank that was acquired in 2008 by nGenera Corporation. The seed ideas of "Wiki Brands: Reinventing the Brand in a Consumer-Controlled Marketplace"[5] was part of a syndicated research program beginning in 2007 called The Net Generation: Strategic Investigation Program, and "Brand Communities: It Takes a Community—Not a Campaign—to Raise a Brand"[6] was part of a 2009 program called Marketing & Sales 2.0. These programs were funded by a syndicate of Fortune 1000 companies, government agencies, and some innovative smaller firms.

In this book, we will explain a step-by-step approach for turning your business into a magnet for customer engagement by providing examples that focus on businesses that use reliable customer-driven business models to make money. Part rallying cry, part support for your own organizational change, the chapters provide guiding strategies and perspectives, helpful rules of thumb, and a pathway to execution from executives and practitioners.

So where do we go from here? Part 2 (Chapters 4 and 5) will identify and explain the six benefits of wikibrands (advocacy, insight, content, support, perception, and serendipity) and describe how companies need to adopt a new mind-set about the brand customer.

Part 3 (Chapters 6 through 10) fleshes out the FLIRT model, which explains how firms need to develop focus, language and outreach, incentives and motivations, rules, and tools and platforms.

Part 4 (Chapters 11 through 14) discusses the roles and responsibilities of managing communities, as well as how to internalize the benefits of a wikibrand philosophy. It also addresses the best metrics for evaluating wikibrand success.

Part 5 (Chapters 15 and 16) takes lessons learned in the corporate world and applies them to the individual, describing how you can crowdsource your personal brand. We make predictions about what social media platforms and relationships between media partners will evolve and how consumers will interface with technology in the future.

Finally, Part 6 (Chapter 17) provides a reference guide to the key ideas in the book, including a fifty-question survey to assess how ready your firm is to build a brand community. In addition, the chapter provides a thumbnail description of twenty of the best brand communities. We have also provided a universe of case studies, thought leaders, opinions, and up-to-date relevant resources to keep the conversation going at **wiki-brands.com**.

PART 2

REINVENTING THE MARKETING PARADIGM

CHAPTER 4

THE SIX BENEFITS OF WIKIBRANDS

Marketing Doesn't Fit in Tiny Boxes Anymore

Many of us learned about the Four Ps in business school. In 1960, university professor E. Jerome McCarthy defined the marketing mix as four elements: product, pricing, place, and promotion. By adjusting these factors, a marketer could manipulate behavior to favor a particular brand. As Brian Fetherstonhaugh, the chairman and CEO of OgilvyOne points out, this model has had a good run but has lost some of its vigor. It defined marketing as a series of instructions rather than a conversation, was dependent on product development occurring in longer increments, and relied on the relative ease of reaching large audiences through one advertising medium.

Fetherstonhaugh likens traditional marketing to speaking to four- or five-year-old children: "They may be rambunctious and misbehave, but they'll eventually do what you tell them."[2] Modern marketing is more like speaking to an eighteen-year-old: "Your best bet is to guide them and make suggestions, but eventually they will make their own decisions."[3] Another cool metaphor he provides refers to fusion cuisine: "During the 'Mad Men' years, a chef could be considered impres-

"Brand building today is so different than what it was fifty years ago. . . . Today anyone, whether it is an employee or a customer, if they have a good or bad experience with your company they can blog about it or Twitter about it, and it can be seen by millions of people. It's what they say now that is your brand."[1]

—TONY HSIEH, *CEO, Zappos.com*

47

sive by adding some vegetables to a skillfully prepared meat-and-potato dish. The new marketing tools are like the new global cooking techniques and hundreds of exotic ingredients. The challenge is not just how to incorporate ingredients, but how to ensure that they interact effectively with each other."[4]

Featherstonhaugh has developed a new framework for marketing, replacing the Four Ps with Four Es:

▷ **Experience:** There is a lot more to the shopping experience than just the purchase transaction. It has many opportunities for a marketer to enter into a conversation with potential customers, including research, comparison, product activation, socialization of the purchase, and after-sale service. Marketers now face the challenge of being involved throughout the journey without being intrusive. As Featherstonaugh explains, "After the cash register rings, that's where you make the money."[5]

▷ **Everyplace:** As we will discuss in Chapter 14, measuring digital marketing is difficult because successful communication affects consumers throughout the decision-making process. Even if customers are questioned about their influences at the time of purchase, they might forget that a Google search, a clever and informative podcast, a perusal of Yelp reviews, an advertisement within a video game, and a discussion in an online forum got them to the point where an effective clerk inside the store finished the purchase. As the marketing mix becomes more complicated, it requires more tweaking to find the most effective way to deploy each tool.

▷ **Exchange:** Using dynamic pricing to ensure that demand more accurately meets supply is nothing new. An umbrella at a kiosk near a train station may be more expensive on cloudy days and hotels in Austin are certainly costlier if the Longhorns are home on Saturday afternoon or during South by Southwest. Companies can more precisely and quickly determine and act on fluctuations in demand. Greater transparency, on the other hand, makes it a lot easier for customers to compare what they each paid for the same product. The concept of exchange goes beyond pricing models though. Fetherstonhaugh urges marketers to ask, "How much do I have to *give* in order to *get* the business outcome I want?"[6] More frequently, customers do not want the marketer to give up margin; many of them prefer to participate in the process, be included in a fan group, or have access to premium product (or even a sneak preview to a new launch).

▷ **Evangelism:** Fetherstonhaugh challenges marketers to "give people an idea so interesting that they want to share it."[7] The old adage of a disgruntled customer describing a bad experience to ten people and a satisfied customer telling three to five gets dramatically amplified when those customers use social media to spread their message. As we will see in Chapter 12, not only are engaged consumers more likely to passionately defend a company's product, but their voices are perceived to be much more authentic. The challenge for marketers is giving up control. Under the Four Ps model, a promotion statement ends with a exclamation point, whereas a conversation with an evangelist ends with a question mark.

Figure 4.1 illustrates how marketers can improve business practices through dialogue, openness, authenticity, and support of advocacy. The center circle displays traditional branding tactics, the middle circle provides examples of methods for improving conversation, and the outer circle shows wikibranding tactics.

With wikibrands, the goal is to develop media hubs where users actively seek content, entertainment, information, and opportunity. A new set of media channels and brand tactics that include online community development, corporate blogs, online applications, virtual worlds (such as Sec-

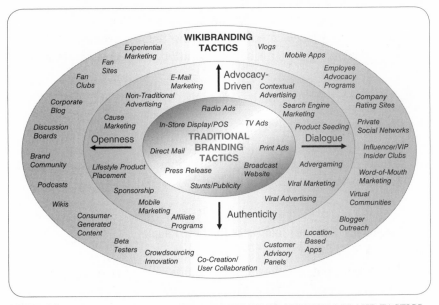

FIGURE 4.1 THE UNIVERSE OF WIKIBRANDING AND TRADITIONAL BRAND TACTICS

ond Life), private brand databases, mobile applications, brand discussion groups and forums, social networks, and message boards have evolved to a sufficient degree that brand relationships can be tailored to self-identified, interested consumers. Unlike traditional, one-size-fits-all branding approaches, these are geared for customer advocacy, dialogue, openness, and authenticity.

Blogs and discussion forums have stimulated dialogue and enhanced levels of trust with fans: some are CEO-driven (Socialtext); some facilitate sales (Dell); some reflect employee views (Hewlett-Packard, Microsoft); some share thoughts on the future (GM FastLane); and some focus on particular topics (eBay PowerSellers, Amazon API developers)

When marketers start with the mind-set of developing brand forums to create "friends" rather than "prospects," they quickly come to realize the ongoing advantages of deeper consumer relationships, business collaboration, word-of-mouth advocacy, and a reduced dependence on expensive media. While building these forums, organizations need to weigh the costs of appropriate levels of brand content development, management, and administration with the need for active and genuine consumer engagement; too often they err of the side of underinvesting and understaffing, leading to unsustainable engagement efforts.

While traditional brand approaches aim to optimize reach and frequency against the broadest possible market segment, wikibrands need not aspire to such democratic appeal. Although inclusive, wikibrands do not give every customer's opinion the same weight. Ideally, the degree of a customer's knowledge, credibility, connectedness, commitment, and involvement should govern his or her invitation and deeper involvement in brand programs.

The Six Benefits of Wikibrands

The next section discusses six benefits of wikibrands and explains how the traditional business paradigm is evolving for each of them.

Brand Advocacy: And They Told Three Hundred People, and So On, and So On . . .

Social tools have put a bullhorn in the hands of the masses. Consider the 2010 Old Spice Guy TV campaign that was adapted to social media and generated more than 10 million YouTube channel views (and more than 150 million downloads from various other places on the Web), 800,000

Facebook advocates, and more than 100,000 Twitter followers in a matter of weeks. Although its potential can be overplayed, the wikibrand Web of connected technologies can undoubtedly spread messages quickly and create excited advocates, lifelong cult followers, and tiny citizen-booster stations that amplify messages.

Since marketers are the primary function accountable for social media and other collaborative strategies, it might not be surprising that creating buzz and traffic are the most popular benefits sought by organizations using these tools and tactics. Generating word of mouth, direct referrals, and brand recommendations; creating ongoing loyalty; amplifying online and offline traffic; and delivering advocacy-driven revenue and sales, evangelical product badging (proud external endorsement through social signaling), and reductions in paid media budgets are the core concerns of wikibrand advocates.

The path to runaway word of mouth is rooted in deep insight into the customer and what the customer wants as an exchange. Some want to be entertained, some want to be educated, some want an experience, and yet others want an escape. This is where companies tend to fall down. The gap between how companies view themselves and how they are perceived by consumers is widening. Eighty percent of business executives believe they are doing a good job building customer relationships, while only 8 percent of their customers agree.[8] Driving this discrepancy is a growing ability by consumers to see through ads and persuasion techniques and critique them for a wide and interested audience.

The future advocacy success of wikibrands will be determined by their malleability. That is, their ability to create a big "tent" of consumer-built benefits, messages, media, audiences, and products, while still maintaining their core essence. Brand malleability provides companies with the flexibility to react quickly to changing marketplace conditions. By pushing for dialogue and genuine user collaboration, firms with malleable brands protect themselves against a fragmenting consumer base.

Brand malleability will allow brands to move more freely into new categories or communication avenues. Customer-centric brand alliances and interesting mashups of benefits and partners (such as Nike and iPod) will become part of the fabric of wikibrands as consumers' need for great, unimagined, and very buzzable brand experiences exceeds the requirement to adhere to a regimented set of brand standards.

It would be a mistake to interpret this type of freedom as brand chaos or anarchy. Five key elements will continue to anchor the brand to its sense of self and consistency of purpose: its logo, name, core idea, belief system, and community. The remaining company activity should focus on driving customer relevance, delivering on benefits promised, and fulfilling customer need—wherever that leads. Mentos, Virgin, Apple, Google, and the Discovery Channel have all blazed new avenues of profit by adopting a malleable brand approach.

The acceleration of continued technological upgrades, add-ons, and patches in video games and entertainment sequels has taught the brand world that sustainable advocacy is driven by an ongoing set of news, tweaks and launches. In a wikibrand world, word spreads quickly, and brands that places a premium on being first, different, or relevant stand to gain the advocacy benefits.

Powerful Brand Advocates—the Influencers. Depending on the tightness of definition, Influencers (people who have significant influence on the consumer behavior of others) are believed to represent 1–15 percent of the population. Various marketing, media, and anthropological experts have attempted to define these unique individuals.

Harnessing Influencers' feedback, involvement, and evangelism for organizations has never been more critical. The Internet has been helpful in identifying and sourcing Influencers, while a variety of new connected media has placed a bullhorn in their hands, enabling them to communicate with significantly larger audiences. What are Influencers talking about? Twenty-seven percent of Influencers' discussions are about brands and products.[9] Two separate studies conducted by McKinsey & Company and Thompson Lightstone suggest that more than two-thirds of today's consumer purchase decisions are primarily influenced by word-of-mouth recommendations.[10]

Canadian athletic clothing maker lululemon is a champion crowd-sourcer. Since its first store opened in 1999 in Kitsilano, British Columbia, lululemon has become renowned for its stylish, lovable athletic clothing; support for environmental and local community causes; and promotion of a West Coast lifestyle—all of which are supported by the praises of its Influencer community. With virtually no money spent on traditional advertising and marketing support, this active fashion icon has more than one hundred stores in Canada, the United States, and Australia; more than twenty-three hundred employees; and annual revenues of more than $450 million, a figure that has tripled since 2007.[11] During the first quarter of 2010, revenue grew an additional 69 percent over the comparable quarter in 2009 and margins increased.[12]

What makes lululemon different? It has largely relied on word of mouth. Thanks to a formalized brand ambassador program composed of local yoga, dance, and fitness instructors, athletes, certified personal trainers, and role models, the buzz continues to build.

Chip Wilson, lululemon's founder, recognizes the challenges of going up against much larger competitors such as Nike, Reebok, and Adidas. "I think there's a difference between a commodity product versus a technical product," notes Wilson. "In our case, formalized advertising isn't the effective way to go." [13]

In return for free and discounted apparel, as well as media exposure as official ambassadors, lululemon's Influencers provide valuable feedback on clothing design and technology, wear and endorse the brand uniform publicly, allow their names and images to be used in the media, and religiously evangelize the brand's products and lifestyle merits to their own athletic flocks. Chip Wilson adds, "When we started out—with no reputation, a new idea, and not a lot of money—it only made sense to invite people we knew and felt were important to get involved." [14]

Each year, the company looks for a new group of five to ten unique individuals per store location who embrace the lifestyle it promotes—"helping people to lead happier, healthier, and more fun lives." The company has anointed 60 elite ambassadors, 900 grassroots ambassadors, with a secondary group of 17,000 registered research and development participants (hundreds per store location). [15]

Community hives of brand zealots are appearing across a wide variety of market segments. Folksy bourbon distiller Maker's Mark has fueled company expansion behind more than 250,000 product ambassadors in what it describes as "marketing without fingerprints," the concept of not invading people's airspace until the company is invited. Sporting goods and apparel retailer The Running Room has incubated a tight-knit group of 320,000+ running, jogging, and walking enthusiasts. [16]

These new word-of-mouth media create a higher order of brand message as technology removes many of the traditional hurdles leading to sales. In a reversal of roles, the key goal of media and marketing could eventually become acting as support mechanisms for driving traffic to collaborative forums. We will explore Influencers in more depth in Chapter 8.

Brand Insight: Better Insight, Innovation, and Feedback

The company arrogance of believing you can't actually learn from your customers is the first hurdle to overcome in order to tap crowd wisdom. Given this corporate insularity, generating brand insight is not surprisingly the most overlooked benefit in wikibrand customer engagement. However, many companies have been successfully learning from customers at a much deeper level of involvement than that of traditional focus groups and survey polling. Organizations are moving more quickly, more economically, and more smartly by tapping customers as a source of idea stimulus, beta testing new products, polling conceptual directions, and generating company/industry intelligence.

Jake McKee, founder and lead strategist of Ant's Eye View and owner/writer of the popular blog communityguy.com, is an original online community evangelist. Involved in the field of community building since 1996, he joined the Lego Company in 2000, where he spent five years creating and implementing the corporation's online community strategy. McKee's work at Lego helped to create Lego Mindstorms, a hugely successful community described in *Wikinomics* as "a flagship for how to get your customers deeply involved in co-creating and co-innovating products." [17]

McKee explains its origins: "When I worked at Lego, I saw that an entirely independent adult enthusiast community had developed, and the company was missing out on it. There were fans meeting up in offline sites, others starting their own photo-sharing websites to display their Lego creations; someone had even created an online Lego shopping mall. And this was all back in 2000." [18]

As Lego's senior Web producer at the time, McKee started spending an extra few hours per week helping to promote and cultivate this community. Gradually, his time commitment to this side project increased to the point where online community building became his full-time job. "Surprisingly, especially for me, nobody told me to mind my own business or focus on my 'real job.' They started seeing the results I was producing and asked me to take on more and more and more of those duties." [19]

The Lego community includes an enthusiastic army of Influencers, ranging from outsourced innovators to advisory panelists to a network of fan clubs around the world. These participants have become involved through the company's Customer Innovator and Ambassadors programs, Lego podcasts and blogs, Lego League (a kids' community), Lego fan clubs and auction sites, and a Lugnuts user group community that has different degrees of community participation. Each of these provides multiple levels of involvement and feedback to the company.

Lego Mindstorms is a programmable robotics kit popular not only with children but also with adult engineers. Mindstorms users can create robots that can solve Rubik's Cubes and identify blue M&Ms. The description of the cube-solving program is as follows (and the video of the robot working can be accessed at **wiki-brands.com**):

An ultrasonic sensor detects its presence and starts to read the colors of the cube faces using a light sensor. The robot turns and tilts the cube in order to read all the faces of the cube. It then calculates a solution and executes the moves by turning, tilting, and twisting the cube.[20]

When the source code for the product was hacked and published on the Internet, Lego did not respond like the music industry and sue their customers. Instead, it engaged the community, supporting the forums and offering prizes for the best inventions. When Lego wanted to upgrade the product, it created a Mindstorms User Panel (MUP) of the most creative innovators, who were selected based on close evaluation of their online reputations and participation in user forums. The original MUPers became de facto employees and had to sign a nondisclosure agreement in order to volunteer their expertise (and pay their own airfares to Denmark). Steve Hassenplug, a software engineer from Indiana, exchanged his time and expertise for plastic bricks and access to an updated, prelaunch product. He explained his motivation this way: "They're going to talk to us about Legos, and they're going to pay us with Legos? They actually want our opinion? It doesn't get much better than that."[21]

One tactic employed by McKee is what he calls "success by one thousand paper cuts." Initially, a single paper cut will go unnoticed, but if you collect enough of them, you can sever a limb. By analogy, employees should start with small projects that don't require extensive approval or resources. If these small projects create success, the results can be shared, and approval for a slightly larger project becomes possible.

Taking such a proactive and bottom-up approach is important in this space. Community building can be placed under any number of departments, such as marketing, sales, communications, customer service, research, or product development. Instead of making community building the responsibility of a single department, the goal should revolve around "facilitating cross-silo collaboration" that allows community to "live everywhere."

According to McKee:

Clients regularly ask me, "Where is the right place for community to start?" My reply is generally, "If you're asking the question, then what part of the company do you work in? There's your answer." At the end of the day, this falls on whoever is willing to do it. Long term, if you're asking who owns it, it really depends on the company—it could belong in marketing, it could be in customer service, it could be in product design. It all depends on what you're trying to get out of it.

If, as an employee, you're thinking, "Wow, our company should really be doing this. Who should be doing it?" then the answer is you. If you're asking the question, then it's up to you to start down that path. A lot of clients will tell me, "We don't have executive buy-in." My reply to them would be to take a proactive approach; go and convince your executives that it's worth buying into. Move one small piece at a time to prove the worth—success by a thousand paper cuts.[22]

Since 1996, Jones Soda has been able to build a grassroots cult following even though it has fallen on some financial difficulties. As founder Peter van Stolk revealed, "People don't need our shit. People get fired up about Jones because it's theirs."[23] Since the company's inception, a continuous stream of consumer-suggested flavors and packaging has become embedded in the product's folklore. The customer community also rates new flavors and label ideas before they are released. Jones enables customization by allowing customers to create their own labels for their favorite existing Jones Soda flavors using their own photos and text. A unique gift for special occasions, such as weddings and graduations, a twelve-pack of myJones can be ordered online. Jones Soda is active in social and digital media; more than five hundred thousand Facebook users "like" the company, and in return the company has put twelve thousand customer photos on its product labels from the more than one million photos it has received over its history. One of the company's more quirky flavors, Turkey & Gravy, enjoyed lots of buzz in the blogosphere when it was released for Thanksgiving in 2006.

Van Stolk summed up his roller-coaster success in an industry dominated by heavyweights Coca-Cola and Pepsi: "We started this company with the philosophy that the world does not need another soda. That forced us to look at things differently. How could we create a new kind of connection with customers, let them play with the brand, let them take ownership of it? Everything at this company is about sharing ownership of the brand with our customers. This is not my brand. This is not our soda. It belongs to our customers."[24]

Brand Content: Sharing the Tester's, Developer's, Director's, and Innovator's Chair

Brands enabling user-generated content have been a driving force behind sponsored brand engagement in social networks. At its basic level, users are extremely adept at providing objective reviews and ratings of products and services. More elaborate platforms have been built to crowdsource customers' content (photos, blogs, video, scoops, and news), creative abilities (campaigns, designs, and merchandise), and collaborative innovations (solutions, technology, and ideas).

Both Salesforce.com and QuickBooks host very active customer forums that enable members to provide feedback on new software releases and ideas for product development. We'll discuss these in greater detail in Chapter 12.

We know people who book travel based solely on the advice of TripAdvisor users, whose ranking systems enable consumers to find a great boutique hotel, an authentic local restaurant, or an enthusiastic Segway tour proprietor (we can't promise that you won't look geeky). Consider Post Ranch Inn, a luxury hideaway in Big Sur. It is a wonderful property. Located atop a cliff overlooking the Pacific Ocean and nestled in a redwood forest, it has won many awards, including Best Spa in the World from *Condé Nast Traveller*. Several of the awards it has garnered are based on consumer participation, including TripAdvisor's Traveller's Choice Awards for Top Ten Best Romantic Hotels and Greenest Accommodations in the World. The TripAdvisor comments are overwhelmingly positive, while most of the negative comments describe a great experience but complain about the prices (many of the rooms cost more than $1,000 per night). It sounds a little like reviewers who, for cost reasons, substitute canned tuna for the main ingredient in a lobster pot pie recipe on Epicurious, then opine, "I was underwhelmed."

The Heritage Marina Hotel came to our attention after it received the dubious distinction of being the Dirtiest Hotel in America according to TripAdvisor consumers. The vast majority of reviewers gave it one star, the worst possible rating, and the narrative of the descriptions reads like a Charles Bukowski novel with tales of bugs, filth, and the drug and flesh trades occurring under the gaze of staff who exhibit an almost-zenlike sense of apathy. In fact, one of the very few five-star ratings for the property included the title line "Run Away, Run Away!!!" and the text included a plea for an intervention from the health department, so we'd suggest that the reviewer struggled a little with TripAdvisor's user interface.

Brand Support: More Answers, Ownership, and Fanship

When the right set of conditions and motivations are provided (see Chapter 8, on incentives), customers will rush in and rally around brands. This type of brand support spans across a full range of benefits, including providing customer service (e.g., answering others' support questions), support-ing value-added experiences (e.g., creating user guides for games), leading industry conversations (e.g., supporting online petitions), and enlisting fundraising support (e.g., raising funds for important causes).

Both SAP Labs and Intuit benefit from the support their brands receive from their community forums, where volunteer members provide effective customer service about their software. We'll explore these communities in greater detail in Chapter 12.

For authors, the ratings and discussions on Amazon.com and other online booksellers are an important method of building a book's profile. An existing community can be very useful in developing an online buzz for a book launch. Keith Ferrazzi followed up his best-seller *Never Eat Alone* with *Who's Got Your Back*. The first book gathered a lot of fans (many peo-ple find Keith's writing inspiring and transformational), and his firm, Fer-razziGreenlight, developed and nourished a community of followers. The result: the launch of *Who's Got Your Back* was immediately welcomed by a huge sales hit and a multitude of Amazon reviews, the vast majority of which were five stars (the perfect score). When a detractor suggested that the reviewers had been "incentivized by Keith's marketing machinery" to post, his colleague Love Streams (which you have to admit is a pretty cool name) responded candidly, "The only incentive we've ever offered for reviews—which we've asked be thoughtful, personal reviews, not puff—is a copy of the book. That's no more or less incentive than reviewers for the *New York Times* get!"

Chase Ansok works diligently to improve gamer experience in the video game Grand Theft Auto: Vice City. For a six-month period, Ansok (his handle is AggroSk8ter) compiled a user's guide (titled *Full FAQ and Walk-through*), by collecting, investigating, and organizing thousands of e-mails and instant messages from users. The end product is a highly organized, comprehensive, and exhaustive thirty-five-thousand-word document that provides maps, game hints, glitches, and a full inventory of assets, proper-ties, and vehicles available in the game. By way of comparison, the "offi-cial" instructions from Rockstar Games contain less than two thousand words, and the instructions provided by Blockbuster for a rented game consist of only twelve words. Ansok is thorough, thoughtful, occasionally pedantic ("Check the FAQ!" he often pleads), and an important member of the Rockstar business Web. How much does he cost? Nothing. Ansok and dozens of others craft these user's guides as hobbies, competing with each other to build the best, most complete, or easiest-to-use guide. In a vein similar to bloggers, AggroSk8ter reluctantly promotes and praises his competition, encouraging visitors to view other walkthroughs with different specializations.

Along with Ansok and his ilk, there are thousands of active members of the GTA community that meet online to discuss strategies, debate the merits of the game, and provide detailed modifications and extensions to the series. There is even fan fiction, not all of which would be rated PG, featuring Vice City's protagonist, antihero Tommy Vercetti. All of this activity adds value to an already immensely successful game; GTA: Vice City was the bestselling video game of 2002, the GTA series franchise has sold 120 million copies worldwide, and its GTA IV launch garnered $500 million in its first week alone, earning more in that first week than the top-grossing movie of 2008 (*The Dark Knight*).[25]

Similar to how soccer moms became an important demographic for politicians, "mommy blogs" have become important to marketers. Julia Louis-Dreyfus's post-"Seinfeld" sitcom, "The New Adventures of Old Christine," invited twelve influential bloggers who wrote about motherhood to visit the set, watch an episode being filmed, and make a video with the actors for their blogs. The bloggers were thrilled, and CBS was pleased with the coverage the show received in their posts.[26] In fact, according to eMarketer, advertising on blogs will top $746 million by 2012, more than twice the figure for 2007. In 2010, popular mommy bloggers were hosted at the Olympics by Procter & Gamble and at the Academy Awards by Kodak.[27]

Brand Perception: More Empathy, Respect, and Culture Changing

Public relations firms were among the first to realize the importance of this new form of external stakeholder represented by connected customers and grassroots journalists. Similarly, one of the leading benefits of wiki-branding has been in how companies get exposed and positively perceived by their audience. The spectrum of customer-driven perception benefits could be in the chatter value (higher awareness, exposure, and search engine optimization), higher affinity for the brand (evoking feelings of "yes, they get me"), greater empathy or respect for the brand ("finally they're listing to me"), and a feeling of industry leadership by exposing issues in a timely, relevant, or intimate manner.

In 2006, no brand was able to rise above its product and implant an idea as effectively as Dove. The Dove "Evolution," a seventy-five-second viral ad, and Dove's umbrella Campaign for Real Beauty have effectively wrapped the brand in the debate about "whether beauty really is skin deep." Janet Kestin, chief creative officer for Ogilvy & Mather, Dove's agency, explains that the seed idea came from a global research group that evaluated women's mind-sets about beauty issues in ten different countries:

> What shocked us was that only 1–3 percent of women around the world were self-confident and described themselves as "beautiful." There was consistency across the board, even in countries we would normally associate with having physically beautiful women.
>
> Campaign for Real Beauty was the first time any beauty company had taken the pressure off of women and told them, "Look after what you have, because what you have is great." We didn't want to replace one beauty dictatorship with another, so there was no finger wagging or preachiness. We threw it out there as a question and let the audience participate. As a beauty brand with a history of being real, simple, and visual, we felt there was a powerful idea/question we could legitimately pose.[28]

The series of ads that appeared in print and digital media—combined with the powerful video "Evolution," which shows a model's flawless beauty manufactured in stop-motion stages, including digital enhancement—has been viewed more than ten million times on YouTube. Dove films showed girls and young women speaking candidly about body image and unrealistic expectations. The campaign, which won many awards such as one at the Cannes Lions International Advertising Festival, was considered empowering to women.[29] In 2006, Dove also legitimized the campaign with the Dove Self-Esteem Fund, which is aimed at helping girls and women feel comfortable with their own beauty and at helping redefine the concept of Western beauty.

The message that all women are beautiful seemed inauthentic when critics pointed out that Unilever, Dove's parent company, also manufactures Axe body spray, which is aimed at teenage and twentysomething males. The advertisements for Axe purported, albeit in a tongue-in-cheek fashion, that the product would make them irresistible to (in some cases) herds of attractive young women. A mashup video of the Dove Campaign for Real Beauty and Axe commercials that showed gorgeous lab assistants swooning at the scent of Axe wearers became a powerful and widely viewed rebuttal to the "Evolution" video. The mashup ended with "Talk to your daughter before Unilever does."

Unilever was clearly given a choice of how to engage the conversation. Dr. Niraj Dawar of the Richard Ivey School of Business at the University of Western Ontario believes:

Unilever is a company with many brands and many brand management teams. Each team manages its brand according to the brand position and the needs and wants of the target market. Dove and Axe both cater to viable market segments, but some consumers may deem them to be incompatible, and that can be a source of criticism for Dove. The genius of the Dove campaign was to take such criticism in its stride, as long as it further fed the marketplace conversation about Dove. In a new media environment, that is gold—to be part of peer-to-peer consumer conversation.[30]

Brand Serendipity: The Unintended and Unexpected Favorable Consequences of Adopting a Wiki Strategy

Some benefits from wikibrands can't be planned or counted on; they just happen. Galvanizing employee interest, seeding far-reaching traditional media interest, being recognized for corporate social responsibility efforts, and creating a web of emotional and captivating customer stories and inspiration are just some of these loosely definable benefits. When efforts hit the right tone at the right time with the right people, wikibrand "wildfire" can occur. Like wildfire, you rarely can predict where it will happen, it usually pops up in unsuspecting places, you frequently cannot control it, but when it happens, it might travel far and impact lives.

No example of brand serendipity and its impact on the war between traditional and new brand approaches is as powerful as that of Mentos and Diet Coke. Cult mint brand Mentos grew its sales by more than 20 percent in 2006 based principally on the engagement and encouragement of user-generated content from funnymen Fritz Grobe and Stephen Voltz and their legions of more than ten million "Mentos-Coke fountain geyser" imitators, fans, and gawkers.[31]

This explosive viral phenomenon was created without an elaborate marketing plan, studio production, or even direction from the brand owners. Whereas Mentos embraced the stunt and fanned the flames of consumer-generated word of mouth, Coca-Cola was standoffish, defending brand purity before eventually jumping on board. Coke's early official reaction included the statements: "We would hope people would want to drink Diet Coke more than try experiments with it," and "The craziness of Mentos doesn't fit with our brand personality."[32]

After months of watching the marketplace's explosive, positive reaction to the alchemical stunt, Tim Kopp, Coca-Cola's vice president of global marketing, provided a turnabout reaction, explaining, "Initially, we didn't have anything to do with the Diet Coke/Mentos video, but the next thing you know, it's on talk shows and all over the Internet. It [viral marketing] will happen with or without you. We really do take it seriously, and we are absolutely committed to reinventing marketing." [33]

On a personal note, when we began this book project, even before we set up a website, we launched a Facebook page, pleased by the fact that twelve hundred people—many from the technology thought leader community— quickly joined. In addition to offering a place for us to test out new material and models with a group of very smart people, it provides a built-in audience for the finished product.

CHAPTER 5

A WIKIBRAND CULTURE

Changing Your Mind-Set About the Brand Customer

Social media acts as an accelerant for good news about a brand as well as bad. Some marketers who are puzzled as to why someone would spend time trashing their brand or wonder how to compensate fans for participating in their brand do not understand the phenomenon. In most cases, winning the contest (and building *their* brand) is more important to fans than a token monetary prize. Even in the case of Frito-Lay, where the winner of a contest to name a new Doritos flavor won $25,000 plus one percent of sales in perpetuity, the prize was probably not as valuable to the winner (a group called Boo Ya Pictures whose "Scream Cheese" was chosen from more than two thousand entries)[2] as the prestige of having their creativity recognized. The exercise was a good investment for Frito-Lay, especially since the company received the creative input of all the other entrants who provided their talent and enthusiasm.

The key point is that everyone has a different concept of what "wasting time" means.

The "United Breaks Guitars" phenomenon is well documented. The short version of the story is that a clever video with outstanding

> "The power is with the consumer. Consumers are beginning, in a very real sense, to own our brands and participate in their creation. We need to learn to begin to "let go" and embrace trends like commercials created by consumers and online communities built around favorite products."[1]
>
> —A. G. LAFLEY, *former CEO, Procter & Gamble*

production value (even though it was created with only $150 and some wonderful volunteer talent) described how a checked Taylor guitar belonging to Dave Carroll was broken by baggage handlers in the United Airlines terminal. The video has been viewed more than nine million times, and Carroll's band, the Sons of Maxwell, has been elevated from a talented but relatively unknown group to a much bigger deal. The song from the video reached number one on the country charts in the United Kingdom, its iTunes sales skyrocketed, and Dave was overwhelmed with media requests. One of his friends took time off from his job to help with the requests, and Dave was flabbergasted when he put Bob Taylor of Taylor Guitars on hold to take another call. Dave told us, "For a musician, it was like putting God on hold. My friend shrugged and said, 'David Letterman's people are on the other line.'" [3]

Dave eventually spoke with representatives from Taylor and was delighted that they offered to repair the guitar. After the success of the first video, United offered to compensate Dave for the damage as well, but he declined, since "negotiations were over, and I'd already agreed to write a trilogy of songs about the experience." [4] He suggested that the company make a contribution to charity instead. So United elected to make a "goodwill donation" of $3,000 to the Thelonious Monk Institute of Jazz. [5]

The second video in the trilogy was viewed more than a million times and offered suggestions about how United could have handled the situation differently and how Dave and "Ms. Irlweg," the reluctant celebrity who gave the final no to his request for compensation, could have been friends. The third video focused on how United's pledge to change was not yet visible. It received less attention than the first two, but context is important. The third video still garnered more than a hundred thousand views; a result that would thrill most independent musicians.

Aside from the huge jump in his success as a musician, Dave has become a customer advocate. Thousands of people have e-mailed him stories about their frustrations with airlines and other companies. He has started an advisory firm that helps companies listen to their customers and lectures frequently about his experience as a frustrated customer and Internet sensation. On the way to one of his speaking gigs, United lost his luggage. You can't make this stuff up.

In the end, United executives met with Dave. He was impressed with their apology; he appreciated that they said they were "sorry" rather than using less sincere verbiage like "regrets." He was also pleased that they changed their policy so musicians may now bring their instruments on board United flights. [6]

But you probably already knew the Taylor Guitar story. The oeuvre of jrdmovimkr, an artist who makes fantastic stop-motion videos may have slipped under your radar. His medium? Lego. Search YouTube for "White and Nerdy and Lego" and you will find a shot-by-shot tribute to "Weird Al" Yankovic's clever music video. jrdmovimkr's work has been viewed more than 3.7 million times on YouTube. For an even more impressive piece of art, search for "Lego Matrix Trilogy," a spectacular re-creation of a scene from the original *Matrix* movie. The artist spent 440 hours creating the eighty-four-second video, which has been watched more than 1.5 million times.

The success of witty, self-created videos on YouTube isn't political or dependent on how rich, connected, or good-looking the creators are—the medium is a meritocracy. Constance Steinkuehler is an assistant professor in the educational communications and technology program of the curriculum and instruction department at the University of Wisconsin–Madison. She says, "It's probably hard to overestimate how much it means to have some of your physical appearance removed. People differentiate themselves and become popular through wit online—being funny, being clever, and being good at what they do. So it replaces the notion of popularity based on looks and wealth (the rich kids are the popular kids and the ones who can afford all the tutoring and extracurricular activities that gets them ahead) with a real meritocracy."[7] If your work is clever and entertaining, it will gain acclaim and you will be famous, at least in the online world and probably for more than fifteen minutes.

You can ask the creators of the Potter Puppet Pals, who post skits based on the denizens of Hogwarts. Their most popular video has been viewed more than eighty million times. Eighty million people, by the way, would be enough to qualify a country as the fifteenth most populous in the world.

Many people are puzzled by how Simon Pulsifer spends his time. One of Wikipedia's most prolific editors, Pulsifer has created or improved more than 106,000 entries.[8] He doesn't consider his Wikipedia activity a waste of time; rather, it's how he relaxes. He also denies that he misses out on a social life; his just manifests in a different way as he interacts with people he considers to be some of the smartest and most interesting in the world. Reading (and writing) an encyclopedia supports his insatiable search for knowledge. Similar to jrdmovimkr and the Sons of Maxwell, Pulsifer enjoys his own version of celebrity. He has his own well-crafted Wikipedia page, which he wasn't involved in creating and has never edited, following the website's rules against self-promotion. Like all Wikipedia's editors, Pulsifer is a volunteer, but his notoriety led to a job offer and numerous speaking engagements. He was featured, along with Wikipedia founder Jimmy Wales, in the issue of *Time* that featured "You" as its Person of the Year.

The following sections will discuss six key ways in which the concept of brand is changing.

Brand Engagement: Moving from Control to Collaboration

In 2007, Absolut Vodka retired its iconic "bottle" print ad campaign after twenty-five successful years and more than fifteen hundred executions. The decision was entirely reasonable. Nina Villsik, Absolut's director of marketing explains, "Our consumers say they want interaction, they want to get inspired, they want to get involved. The media landscape has changed so much. Only ten years ago, we could reach all of our consumers in print. That is not possible today. You need to talk to them in an entirely different way."[9]

Revelations like these are being repeated in executive, marketing, and agency boardrooms around the world. Engagement, interaction, user-generated content, and citizen marketing are the new building blocks of the wikibrand economy.

A new generation of Web-enabled marketers, with a roster of new technologies and tactics, has tapped into what entertainment acts, sports teams, religions, political movements, and various innovative marketers like those for Harley-Davidson, Wheaties, Ben & Jerry's, Converse, and Saturn have known for some time: people value the time they spend engaging with family, friends, and, yes, even brands.

Wikibranding requires a shift in company focus from top-down consumer communication to consumer collaboration. Consequently, a marketer's job is becoming less about what to communicate and more about how to engage people. In this new brand paradigm, customers become less like the objects of your communication, predisposed to being targeted and conquered, and more like extensions of your company, ambassadors with valuable insights and enthusiasm to contribute to brand value.

Some business leaders argue persuasively that customers do not want to engage with brands, believing that consumers are tired, cynical, and overwhelmed by them. In some cases, this viewpoint is not misguided. After all, not many people desire a deep relationship with their dishwashing soap. However, three significant caveats suggest that marketers who follow "brand burnout" theory will do so at their peril:

1. Passion for brand engagement and collaboration is not evenly distributed across the entire consumer population; rather, it is concentrated in small pockets of activist consumers whose influence can sway public opinion. Research shows that 1 percent of a target audience typically creates a majority of the content and interaction; 10 percent typically trades, contributes, and spreads it; and most of the remainder merely consumes it.[10] This reality can lead business decision makers to believe the influence of user collaboration is a niche, or fringe, activity with little impact on their core markets. But these 1 and 10 percenters blaze trails of enormous influence and make it their business to market to others.

2. Historically, marketers have not been very good at incubating brand engagement, so it's not surprising that consumers are cynical. Real brand engagement requires a different platform, skill set, and orientation than what traditional marketers have been taught. A conversation cannot happen unless companies and customers talk and listen to each other as equal partners. Marketers may believe they are producing engagement by spending money on researching and polling consumers, offering forums on their website, or providing viral advertising for public consumption, but this falls well short of real consumer engagement. What's missing is a relationship and feedback loop.

   Watch out: when consumers feel they are being superficially involved in conversation, they tune out quickly or, even worse, engage in negative behavior directed at the brand. This phenomenon was witnessed by the negative reaction to the Chevy Tahoe consumer-generated ad competition in 2006, where people overlaid the provided video of the product with audio illustrating its negative impact on the environment.[11]

3. Collaboration with brands is a core trait of the Net Generation. It should come as no surprise that the initial surge of popularity of social networks MySpace and Facebook began with concentrated groups of young people focusing on their key interests: music and university friends. The marketer's new role is to get this group's involvement in motion, start the conversation, get out of the way (although not completely), and let members talk and produce. As their generational influence widens, so will widespread digitally enabled activism across all age groups.

By open sourcing the involvement of customers in the development and execution of advertising, marketing, and operational initiatives, companies can also develop better real-world insights, produce superior products, and incubate word-of-mouth evangelism among these participants.

Many big brand marketers have yet to embrace or internalize this thinking. On the contrary, in a Brandchannel survey, senior marketers viewed "consistency" and "message/communication" as the key elements of strong branding.[12] Meanwhile, "relevance," "key stakeholder buy-in," and "connection to customers" appeared much further down the list. As if to dispel this misunderstanding in one fell swoop, an upstart maverick rose from the ashes of Netscape. Mozilla Firefox has brought the concept of brand engagement full circle and proved its worth as a core business driver.

Mozilla Firefox is an open source, peer-to-peer marketing pioneer with approximately 25 percent of global online browser users;[13] it is driven principally through the power of its developer and enthusiast audience. Since 2004, its most passionate adopters have congregated online at Spread Firefox.com and actively put themselves to work. The company reports that there are more than 350 million users of Firefox around the world.[14] As the highest tribute to the power of brand engagement, 30 percent of the code for its Firefox browser was built by its network of unpaid contributors. Firefox chairperson Mitchell Baker observes, "We want users to feel involved from the very beginning and not [for us] to be controlling. When users get involved, something magical happens."[15]

Asa Dotzler, head of community development, enthusiastically adds, "It starts with a genuine Firefox mission of building, above all else, the best experience for the Internet user possible. We then provide the infrastructure, leadership, and support to empower users to get involved in this cause."[16] This is no platitude—a volunteer community of five hundred thousand people is engaged in a wide range of Mozilla activities:

▷ **The Mozilla Developer Center:** An open source developer platform focused on building and testing new code and reporting bugs and feedback

▷ **SpreadFirefox.com:** The home of Firefox community marketing and a base for evangelists around the world to promote and support community development and localization efforts

▷ **Get Firefox:** An exposure-building referral program that acclaims the world's very best referrers

▷ **Firefox Flicks:** A user-generated, content-driven site where submitters post their best thirty-second video clips expressing the virtues of Firefox

▷ **For the Record team:** A quick and mobilized group of advocates to defend and debunk media buzz

▷ **Firefox Got Your Back:** A community pixel wall of member profiles

At the risk of appearing like the brand "barn doors" have been completely thrown open, Dotzler emphasizes that the community has developed as a "meritocratic hierarchy—the more you engage, the bigger your reputation, the more you're given access, and the more you're listened to."[17]

This self-governing community system feeds the curiosity, passion, status-seeking ego, and sociability of its "ambassadors" who, as unpaid members of the Mozilla community, can approve new developments, speak to the press, and host parties on behalf of Mozilla. It also allows Firefox to compete effectively on a threadbare budget. This is significant given that Microsoft spent $500 million launching the Vista browser alone.

How deeply engaged is the Mozilla community? A large percentage of the site's original employees were experts, enthusiasts, and hackers who joined the firm's evangelist communities. A group of Oregon students created a 45,000-foot crop circle of the Firefox logo. Another advocate tattooed the logo on his head. Incredibly, thousands of the top Firefox referrers also became donors to underwrite a two-page ad in the *New York Times*, spurring further Firefox adoption and buzz. Similar fund-raising programs have been developed in other Firefox geographies around the world.[18]

For those wanting to replicate this kind of success, here are some key questions Mozilla regularly poses before pursuing a course of action:[19]

▷ Will our developments truly benefit our users (as opposed to merely serving our company)?
▷ Will the product enrich users' experience and not mess up what's already working for them?
▷ Does what we're doing have consensus among our community of users?
▷ Is our behavior consistent with the values of our audience?
▷ Have we maximized the amount of authenticity and transparency to deliver participation, accountability, and trust?
▷ Are we letting our passion show? (It's all right to be eager and occasionally wrong because of it.)
▷ Do we start with these questions to our audience, "What do you think and why?" and "What value could we provide you?"

Brand Orientation: From Communications Genius to Customer Experience Management

The ascendancy of creative strategy and the communications genius has ruled the marketing hallways for a good half century. CEOs have routinely looked at marketing as the "advertising and promotion" department. While a strong and consistent viewpoint on brand essence and design consistency is still very important, significant value is no longer generated by slavish adherence to repetitive selling lines, increased media frequency, or brash creative.

This transition from communications genius to customer experience management implies managing each and every touchpoint as an organizational branding strategy and helping to elevate the brand role played by front-line company staff and key customer experience partners. Successful brands will reflect their brand culture and consistency in each important interaction between company, consumer, and brand—from consideration stage to purchase environment, to delivery and distribution, to receipt of product, to product use and post-product service—via customization and the overall impact of the customer experience.

Providing superior engagement at each stage of a customer's experience is already a key discussion point at boardroom tables. This discussion is quickly becoming one of brand. If they are to own customer engagement, however, marketers will need to become generalists in orientation and much more invested in facilitating dialogue. Expertise in the development of better branded experiences will need to reach deep into company functions. Improved real-time and collaborative systems and incentives will need to grease the internal "collaboration wheels," bringing down structural and behavioral barriers that currently exist in firms that are organized into silos.

Starbucks has courted coffee drinkers and converted them into repeat customers by expertly managing the brand experience. With more than 17,000 stores and 128,000 employees spread across fifty-five countries, maintaining a consistently authentic brand experience is no small challenge.[20]

Rather than applying an army of tactics that do little to support the product, Starbucks has understood and executed its brand deftly through experience. Joe Pine, the author of many excellent business books, told us, "Starbucks innovated a scalable coffee-drinking experience, taking beans worth $0.02 to $0.04 per cup and creating an experience worth $2.00 to $4.00 per cup. It created places with a unique ambience and a process with a distinct sense of theater that engages people and gets them to spend time with the company—the true currency of the 'experience economy.'"[21]

The heartfelt association loyal customers feel with Starbucks has little to do with its scant print and outdoor advertising around key commuting locations. Rather, its success stems from the experiences and associations of indulgence, craftsmanship, and the comfort of a "third place" that Starbucks deliberately fosters. It keeps customers coming back with habitual predictability; its average patron will return more than twenty times a month.[22]

As Mary Graham, Starbucks' vice president of marketing, sees it, "We're not selling transactions; we're in the business of interactions." She suggests that the reason consumers keep coming back and paying much more than the commodity value of the product is rooted in the authenticity of the company's values. These are brought to life every day for its customers and reflected by everyone from the company's top executives to its baristas:

> Passion to improve the world, a daily inspiration, an uplifting experience, and core motivation to produce and sell great coffee are our reason[s] for being. Creating this theater is reinforced by expertly trained staff; a welcoming in-store environment; and a combined sensory experience of music, coffee aroma, and great taste. You'll also note that whether you're just passing time or having a long business meeting, you never get the feeling your time is up in Starbucks; it just wouldn't happen.
>
> Although anything but coffee is clearly secondary—our music, books, and programs appeal to our audience as a cultural portal to experience new things and support the brand experience goal of creating memorable moments of discovery—this discovery appetite is also why we spend enormous organizational effort on developing, training, and producing eleven new product-based programs each year. [23]

Graham confesses that the ability to achieve success in a fast-moving company with an increasingly demanding consumer base relies on a nexus of international task forces, global teams, and local commercial groups to build a consistent and relevant experience. She emphasizes, "We must always remember we're not in the coffee business selling to people; we're in the people business serving coffee." [24]

As opposed to spending large amounts of money on mainstream advertising that lists its values, Starbucks lives its values by providing good deeds, although this is a somewhat unseen and underappreciated part of the overall company experience. A full 4 percent of pretax earnings finances social responsibility programs for causes such as promoting the environment and literacy.

MyStarbucksIdea is a crowdsourcing program that encourages the public to make suggestions about products, promotions, and operations. It has been a major success, collecting, by most counts, seventy-five thousand ideas in the first six months of operation and winning a Groundswell Award from Forrester Research. BillMac, one of the community members, came up with the idea that each voter in the presidential election of 2008 would receive a free cup of coffee. A sixty-second ad about the program appeared on "Saturday Night Live," then was viewed by more than 480,000 people on

YouTube. The awareness generated by the idea was impressive, even though the concept turned out to be illegal (it is against the law to provide an incentive for voting).[25]

Denis Hancock, the research director of nGenera's Marketing Insight program, says:

What Starbucks implicitly understands is that building a wikibrand isn't necessarily about the wisdom of crowds. Instead, it is often about leveraging the insights and contributions from a few uniquely qualified minds within the crowd, if (and when) it fits into the company's strategic objectives. While the BillMac idea got a few votes from the community, there were many others that had many more votes at the time when his was selected. But this one fit nicely with the company's overall branding objectives and the mood of the nation at the time. Starbucks selected it; explained why on its Ideas in Action blog (crediting Bill and those who had voted for it); and then used platforms like YouTube, Facebook, and Twitter to get the message out in a very cost-effective manner. That they could source a great idea so easily and communicate it to millions so cheaply (and quickly) is exactly what marketers should be thinking about when considering their own social media strategies.[26]

Brand Tone: From Incentive, Hype, and Branding to Authenticity, Transparency, and Idea Planting

In daily life, we are attracted to people who are trustworthy, have integrity, tell the truth, are modest, make us feel important, and are entertaining. In a world where collaboration is a tenet of social, work, and educational life, brands need to play by the same relationship rules.

Wikibranding places a premium on authenticity and transparency. Consumer cunning and filtering tools are increasingly screening out hyped-up messaging and "carrot-and-stick" brand incentive schemes. A rise in public activism, aided by investigative citizen bloggers and journalists, has caused consumers to banish untrustworthy companies from their brand consideration set, shopping bags, and investment portfolios.

Engaged customers want openness in their dealings with companies. With their current level of connectedness, they can police and govern cloak-and-dagger marketers more easily than ever before. In a business environment where little can be hidden, the idea of openly sharing knowledge about the inner workings of a brand, warts and all, seems considerably less frightening than the headline-stealing leak of an embarrassing internal memo.

Authenticity is important while building a brand; building an inauthentic grassroots campaign (known as *astroturfing*, as in fake grass) is usually counterproductive. The blogosphere is very good at spotting a fake, such as when Sony promoted the PlayStation Portable in various American cities by hiring graffiti artists to spray buildings with images of people playing with the device.[27] Local graffiti artists fought back with tags of their own, including "Fony" and "Get out of my city." Sony ran into similar problems the following Christmas when its advertising agency staged a guerrilla marketing campaign in which its representatives posed as young bloggers desperate for a PSP.

The development of corporate blogs, sponsored forums, video uploads, and virtual-world universes has enabled some companies to bypass media filters altogether and connect directly with their intended audiences. The early returns of this approach are promising, but companies must be fully transparent to realize the benefits. Disclosure of one's identity, intentions, and relationships is a baseline requirement.

At the same time, the key to commanding any kind of sustainable price premium in a marketplace in which people are actively trading up and down and product-based differences are being marginalized is to authentically provoke passion and improve customers' everyday lives. Wikibrand marketers are redefining the purpose of their brands by helping their customers congregate around ideas and issues, transcending product features and elevating their brands as touchstones of culture and opinion that audiences can shape and own for themselves.

For some companies, a new wikibrand tone requires a 180-degree shift in the use of brand assets and information. The implications are significant and include rewarding openness, removing hurdles that separate companies and their employees from their audiences, achieving authenticity in motives and practices, creating new customer-centric forums, and implanting ideas for a passionate discussion around the brand that will make people want to participate.

The Marketer's Changing Role: From Decision Maker to Dialogue Facilitator

Thanks to the expansion and sophistication of sales functions, organizational customer relationship management (CRM) programs, customer service, and e-commerce/online groups, conventional marketers are often seen as out of step with both the consumer and the rest of the company. Even so, old-school marketers are still given the keys to the final brand decisions, and this is problematic.

Wells Fargo's chief marketing officer, Sylvia Reynolds, has christened marketing and the decisions remaining in its bailiwick the "make it look pretty" department.[28] Although brand expression rests with marketing, the department and its agencies tend to develop creative ideas far removed from the customer experience. The result is that 80 percent of present-day marketers don't influence a critical customer service function.[29] To provide organizational value, the traditional roles of marketer and supporting agency will need to change fundamentally.

The Role of Brand Positioning: From External to Internal

Traditionally, brand positioning statements have driven marketing communications and enabled companies to manage customer perceptions. Now, as organizations become more transparent, the core associations emanating from a brand will increasingly be derived from the firm's own internal philosophy and business dealings. This may be problematic for companies with skeletons in the closet or whose portfolios contain brands with competing values.

Under the wikibrand model, positioning statements will continue to affect the internal values and guidelines to which a company adheres. In the future, a brand positioning statement will be as helpful in governing key internal processes—such as employee recruitment, performance management, and desirable company practices and behavior—as for guiding external communications.

Vancity is Canada's largest credit union, with $14.4 billion in assets, more than 414,000 members, and fifty-nine branches throughout Greater Vancouver, the Fraser Valley, and Victoria. Its successful brand is based on a corporate culture guided by a commitment to improving the quality of life in the communities it serves.[30] Broadcasting its brand values and leadership is more an announcement of its "heart characteristics" than any form of strategic campaign. The organization is as interested in making its community work as it is in making money. Adherence to its principles has generated positive publicity in the form of its rank as the second-most respected company in British Columbia and the best workplace in Canada, according to *Canadian Business* magazine.[31] As a complement to its advertising campaign, Vancity has also established an online community called ChangeEverything.ca, a site for people in Vancouver, Victoria, and the Lower British Columbia Mainland who want to change themselves, their communities, or their world. This extends the company's real-world community orientation to the Web.

As part of what is perhaps the first cause-related social network ever sponsored by a financial services company, ChangeEverything.ca links people and causes that might never otherwise connect. Instead of discussing mortgage or investment rates, users actively participate in collaborative efforts to improve life by discussing initiatives online in tags and postings. One blog post within the community led to a campaign called Got Socks, in which Vancity branches were used to collect socks for the homeless population of Vancouver.

The credit union's director of web engagement and branding, William Azaroff, notes, "All social Web projects should start with being authentic and honest. Members of ChangeEverything don't have to be bank customers, and Vancity's branding is intentionally minimal. We don't want this to be a vehicle we can monetize, but hopefully, it can get people to think about genuine change. Indirectly, if during the process they consider financial security, that's great too." [32]

Vancity is putting its money where its mouth is. As part of its environmental plan, it has established a mission to become carbon neutral. It has also provided a platform for one of its customers, EnviroWoman, to tell the story of her quest to remove plastics from her life. As part of its social responsibility plan, Vancity provides a rigorous social audit of itself every year, returning 30 percent of net profits to members and local communities. More than twenty-six hundred nonprofit organizations have received more than $46 million in grants and community contributions since the credit union's launch in 1994. Internal brand positioning that aligns with integrity and collaboration can indirectly produce large returns. Not surprisingly, Vancity's membership continues to grow at a healthy pace.

Brand Monitoring: From Counting the Eyeballs and Clicks to Putting an Ear to the Ground

To a traditional-age marketer, the concept of listening may sound motherly and granola, but you must know by now that it's critically important to an engaged business. Our 2010 "The Buzz Report" suggests that of sixteen different elements, "Not listening—not staying tuned in and responding to what members/customers want quickly" was considered the *biggest sin* for not building an engaged, collaborative business. More than 53 percent of our panel ranked the seemingly simple act of listening as the first step and top ingredient for doing well in social business.[33]

Marcel Lebrun, CEO of Radian6, understands this world well. His company records, tracks, and measures these "digital bread crumbs" of conversation through Twitter, blogs, and forums, to help change how companies are organized and how they communicate. He mentions that listening has a "yellow brick road of maturity from listening to responding to participating to sharing your story and contributing. The key principle being: don't start saying before you understand."[34]

Organizational behavior experts will tell you that changing company culture is sometimes a difficult effort to shepherd; it can move slowly and can be tough to maintain. Contemplating structural changes in how organizations (of any size) work is a must. Opening up to brand conversation/engagement practices, building a stronger customer experiential orientation, establishing a more transparent external tone, encouraging dialogue-driven customer departments, creating an internal culture that lives the brand, and fostering a responsive listening culture across the organization are the antecedents of a wikibrand strategy and practice. With a commitment to getting these conditions in place, choosing appropriate wikibrand strategies and tactics is the next step.

THE FLIRT MODEL— BUILDING A WIKIBRAND

FOCUS

If I Don't Know Where You're Going, I Don't Want You Getting There Fast

Imagine the small ripple of a movement that starts with thirty close friends and is then embraced and evangelized by an army of thousands of men globally, all galvanized by the same idea. A powerful blend of social activity and testosterone—that is exactly what happened with Movember, a word-of-mouth juggernaut and a charity dedicated to raising the profile of and much-needed funds to fight prostate cancer worldwide. Australian founder of Movember Adam Garone humbly remarks, "Movember grew sort of by accident, but we always had a clear mission from the beginning of changing the way men think about, discuss, and treat their own health issues. We also wanted to create a charity experience that didn't count on a big celebrity, a megawealthy individual, or a corporate cause—to provide a new role model for how not-for-profits and fund-raising work.

"Back in 2003, when we started, and even now, when we expand into new countries, we've had to rely on a small, passionate base of guys who buy into our mission deeply and spread it with conviction, originally through face-to-face and now accelerated through

"Tossing up a brand community without an understanding of the general concepts, specifics of your mission, and needs of your participants is a shot in the dark."[1]

—JENNY AMBROZEK,
founder, Sagenet

social media."[2] Even in a difficult economic environment, a simple, clearly stated and passionately felt business objective and purpose has helped Movember raise more than $100 million for prostate cancer worldwide and still grow at a clip of 48 percent annually.[3]

Noble missions are one thing, but Garone readily admits that fund-raising is one of the most competitive, political, and crowded industries around. Why did Movember take off while other worthy charities fail? Owning a simple, iconic community idea that people understood eas-ily and found motivating was a special ingredient. The initial, irreverent idea was to "bring the moustache back" and use it to give men the "door opener"; a tangible reason to talk about and raise awareness of health issues as women have done so successfully with breast cancer and the pink ribbon over the last couple of decades. The moustache, a popular mark of 1970s culture, had lost favor. Movember's vision was to revive the mous-tache and make it *the* icon for prostate cancer.

The method for raising funds in Movember's world is to get regular guys, grassroots Influencers, and concerned others to grow moustaches—or a "Mo"—over the month of November. Garone remarks, "Initially, we didn't know how broad or how global this idea of growing a moustache was going to be. It's a huge task, not only to get people to raise money, but to also get them to change their appearance, particularly men. But regardless of country, stockbrokers, designers, military personnel, policemen, techies, and office workers all enthusiastically embraced our Movember cause and, perhaps, this larger shared idea of reclaiming masculinity and showing the women in our lives that men do care."[4]

The community motivation is so powerful that fully 88 percent of partic-ipants consider getting a checkup during the campaign, and 82 percent of normally tight-lipped male campaign participants talk about men's health issues with people around them as a result of Movember involvement.[5]

Movember has also developed an exceptionally clear understanding of its stakeholders that, at its core, began with highly socialized members of the hospitality, technology, creative/design, and surf/skateboard indus-tries. The organization realized these participants get involved for three different reasons:

▷ **For a good cause:** Given that one in six men will be diagnosed with prostate cancer, people typically have first- or second-degree exposure to the cause. Movember provides a simple mechanism and validation for growing a mustache, which they would otherwise find difficult to justify.

▷ **Social acceptance/sense of togetherness:** By participating in a very public display of support online and offline, men feel they are bonded as a group to a larger cause.

▷ **Fun:** It's about the friendly conversation, banter, and reactions among people during the course of the campaign, while encouraging men to tell their stories online through video.

Through online stories and offline experiences, the Movember team has reinforced and strengthened these motivational elements.

Finally, Movember's team and company culture zealously embraces what it does at every touchpoint. Even with a small office of people, Garone says, "We have a clear philosophy that every Mo Bro counts. We want to make them heroes; they become our champions. It's not about the number of people we engage but how engaged they are and, consequently, how engaged we are."[6] Movember's team reinforces its focus in practice every day, whether it's using social media as a tool to build relationships; using Facebook post templates, e-mails, and tweets to spread the news easily; limiting pressure on its database by having no minimum fund-raising standards so people feel comfortable; or never underestimating the power of even one customer interaction by actively listening and responding to each post. It's why four hundred thousand men will gladly grow a (perhaps not great-looking) moustache this November and are stoked about doing it.

Movember's continuing expansion and global success has three important lessons for their peer not-for-profit organizations and for-profit peers:

1. Having a precision level of focus is required for wikibrands to cut through the muck and clutter of a competitive marketplace.
2. A smart focus needs to consider business objectives, a motivating community idea, a solid understanding of customer and stakeholder interests, and an organizational alignment of resources committed to succeed.
3. Looking at a brand through a different prism—more as a cause than as a collection of products or attributes—is extremely powerful.

Taming the Wild West of the Social Web and an Appeal to Reason

Although later chapters in this book will describe a variety of wikibrand principles and tools that operate much differently than traditional business practices, being strategically smart isn't one of them. Having a smart strategy, an effective planning process, an understanding of your organization's capability, and expert insight into the customer is still as integral to the wikibrand world as it has been to corporate circles throughout history.

Designing effective, engaged businesses for today's marketplace—whether it's a pilot program of 150 members, a grassroots brand initiative of 5,000 members, or a customer community of millions of people—is an essential skill that CEOs, CMOs, and their organizations must master. It takes strategically sound guidance, an aligned company effort, and smart relevant tools. In truth, even some of the most well-intended wikibrand efforts are doomed to fail before they even get off the tarmac for lack of intelligent focus.

From a traditionalist critique, organizations approaching social Web initiatives are using overly aggressive expectations, rigorous standards, and simplistic views on what customer audience they're serving. European-based engagement marketing expert Alan Moore, co-author of *Communities Dominate Brands*, sums up the issue: "We've tried to put the furniture of previous media online. It simply doesn't work. We need companies to become more permeable and flexible to absorb flows of information and people. Organizations need to adapt more quickly and become more organic in thought and deed. A new culture needs to exist that requires a different type of customer intelligence that informs our judgment and accommodates not only behavioral and demographic intelligence, but also social intelligence to tap the true value of a networked economy."[7] We liken the traditional way of building strategy to a *focus of stone tablets*—"These are our commandments, so it shall be done." We have seen enough evidence that people resist being preached to in a modern participation economy.

According to the new age media critiques, corporate use of social media has had a dubious track record. An article in *BusinessWeek* titled "Beware Social Media Snake Oil" claims that an entire industry of consultants has arisen to help companies navigate the world of social networks, blogs, and wikis and are leading clients astray.[8] The numbers speak volumes: if you consult Twellow (a type of Yellow Pages for Twitter), more than forty-five thousand people claim to have some level of social media expertise or self-certification; some of them are well qualified, but most are not.[9] A large group of corporations that took the plunge into enterprise 2.0 and social media are now sitting on loads of expensive, uninstalled software. The International Association of Business Communicators (IABC) claims 62 percent of top executives don't use internal social media.[10] Employee adoption of corporate internal social media tools lags far behind the widespread consumer adoption and skyrocketing growth rates on external networking sites like LinkedIn.[11]

Many popular social Web advocates issue platitudes such as "burn the ships," "unlearn your ways," and "your customers rule," looking at the rest of the world as Luddites who don't quite get it. We liken their method of strategizing for success to a *focus of Etch A Sketch*—"Let's shake everything up, erase, and start over." In most business environments, this type of approach lacks practicality, leads to resistance, and develops organizational silos. We actually think building a true wikibrand focus should be more like *Silly Putty*—pliable, malleable, influenced by user input, but still with some very identifiable traits.

When it comes to the social Web, it has become a bit like the Wild West. Technology companies are selling collaborative platforms, and why not? With a global IT industry accelerating past $1.6 trillion, there's social gold in those hills. Established Web firms IBM, Microsoft, and Oracle have entered the space with their own software platforms. The Software as a Service (SaaS) companies such as Jive, Socialtext, Lithium, and Kickapps are showing double-digit growth, with content, communication, collaboration, and customer relationship platforms leading the way. Open source content management systems like Joomla and Drupal are also becoming the darlings of independent Web developers. Communication agencies are rushing to cash in out of either crisis or growth prospects. Social media hothouses are mushrooming up, tapping into the zeitgeist of a marketplace that can't talk enough about "social media." Consulting companies are cashing in. Staffing and promotion companies are trying to backward-engineer the digital experience. The trend toward outsourcing to other firms is enhancing the boom of external experts. In the race to mine this new frontier from all sides, one of the unfortunate residual effects is that little time or talent is being spent on creating an appropriate strategic focus for these efforts. Engagement expertise on the social Web is being separated from people who work inside the companies, causing a lot of square peg strategies with round hole solutions.

Poor strategy plays an equal part in the failures of engaged business building, on a par with bad execution and misapplied technology. In our annual survey of trends, beliefs, and opinions, we queried top marketers and media and digital executives about where people go wrong in new media. Lack of "strategic focus" and "customer focus" were the third- and fourth-biggest sins in building social media and online communities/business-customer collaborations (behind "listening/responsiveness" and "engaging content," which we will cover in subsequent chapters). If there is anything both wikibrand adopters and the gray-haired traditional establishment should be able to agree on, it is that bad strategies equal bad plans.

Adoption issues and silos are two of the big hurdles in getting companies to move in the right direction of customer engagement. Here are some common objections posed by critics:

▷ "This feels more like play than work."
▷ "We wouldn't be open to that; our culture won't accept it."
▷ "We just don't have money for this."
▷ "I question the value of this for our business."
▷ "Unless IT/legal/executives buy in, this is going nowhere."
▷ "Let's keep this under the radar."
▷ "Who has extra time in the week to do this?"

Wikibranders don't shrink away from resistance easily. Defining a focus and strategy allows you to tackle the executive-level conversation more easily and anticipate objections. Finding executive champions who "get" the social Web can also help translate executive feedback and concerns into a coherent wikibrand direction.

The Conundrum of Why, How, and What

Consultant Simon Sinek presents an interesting thesis in "The Golden Circle." [12] He characterizes the thesis as a simple leadership theorem based on concentric circles, moving from "why" in the center, to "how," and then to "what" on the outer edge. His theory is that most companies operate from the outside to the inside, focusing on what they do ("We are in the technology business." "We sell cheese." "We market hedge funds.") instead of why they do it.

He suggests that larger, successful companies—such as Apple, Patagonia, and BMW—and many impressive smaller ones operate from the inside outward. In the face of a fairly even playing field of access to resources, funding, and people, they recognize that customers make purchase decisions, employees are motivated to join communities, and media are more willing to publicize companies based on why they do things versus what they produce. It's the reason people wait in line for hours to buy the new Apple product the day it's launched, even though they could wait considerably less time if they purchased it the following week. Can you imagine buying a Toshiba PDA? Probably not. Yet we gladly embraced Apple's launch of the iPod, iPhone, and iPad. It's not what the company normally produces—computers, in Apple's case—but why it does it—"smart, simple, design-friendly technology from and for people who think differently."

In wikibrand circles, this philosophy holds water. The companies and brands that lead in customer collaborative spaces tend to have a driving ethos that makes their people and fans go the extra mile. It's likely why Martin Luther King, Jr., said, "I have a dream," rather than "I have a plan." It's also why Barack Obama rallied around a populist sentiment ("Yes, we can") as opposed to John McCain's roll call of "Reform. Prosperity. Peace." As charismatic and well spoken as these men were, most people didn't buy into their philosophies because of their singular personalities. People bought into ideas that would serve their own best interests.

Given the choice, self-selection, and scrutiny that exist in the collaborative business game, the most successful efforts are based on strong understanding and successful communication of the why. Nike Plus's community partnership effort with Apple for runners asks why joggers run; the companies have built a platform and tracking, social, and competitive applications that build customer commitment. Cisco's One Million Acts of Green asks why people change their habits to take advantage of greener technology and builds a challenge-based environment for members to achieve their goals individually and collectively. Intuit's Love a Local Business asks why people frequent local companies and has built a platform that recognizes and financially rewards top businesses. All of these examples show a range of successful efforts that marry a well-defined why the company got involved to why customers and others got involved.

One overriding question you should ask to build a strong, sustainable wikibrand is "What if our business were a cause?" Forget superior product performance, the funkiest advertising, and the best-positioned set of features. Stripped to its core, what is your brand's defining DNA and raison d'être? What legacy would it leave? What would be the best way to get your audience involved in building that legacy?

A Quick FLIRT Overview: A Primer on Building Wikibrands

Since the art of building brands in a collaborative social sphere is so new, there are few blueprints to follow. As much as we love personal brand examples, they tend to live and breathe based on the whims and passion of their celebrity business leader. These examples are tough to replicate in large corporate settings where there is a great diversity of people involved and so many solutions are required. One promising social brand architecture is Finnish community expert and planner Sami Viitamäki's crowdsourcing model: FLIRT.[13] This model is inspired by, among others, Eric von

Hippel, James Surowiecki, Chris Anderson, and Jeff Howe—thought leaders in the field of collective intelligence. Here, we adapt the FLIRT model for building wikibrands.

We've used FLIRT as an acronym for the strategic, executional, and technological processes involved in building an effective engaged brand. The five elements for building a wikibrand are as follows:

▷ **Focus:** The strategic imperatives of your engagement efforts, in which you also determine the specific areas, depth, scale, and exclusivity of collaboration you want to achieve with your intended community. These organizational and strategic considerations come before you make a single decision about technology or execution.
▷ **Language and content:** The "face," tone, and context in which you present the brand to your potential audience, as well as the stream of posts, apps, e-mails, photos, and video that generate "wow" reaction and sociability.
▷ **Incentives, motivations, and outreach:** The intrinsic, extrinsic, and explicit rewards, motivations, and outputs that members/fans/followers/customers/prospects earn for their participation in the community and the tentacles that extend out to prospective members.
▷ **Rules, guidelines, and rituals:** The explicit laws, general principles, and loose customs and traditions that govern accepted engagement and community brand norms and activity.
▷ **Tools and platform:** The technical infrastructure, collaboration, engagement and community features and activities, and social extensions that optimize user experience and wikibrand performance.

We've added four additional components to the original model to help build a wikibrand as well as maintain one:

▷ **Metrics and insights:** The key measures and feedback required to track progress and support wikibrand investments.
▷ **Internalization of benefits within the organization:** The steps to optimize and bring the value of customer engagement and collaboration inside the company.
▷ **Life cycle of the community:** The phases and recognition of constant maintenance and updates that are required to keep engaged brand communities fresh and organically growing.
▷ **Community management:** The need to staff up for dialogue and exchange and moderate wikibrand activities.

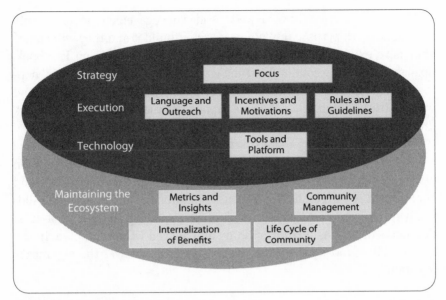

FIGURE 6.1 THE FLIRT MODEL

The FLIRT model, depicted in Figure 6.1, appeals to our intuitive sensibilities in building and sustaining a wikibrand across stages: developing strategy before execution, considering execution before technology choices, and developing technology considerations before wikibrand incubation. Unlike ad campaigns or promotion efforts, wikibrands have a much longer "candlewick." In order to prolong the longevity of effort, the four elements of "maintaining the ecosystem" are critical engagement considerations for engraining success.

Focus

"Any brand's objective is to strike an emotional chord with the consumer, [and] there is no better way than to get them involved in the design and positioning of the brand."

—**GILES POYNER**, *Managing Director, Hollman Group*

Successful wikibrands are built on solid strategies. They have a core business aim, a brand idea that motivates consumers, and links to an organizational culture and capabilities that can support that idea. Perhaps most important, successful wikibrand communities deliver what their prospective members and customers want.

Many organizations have viewed the idea of engagement or community as a tactical, or "perpetual pilot," exercise of "build it and they will come." They have experimented in building profiles or fan pages on Facebook, uploaded Twitter accounts, YouTube channels, and corporate blogs, hoping to achieve customer gratitude, cost-effective database building, and wholly positive interaction. It didn't happen. They learned that things work differently on the collaborative Web.

The task of building a smart strategy for a wikibrand uses the same tenets as the smartest business or operating plan. Any organization worth its salt recognizes that, in a world of unlimited possibilities and constrained resources, having a focus is paramount. It's as true for building a capital asset management plan, an operating budget, or a sales development plan as it is for building an engaged wikibrand plan. In the case of wikibrands, you need to understand and answer the big, meaty questions:

▷ What is the underlying motivation for any engagement strategies and activities? Are we doing this to achieve bottom-line success, operations improvement, or top-line performance?
▷ What are the objectives and goals behind the effort? What will success look like? Will we be happy with ten thousand or a hundred thousand fans or followers, and what does that objective mean?
▷ What efforts will be consistent with our key customer and target customer values and needs?
▷ Does this constitute new spending and incremental new work? Who is going to lead and do this work? How will we resource it incrementally for sustainability?

In the majority of organizations we surveyed, companies that hadn't been diligent enough to define the "why" mission and objective and the "what" strategies behind these initiatives ended up viewing wikibrand efforts as busywork projects that never really impacted how a company transforms its external face—certainly not as a tool to radically embrace audiences and transform internal work operations. Joe Cothrel, chief community officer for Lithium, is wary of these piloting exercises: "Pilots are not always bad, but they should be used to test a larger investment or idea. In too many cases, they are used to kill a project before it can evolve. Getting strategic-level commitment on external communities, even pilot ones, is essential for long-term success."[14]

The best engaged brand performers don't try to bite off too much, at least not all in one place. At Comcast, it's clear: Comcast Cares is all about customer service and remedying customer problems. American Express's business-to-business content platform Open Forum is designed to inform and help small businesses promote themselves and change AMEX's brand perception to that of a company wanting to improve the life and business of small-business owners. Given the wealth of countries, languages, and products that Microsoft supports, the corporation's work in user engagement communities needs to be focused. Microsoft is looking for three very specific wikibrand benefits: (1) product feedback on existing products and emerging issues; (2) brand advocacy among their best Influencers and sharing among their customers; and (3) customer service support on both break-fix issues and individual customer issues.

Before embarking on a wikibrands development and alignment exercise for your situation, let's presume there are a number of preconditions already in place before deciding on a focus. First, we'll assume you are looking at engagement and collaboration as a key corporate driver that warrants the time and effort you will need to devote to it. You see this as a project with longevity and not merely this season's campaign. Note that it is important to get senior management onboard, given the need for sustainability. We will also presume you've already established a strong listening, customer-centric culture as outlined in Chapter 5. Finally, we'll assume that you are planning to build an ecosystem of content, activities, dialogue, and relationships across a number of platforms, including both owned platforms and external communities and networks, which requires making some prudent choices.

Two Cardinal Rules of Focus

Two rules override all others in building a community focus.

Putting Your Focus Before Technology and Tools

Frequently, engagement platform decisions are based on what might be conveniently available through an enterprise-wide technology decision. This is a recipe for failure. Gartner Research predicts that IT-led social media initiatives will only succeed 20 percent of the time and that when these initiatives are led by the business and customer side, success rates more than double.[15]

Even a large $14 billion technology company like EMC understands the idea of building focus before technology. EMC has been able to leverage the power of global genius through its forty-five thousand employees in eighty-five countries; 75 percent of those employees participate actively in their EMC One community.[16] Jamie Pappas, EMC's social media strategist, and Polly Pearson, its brand storyteller, have designed the perfect "open" employment brand through engagement, allowing employees to communicate and socialize both inside and outside the company.

Started in 2007, EMC One is designed for user behavioral paradigms and "make it, break it" strategic agility. EMC is more concerned about collecting use cases that demonstrate the community's value to its audience; supporting the community with five hundred-plus mentors; building a mix of business and social use that creates audience commitment; and linking back to the objective of unleashing employee initiative, creativity, and passion through 2.0 technologies. In EMC's rollouts, the tools are simple at the outset, designed for ease of use (and, importantly, based on user behavior rather than what's sitting on the tech shelf). As proof of its "simple-first" approach, EMC One took only five weeks between technology selection and deployment.[17]

Len Devanna, director of EMC digital media, says, "While most technology implementations require an extensive gathering of requirements and up-front engineering, social software works best when you keep things simple and let the community itself determine how it should evolve."[18] EMC has discovered that hives of users organize around values and efficiencies over time and that technology needs to accommodate these changes gradually. The company's results are tremendous, with 156 active subcommunities on its internal community, seventy-eight thousand registered users of its external customer community, and eighty thousand members on Twitter.[19]

Putting Your Customer Before Your Company

The other danger zone in building a community focus is misplaced priorities. In a profit-driven world, this may seem paradoxical, but wikibrands actually come out ahead by putting customer benefits ahead of their own brand or company needs.

Intuit has built a thriving community for its flagship product Quick-Books based on this principle of putting customers first. Back in 2006, Intuit employees were not even allowed to talk to bloggers. In four short years, they have become the leaders in business-to-business engagement online. The whole idea of the corporation's base community and various appendages like Small Business United and Love a Local Business is to make customers successful wherever they exist online. Kira Wampler, group marketing manager for online engagement, says that Intuit's business goal is to build community by unleashing fans in a positive way.

Customer centricity was rooted in the community development, with four months of intense listening to customers in what the company referred to as "follow me homes"—watching small business owners and their spouses at the kitchen table and analyzing what made small business successful. Wampler mentions that the exercise led to "instant agreement on how we needed to approach our core audience as a company, from top leaders to the front line, and also helped us appreciate feedback and dialogue with customers as our best gift." [20] The results are online communities that have built millions of dollars in value through small business customer and revenue acquisition; millions of unique community visitors per month, with engagement of users ten times the expected average; 40 percent participation rate among new visitors; 90 percent positive impression on promotional community experience; and referral traffic that spends seven times as much time on the site versus the average. [21] These customer-driven efforts have changed Intuit from the outside-in, embedding collaboration into the Intuit infrastructure for building and launching products, heightening employee involvement, and delivering on the real perception among small business owners that Intuit has a genuine stake in making them successful wherever they are. Intuit does not sell within a majority of its community environments, but by exceeding customers' expectations, it achieves its company sales goals anyway.

The Four Focus Legs of the Wikibrands Couch

The failure to answer the fundamental questions "Why are we doing this?" and "What are the key strategies for achieving value?" in customer engagement efforts is putting the proverbial cart before the horse. The critical phase of "focus" in our FLIRT model guides resource allocation, content development, decisions on the types of activities to engage in (online and/ or offline), governance of community, and choices of tools and platforms (owned, earned, shared, external).

Consider a couch as a metaphor for wikibrands. A couch is something many of us spend a lot of time on; it is built for a number of people; it is where we socialize, entertain ourselves, and spend our free time; and it is comfortable. Simple physics suggests that the couch must have four legs;

otherwise, it tilts and the user's experience suffers. In wikibrands, the couch's legs represent the four essential elements of focus.

Not having a *strategic focus* tied to business needs dooms wikibrand experiments to attacks on credibility and criticism of potential business value generation. Not having a *customer focus* that identifies and taps real, deep-seated customer wants, leads to apathy and dashed performance when member or fan expectations go unmet. Not having a *resource focus* that creates a passionate and accountable group of people willing and able to steer customer engagement efforts leads to eventual "ghost towns" of ambivalence, if not criticism of underlying business motives. Not having a *brand focus* leads to a failure to inspire a reaction and generate customer enthusiasm aligned to the rest of your brand and business-building efforts.

The wikibrands that get it right from the outset generate the results. Before committing budget, resources, and risk, they carefully identify and build around the following four legs of the wikibrands couch:

▷ Business objectives and goals
▷ Member/customer values, lifestyle, and desires
▷ Brand community idea and purpose
▷ Organization, culture, and resources

These are the strategic guardrails that guide wikibrand development.

Business Objectives and Goals

Be clear about the purpose of your wikibrand engagement, collaboration, and community efforts. Being viewed as an experiment within the company is not a recipe for long life. A study of brand communities indicated that the prime motivations were (in descending order): innovation, new media/communications publishing, customer care, learning/training, marketing/sales, and product development.[22] Today, with broader participation and social media creep within enterprises, marketing and communication goals are much more likely to drive the use of collaboration and community goals.

Unclear business objectives make it difficult to align the organization and justify performance later. It's easy to pay lip service to this, but when you work within a company of more than fifty employees, it is no longer simply a meeting or a conversation requesting commitment. Wikibrands require a clarity of purpose to ensure that the corporate version of Broken Telephone doesn't take over. One of the biggest problems with brand communities is a mismatch between the objectives for a community and the metrics that the company subsequently tracks.

The temptation to overwhelm the community with multiple objectives is also a mistake. Instead of burdening a single community with every corporate objective, it's better to follow the lead of Dell and Mozilla Firefox: establish multiple community platforms to support different business objectives.

The ability to define business objectives and goals can be adopted directly from company values, mission statements, or operating plans. If time and process allow, interviewing a cross section of your company's leaders can not only help you identify the proper shared objectives and goals, but also build organization-wide commitment, participation, and eventual adoption.

Member/Customer Values, Lifestyle, and Desires

Brands too often focus on the value a community can bring to the company rather than investing in the community itself. Home Depot's digital manager, Nick Ayres, reflects on growing the company's digital orange apron: "You can learn a lot by just paying attention to what's already being said about you. I'm a big fan of approaches that start with customers and their expectations and work toward technology instead of the other way around." [23]

Your first job is to make sure your customers understand the purpose of your community and can get what they want out of it. EMC calls this WIFA (What's in it for the audience?). Brand owners tend to have an exaggerated view of their brand's importance in the world. The reality? There is so much digital noise and competition for attention out there that prospects must immediately be excited about the community or they will leave. Members of online communities vote quickly with their mouse, and you want to ensure that they have an immediate and ongoing positive experience.

The most successful communities listen, observe, and offer a less corporate and more relaxed setting for participation. They also listen to customers and engage them on their own turf, in their own way, to help them solve problems. These communities are transforming strangers into members, members into customers, customers into contributors, and contributors into powerful competitive advantages such as content developers, distributers, and scouts.

With the wealth of online monitoring tools and applications (including both free and paid services), the world is your oyster when it comes down to evaluating your current customer, prospect, Influencer, industry, and cultural ethos. Monitoring conversations about your communities, company, brand, product, and people is a click away. An online distillation of insight is a great first step but, of course, no replacement for live dialogue with your best Influencers or ongoing collaborations with target advocates, both of which can bring insights to life. As a midway point, companies like Communispace have set up effective moderated communities, extending the role of the traditional focus group online to gain insight from an ongoing set of Influencers.

Brand Community Idea and Purpose

If customers don't join and participate in a brand engagement effort, all the money and creativity in the world won't make it a success. But it's a routine mistake to think that wikibrands are entirely about customer-driven motivation.

In a commoditized world, brands are still essential shorthand for products and services. In the past five years, everything the Apple brand touches seems to turn to gold. Ice cream brand Ben & Jerry's was purchased by Unilever nearly a decade ago, yet it still engenders high levels of brand loyalty among its grassroots enthusiasts. And witness the customer reaction to the design overhaul of trusted brand Tropicana; sales dropped 20 percent.[24]

As it is with financial markets, so it is with community building. Brand communities derive value from strong brand differentiation. A starting point for a brand community is the same as for a brand in any media arena—you need to have a well-articulated point of view and a promise that will engage and excite people. Method's People Against Dirty is a great community extension of an already healthy brand. If you don't have a strongly felt brand promise to attract community participants, you can establish one as the basis for your community that may rise above your brand.

If your brand is all about high-quality, luxury products, make sure that the access, services, and tone you use with your community audience reflects that (such as with lululemon's ambassadors). If you make a low involvement or commodity type of product, invest in an idea larger than your brand (such as Dove's Campaign for Real Beauty).

In their book *Made to Stick*, Chip and Dan Heath identified a number of key principles on what made some ideas flourish and not others. We investigated *Made to Stick*'s tenets and reapplied them to building engaged wikibrands:[25, 26]

▷ **Simple:** Find the core of the community and present its essence (for example, WD-40 fan club's pursuit to find more product uses).

▷ **Unexpected:** Grab people's attention by surprising them and exceeding their expectations (as with Skittles open source website).

▷ **Concrete:** Make sure a community cause or mission can be grasped easily and remembered later (such as the website Will It Blend?).

▷ **Credible:** Give a community believability and a reason for existence (as Livestrong does).

▷ **Collaborative:** Get people deeply involved in the community (like open innovation platform InnoCentive).

▷ **Emotion:** Help people see the importance of a community (as with Vancity's Change Everything).

▷ **Escape:** Invite people to become deeply, frequently, and intimately immersed in the community (such as in Mozilla's 150 community areas).

▷ **Evolving:** Ensure that the community changes and adapts based on members' involvement (as Intuit's Quickbooks community does).

▷ **Stories:** Inspire people to use a community through a great narrative/ manifesto and ensure its relevance (as with Zappos's quest to provide the best customer experience possible).

▷ **Social and sustainable:** Get people talking and connecting with each other (as Nike Plus does).

In our Procter & Gamble lives, we might have called this the billboard test. In our Threadless lives, we might have made it the T-shirt test. Given the absolute volume of media and factors competing for consumers' everyday attention, the compelling nature of your core Wikibrand proposition cannot be underestimated. Can you build emotional and rational interest in your proposition with one simple statement or visual that instantly captivates? This is the litmus test for getting noticed and talked about on the social Web.

What triggers your wikibrand might not be merely a function of a brand equity or product attribute. You are conning yourself into brand self-importance. As proof, John Gerzema and Edward Lebar of Young & Rubicam conducted a landmark study and wrote a book (*The Brand Bubble*) that flipped what marketers have always thought about brand drivers on its head.

Historically, people have acted on attributes that instilled trust and were linked to a product's inherent value. In an attention-starved economy with similar-performing business models, these leadership qualities are either considered at par with competitors' or too difficult to prove to customers. Customers are more motivated to act on things that make brands appear different from others; Gerzema and Lebar call this "energized differentiation." Of the fifty attributes they tested, the most valuable ones were considered high quality, trustworthiness, good value, reliability, originality, simplicity, fun, and leadership—a great list to be attributed to a brand but really not much to talk about and tough to prove. However, the intriguing part of the study was what qualities made brands appear different and truly talkable: unique, dynamic, different, distinctive, innovative, visionary, daring, and progressive. The real question you need to be asking yourself is, "Does our wikibrand proposition address these latter attributes and hit prospective customers between the eyes?"

Organization, Culture, and Resources

The core value of an organization should be the heart of its community strategy. Make sure your company can actually deliver on some type of real, special, unique, or obvious value to your target participants.

If your company has a culture of being closed or conservative, start small, keep it manageable, get an executive champion, and engage in little experiments. If your company needs to capture benefits in a large-scale fashion, find internal champions and get alignment across all key functions.

As Gary Koelling from Best Buy says,

> First ask yourself, "What kind of relationship do I (not *we*) want to have with my employees or customers?" Give yourself an honest answer. If it's a purely transactional relationship, that's fine. If it's something else, try to plot it on a line of intimacy somewhere between "someone I see a couple of days a week in the elevator" and "soulmate." Hopefully, for their sake, it's somewhere in the middle. Then practice. Keep it small. Say hi. Get to know each other. Try things. Learn.[27]

A great wikibrand needs to inspire employees first. Given current corporate health, this could be the hurdle you and your community managers spend the most time cultivating. In current business environments, only 37 percent of employees know what they are trying to achieve in their day-to-day roles, just 20 percent of staff members are enthusiastic about their jobs, and a mere 15 percent feel empowered in their jobs.[28] Employees and customers live in these parallel but shared online worlds. Customers won't feel ownership until the company does. Creating internal advocates and investing as much company enthusiasm as possible for your wikibrand's effort inside your corporate walls is not only a requirement, it can be a real competitive advantage, especially for larger companies.

Bridging the Divide Between Strategy and Execution

So you have made some tough calls and aligned your company based on a sound foundation of business objectives, supporting resources, customer needs, and motivating ideas. Great. Now you need to bridge what the executive office has signed off on and what your project team needs to chase down. An additional four elements will help you determine how big an effort you have in front of you and who needs to be involved.

Benefits of Community/Engagement

Anticipate your benefits using the six categories we discussed in Chapter 4 (advocacy, content, insight, support, perception, and serendipity). The types of benefits you seek drive your community's features, incentives, and content. Remember that your brand community cannot deliver all possible benefits.

Scale of Community/Engagement

A pivotal question to address is "How large does this community need to become?" The answer drives ongoing support, staffing, executive involvement, features, and technology choices.

▷ **Small-scale communities (two thousand or fewer members):** Most communities, by design or failure, fit here. With so much competition for Internet attention, it is tough to scale active, engaged communities. There are many situations, however, in which small-scale communities can succeed. A brand community in the tens to hundreds may be the best option if your brand is under-resourced, your market is small, your brand or the community idea is exclusive in nature and targets hardcore fans, or the community's primary motivation is research. Communispace effectively manages hundreds of brand networks/panels, and most of its communities have considerably fewer than a thousand very engaged people.[29]

▷ **Midscale communities (two thousand to ten thousand members):** Midsized communities reach sufficient scale for brand support or brand content needs. This typically happens when there are enough resources to handle the traffic and when a registration or qualification requirement profiles target candidates from a larger pool of people. Business-to-business communities operate very successfully in this category.

▷ **Large-scale communities (more than ten thousand members):** Companies looking for brand advocacy, thriving social network interaction, or e-commerce–driven brand support need to build very large communities to deliver mainstream brand awareness, pass along referrals, and encourage deep interaction. IBM, Dell, SAP, Nike, and Mozilla are all in this stratum of large, sophisticated communities.

With few exceptions, communities start small. Here is what you need to do to scale up a community:

▷ Ensure that your first members are very committed and motivated.
▷ Support the community with rich content and significant outreach until it achieves a degree of self-sufficiency.
▷ Provide and support a strong suite of member induction activities.

Depth of Member Involvement

Depth refers to both members' collaborative activity and their commitment to the community and brand. Greater depth means members exert greater control. Less depth makes the community easier to manage, but at the expense of higher-order benefits such as brand evangelism, shared purpose, and collaborative development of content. Too little opportunity for involvement may hamper members' creativity and limit influence and appeal; too much choice can be overwhelming, tough to administer, and daunting for new members.

Three basic depth levels are possible:

▷ **Shallow:** Marked by simple voting or rating, episodic contact, and members consuming content. A connection with members is established.
▷ **Middle:** Marked by some type of content development and active contribution, periodic contact, and an expectation of group participation.
▷ **Deep:** Marked by immersive offline and online contributions from members, almost daily contact, and a sense of shared ownership.

We will consider these aspects of depth in Chapter 10.

Exclusivity of Membership

Exclusivity refers to the degree of private access that members have in the community. One theory of social media suggests that everything should be open, transparent, and perhaps even best developed without company intervention (as with IKEA fan clubs). While most brands could benefit from being less controlling, a number of industries and brands thrive based on communities that have some qualification standard for joining (for example, Ford Fiesta Movement).

A more open community can capitalize on reach and promote the feeling of a brand that has nothing to hide. A more closed community increases its cachet and intensifies the social glue among members who have earned their place. But people must be able to see clear and tangible benefits of exclusivity before they'll attempt to qualify.

There are three levels of exclusivity:

▷ **Low:** Simple registration process; does not require experience with the product
▷ **Middle:** Requires some level of registration or qualification, previous experience with the product or referral
▷ **High:** Requires some level of appointment, nomination, or self-identification as a real devotee of the brand or Influencer in the industry.

Frequently, brands may use a combination of all levels of exclusivity to segment members and create motivation for getting closer to the inner sanctum of the community without being seen as elitist or cultish.

As Seth Godin mentioned in his book *Tribes*, "The market for something to believe in is infinite."[30] The challenge is to find it for your company. Before embarking on what needs to be done to create these environments, you need to ask the tough question, "Why do we want to do this?" Given a clear focus on the business objectives, organizational resources, motivating brand idea, and—perhaps most important—customer needs/wants, you can build an effective plan around your desired wikibrand.

CHAPTER 7

LANGUAGE AND CONTENT

Business Gets Humanized and Presses the "Awesome" Button

In a blog post celebrating its two-year anniversary, community-based apparel design company Threadless proclaimed, "In the beginning, there was awesomeness. Then, that awesomeness begat more awesomeness. Behold, some of the awesomeness that set the bar of awesomeness we still live up to today."[2]

Now ten years old, Threadless is a standard-bearer for great wikibrand language and content. It works like this: each week, in the truest form of crowdsourcing, designers from all over the United States and around the world create and submit up to fifteen hundred smart and sometimes smart-alecky T-shirt designs. Visitors to the Threadless site vote for their favorite designs, and the company then produces, markets, and sells those designs. It's a $30 million business that has attracted the attention of millions of people on the Web and a number of much larger corporate partners (in 2009 and 2010, it teamed up with Shutterstock and Twitter to advance its growth).[3]

How has Threadless remained consistently relevant to an audience of designers and creatives who crave novelty and are usu-

> "It doesn't matter what you say if I don't like the way you're saying it."[1]
>
> —JAMES CHERKOFF, *Director, Collaborate Marketing*

ally gone before a trend becomes part of the mainstream? The company has eschewed marketing puffery and instead communicates its essence in everything it does—from its Web face to its events, through its employees and (of course) through its designs and products. Visit the Threadless website's home page, and you are immediately immersed in something very different. It's colorful and interesting and has a simple menu: "Shop," "Participate," "Community," and "Info." Each month, it gives its audience a new roguish design challenge that encourages community members to participate in and return to the site. By highlighting its star designers, the company gives community an authentic presence on a par with the rest of its operations. Threadless has extended its cheekiness and engagement across the social Web, turning Twitter captions, Shutterstock photos, and Society6 art into apparel and creating a funnel that brings people back to the Threadless community hub.

People simply love Threadless. Millions look forward to each week's new designs and applaud their favorites on various well-populated Twitter and Facebook pages and fan blogs. Jeffrey Kalmikoff, former executive at parent company Skinnycorp, explains, "The community changes the brand to suit them. We don't have expectations of what Threadless will be. We just manage the parameters."[4] It's tough to emulate the Threadless business model—its community-based orientation and intimacy with its audience has been part of its DNA from the beginning—but it's worth paying attention to the language and content concepts that have made it one of the social Web's best performers.

Why do some businesses, like Threadless, achieve cultlike status in their internal and external communities while others are ignored? Why do some product or marketing ideas "tip" and spread virally while others die? Why does your favorite blogger's post generate nonstop traffic while similar material you posted a week ago drifts into the digital weeds with no comments or retweets? Let's be clear, there are many factors, but one of the first considerations is your language and content. On a Web driven by search engine optimization (SEO) and social media optimization (SMO), content plays an integral role in getting found—and getting a fan base—online.

In a study by Agent Wildfire, lack of appropriate content was found to be the second biggest sin committed by brands engaging in social Web environments.[5] Those who frequent social media sites expect fresh, high-quality content, but many corporate blogs are just stale repositories of "press releases in a different format." You can't assign your blog to the most junior staffer or tack it onto the end of someone's to-do list and expect it to make a splash.

Finnish user experience expert Sami Viitimäki argues that what counts on the social Web is the way you communicate about your products (language) and the things you attach to them (content). "No matter how sexy and hip you think your company or brand is," says Viitimäki, "they both are very likely to be dramatically less interesting or cool to your customers than they are to you."[6] With the possible exception of Apple and a few others, products and brands themselves do not inspire large groups of people to get involved with them. If you have built a solid focus and purpose for your brands in the social Web, your next task is to get the customer communication and dialogue aspects right.

The Human Instinct to Buzz

Well-known Internet commentator Clay Shirky believes we're living in a period of transformation rivaling those surrounding the invention of the printing press, the inception of conversational media (the telegraph and telephone), and the invention and use of recorded media (photos, sound, film, TV, and the Internet). Shirky argues that we are experiencing the largest increase in expressive capability in human history and points to three new media innovations to prove his point: (1) people can now have Web-enabled conversations with groups, allowing many-to-many conversations for the first time; (2) in a world of hyperdigitization, media is less a source of information and more a coordinated site where like-minded people can meet; and (3) members of the audience can perform the role of producer and consumer, sometimes simultaneously.[7] But let's pause for a second. The media and technology trees have shifted, but the customer forest is still there. Human behavior changes slowly; some tendencies that have been programmed in over millennia are tough to reboot.

One of the most important is our need to socialize. As Emanuel Rosen argues in *The Anatomy of Buzz*, from the primitive days of sitting around the fire circle to the Starbucks coffee chat to the Second Life room visit, six key needs have motivated people to congregate as a species and share what they know with others. We chat, gossip, kibbitz, discuss, poke, or commune for six key reasons: to survive, to connect, to make sense of the world, to reduce risk and uncertainty, to benefit economically, and to relieve tension.[8] The relative importance of these communication drivers has changed over the course of history, but they all still exist as inbred instincts that can now be expressed digitally.

Every part of an organization has to socialize—that is, communicate internally and externally. At some point, the language and tools of social media will become as ubiquitous as e-mail or the phone call is today. But before that can happen, organizations will need to master what makes people tick and click in culture at large. Do your business and its communications tap into the six drivers of human communication? If you are like most businesses, probably not.

The following are examples of social Web phenomena that have figured out how to tap into each of the six key drivers of communications:

▷ **Survival:** Kiva.org is a social lending platform that has shared more than $140 million of microcredit loans with people in third-world countries, helping to raise the standard of living for tens of thousands.[9]

▷ **Connection:** We have a latent need to connect and show our peacock feathers to our peers in the form of updates, photos, and videos via Facebook, the world's top social network with enough members to become the third-largest country by population.[10]

▷ **Making sense of the world:** Consider Wikipedia's mission to make sense of the world by harnessing the wisdom of thousands of unpaid contributors to produce its unofficial knowledge.

▷ **Reduction of (purchase) risk and uncertainty:** Amazon offers less risk by allowing users to rank, rate, and comment on its products, providing a more informed purchase environment and helping to make it America's largest online retailer with a market capitalization larger than all retailers except Wal-Mart.[11]

▷ **Economic benefit:** eBay, the world's largest auction marketplace, pairs up ninety million buyers and sellers from around the world and enjoys a $30 billion market capitalization.[12]

▷ **Tension relief:** Consider YouTube's unique ability to relieve tension and entertain, whether it's Judson Laipply's wacky Evolution of Dance, OK GO's grassroots breakout hit "Here It Goes Again," Lady Gaga's massive hit "Bad Romance," or the slightly macabre "Charlie Bit My Finger Again." Even if it's not your cup of tea, two billion views per day prove that your neighbors are watching.[13]

None of these sites or companies existed twenty years ago, and several have only gained prominence over the last five. When you consider that all but Kiva are among the twenty-five most popular sites in the world[14] and represent both a considerable redistribution of corporate wealth and a massive dent in how consumers spend their time, you start to understand the power of tapping the deep-seated human instinct to connect.

If we can agree on what makes people talk, perhaps we can discover how business can do it. Because although companies can see the growth and success of social business models and technologies, they're stymied by how to use them. Among the millions of websites, blogs, pages, and apps, how does an organization find its voice and use it to connect with a network of customers it wouldn't otherwise have been able to reach?

The Language of Wikibrands: We're Human Too, Just a Little Different

Consumers view brandspeak and corporate messages with suspicion at the best of times. Over the last half century, businesses and their customer-facing functions have lost the ability to talk persuasively to their customers. They broadcast a series of messages to the customer and see what happens. When these messages fail to stick, they broadcast even louder in an attempt to rise above the cacophony. The tide of media clutter and advertising bravado rises, but advertising recall is at unprecedented lows.[15]

Even under ideal conditions it's hard to transform the way people think, act, and buy. Doing it in an environment where consumers distrust most ad messages is especially tough. Communicating persuasively in an inflationary ad marketplace where savvy customers and prospects have tools and technologies to filter out your messages is next to impossible. But don't despair. There is a tone and vernacular behind wikibrands that can engineer goodwill and participation. It's not all about ceding your voice to the audience or inundating your audience with incentives to buy some love. Good wikibrand efforts represent a mixture of an organization's perspectives and a mosaic of customer views. It's about encouraging customers, prospects, and sometimes even naysayers to join your marketing efforts.

The PEMCO Insurance Story: We're a Lot Like You. A Little Different

Rod Brooks, CMO for PEMCO, is a rare breed. He's built like a linebacker and pursues his business, the customer, marketing, and new media as if they were a scrambling quarterback. He sees opportunity everywhere, exudes positivity, and has a humble and childlike fascination with social media. He's also a shrewd businessman who has the ear of his CEO and is a natural leader for his Seattle-based insurance company's effort to become an engaged business and exciting brand.

Just about any resident of the Pacific Northwest can recite PEMCO's campaign slogan: "We're a Lot Like You. A Little Different." In coffee shops and microbrew restaurants across Washington State, people compare themselves to the campaign's characters (which include the Snowflake Freakout Lady, the Roadside Chainsaw Carver, the Sandals and Socks Guy, and the Ponytailed Software Geek). The campaign has garnered PEMCO a national reputation for brand engagement.

How has the company done this in an industry that is highly commoditized and super-regulated, that has historically had low customer involvement and competitors that spend heavily in mainstream advertising? "It's about adopting the voice of the customer," says Brooks. "Customers can share their testimonials and reviews online. We put it at the heart of everything we do." [16]

Part of this strategy stems from the belief that providing the best customer experience possible is paramount. Knowing that its competitors could outspend PEMCO in conventional advertising, Brooks decided in 2007 to move to the "conversation hill" and focus instead on customer advocacy and confidence. Through comprehensive ethnographic research, PEMCO discovered the values, landscape, and language of its customers. It tapped into the unique and quirky Northwest humor and sense of individualism, focusing on a deeply rooted local positioning and building meaningful two-way communications with customers through brand ambassador programs, community events, and a progressive stream of social media outlets. PEMCO and its nine-person marketing team have thus created a word-of-mouth juggernaut and a challenger brand that beats out its much larger national rivals.

As the PEMCO story demonstrates, knowledge, passion, and time are essential for embedding yourself in your customers' lives. There are no substitutes here: you may be able to pick and choose language tactics and techniques, but authoritative knowledge, unbridled passion, and dedicated time underpin all successful wikibrand efforts.

Insufficient knowledge will lead to a credibility gap with external audiences. The ability to create sound, well-reasoned arguments requires a significant base of learning and continuous upgrading. See, for example, C. B. Whittemore's Flooring the Customer blog. Whittemore has turned her niche knowledge of flooring and a passion for the customer into her own consultancy. Online, she is *the* authority on flooring, and her subject area mastery has given her credibility as an authority on the overall customer experience.

Insufficient passion will leave your intended audience cold. We can all think of companies that seem soulless. Too often, many of the right elements are in place, but companies fail to connect emotionally with their customer base. If your business is involved in new forms of customer engagement, you may not have great wealth or connections, but do you have passion, tenacity, and sweat? That's the mantra of Gary Vaynerchuck of Wine Library TV, who has turned his hustling attitude and passion for wine into a $60 million business.[17]

Insufficient time will keep your wikibrand pilots on hold or in perpetual beta status. Many larger brands' customer engagement ventures are understaffed and under-resourced. If that's your challenge, try crowdsourcing a group of enthusiastic experts who live the life of your customer. Consider garden and craft manufacturer Fiskars: the Finnish company supports a community where ambassadors called "Fiskateers" generate daily content with significant interaction and goodwill.

Seven Key Language Principles

Overcoming our tendency to make sales pitches takes some conversational creativity and patience. Successful wikibrands follow seven key language principles to instill trust and develop participation among communities of interest.

Develop an Expert Understanding of the Target and Context

Smart companies spend three to six months learning what resonates with customers before undertaking any wikibrands initiative.

Start with prospective customers' values: what do they care about? Pay attention to context. What do they talk about, and what kind of language do they use? Where are their pleasure and pain points in life and in their experience with your company? Understand the community's accepted cultural norms, values, fashion, idioms, and current topics of interest. Live among the "tribe" to understand them or hire people who are already members.

Alcoholic beverage companies are not known for creating effective two-way engagement with their fans. That's what makes Molson Coors's efforts so intriguing. After a challenging early foray into Facebook in 2007,[18] chief public affairs officer Ferg Devins led a complete 180-degree reversal in Molson's social media strategy. The company has gone from being a social media hall monitor—interrupting and broadcasting messages—to practicing what Devins calls the "LIAM" principle":[19]

▷ Leveraging what we see in conversations
▷ Initiating discussion and dialogue
▷ Acquiring people for our community
▷ Managing our communities

Have a Belief System, Develop a Common Voice, and Rally Around It

Many employees may touch your engagement initiatives. Although these community managers and staff should not be clones, they should sound like they came from the same parent. In every touchpoint, link to "why" you're doing what you're doing. Establish broad guidelines for what your wikibrand DNA is all about and free your employees to talk off the script. Vancity is a great example of logically and naturally building a community platform based on the triple bottom line of its business operations—healthy people, profits, and planet—and letting the conversation flow freely from there.

Listen to People and Acknowledge What They Have to Say

Wikibranding is a two-way street; it's effective because it's truly collaborative. People enjoy and pay more attention to your words when they are in a "tennis match of conversation" and have to—or want to—keep up their end. Check out Whole Foods's Twitter strategy: the company has a top-ranked national account, various topical accounts, and accounts for each local outlet. These accounts have an extraordinarily high (as much as 90 percent) ratio of replies to and retweets of customer versus promotional content. By treating customers as valued fans, Whole Foods allows them to feel more ownership in the discussion.

Establish a Humanizing Tone

We are all customers, and as a rule, we want the human touch and will usually pay more for it. Think about that restaurant that treats you like a VIP and provides extra-special touches; you probably tip more there than you would elsewhere. So whether you specify the real names of front-line wikibrand representatives or not (there are arguments for both sides), have them speak as people, not as "the company." If you wouldn't say it in real life, do not say it in community. The relationship you want to develop with your customers is somewhere between a best friend and a person they see on the bus each day, depending on your focus, desired tone, and resource bandwidth.

Let communication be natural; the best exchanges are unplanned, unrehearsed, and consistent with your personality. Learn from the Austin-based Sweet Leaf Tea and its belief in laughter, high fives, and good music. People love the company's various folksy video uploads, "Ask Granny" advice areas, and 1 percent donation to members of its Communi-Tea. Allow people to play, use slang, and be spontaneous; let your mess show. And don't try to be perfect. Connect with minds and hearts equally. More than half of customer choice is based on emotion. Appeal to customers' hard-wired social instincts, as well as to facts.[20]

Embrace Your Role as Ringleader, Facilitator, and Expert

Wikibrands is truly for lovers. Great brand evangelists and front-line managers embrace their roles as experts, social glue, or trendstarters and are motivated to share their experiences. Most successful wikibrands also have a senior-level executive champion who enthusiastically leads the community effort (see Chapter 13 on community management). These executives are eager to share what they know and don't feel threatened by other people's expertise. Lionel Menchaca, chief blogger at Dell, with his extraordinary ability to disseminate knowledge and provide customer service in an informal but authoritative manner, is a great example. His commitment is a key factor in the successful outcomes of Dell's Web-based discussions and issues.

Demonstrate Authenticity, Humility, and Transparency

Be real in practice and principle and stick to the Word of Mouth Marketing Association (WOMMA) "Honesty ROI" code: honesty of *relationship*—say who you are speaking for; honesty of *opinion*—say what you think; and honesty of *identity*—say who you are.[21] One bad fact or overstated truth is like one bad coffee bean in espresso; it ruins the whole brew. Word of mouth is built on the stilts of trust; when trust breaks down, the message falls apart. Besides, in a hyperconnected world, somebody somewhere will find out the truth and spread it around the world in a matter of hours.

Even if you are not lying, things can go wrong, as Johnson & Johnson's Motrin brand found out in 2008 when it launched an online video about baby-wearing moms that was viewed as insensitive (more on this story in Chapter 14). In the span of a weekend, before Motrin could make a formal response or retraction, tens of thousands had voiced their displeasure. The lesson? If something goes wrong, admit your mistake immediately. Denying or defending the mistake will just damage your corporate image. Even though admitting mistakes may run counter to traditional corporate practice, the public forgives a repenting friend but beats up on obstinate defenders.

SEAN'S EXPERIENCE WITH GUINNESS

Back in 1998, I did not think much about the value of content. It may seem foolish now, given the Web expert mantra "content is king," but back then, I believed that as long as a brand had a solid, well-executed strategy, content just came out the other end of the sausage grinder. If the content you were pushing was accurate, sometimes you could win a little with better content, sometimes you could lose a little—but there wouldn't be a big swing either way. In truth, what I have learned about content comes from the bottom of a Guinness glass.

As the former shepherd of Guinness marketing efforts in Canada, my job was to build a geographic market for parent company Diageo by creating more adorers and admirers of Guinness in a market that barely knew the brand. What the market did know about Guinness was off-putting: it was a "meal in a glass," the "best Guinness was served in Ireland," "it was served warm," and it should be consumed only on St. Patrick's Day. This was more than a pint-sized problem.

One of the best things we did was challenge those myths with an integrated campaign: "One St. Patrick's Day, 364 Practice Days." We took the message to the streets and had eight-foot Picketing Pint mascots protesting their single annual day of celebration. We mass-produced T-shirts for bar staff with cryptic numbers (3-5°, 196, 53°N, 6°W, and 116) and a harp scrolled on the chest. The numbers—the actual temperature, calories, brewing location, and number of Guinness pints sold every second in the world—became conversation fodder in bars across Canada. People took pride in knowing the answers, which provoked further buzz. We had a marketing

In the age of social media, transparent language is important. Transparency in itself can act as a powerful incentive to participate. Credit people for their contributions and shine a spotlight on them. It creates a feeling of "we-ness" and of actually making a difference. People are also interested in the progress of the collaborative projects in which they participate, so unless you have a good reason to keep something a secret, such as stock market rules or restrictions related to litigation, disclose it.

Feed the Personality

Triage people according to their interests. Make it easy for consumers to find or get what they want. Tailor content to the interests and past experi-

---

meme[22] on our hands. Whether we knew it then or not, we had successfully engineered content for word of mouth; we gave a few well-placed pushes and watched it go. Business grew by 25 percent, and we became the lead growth geography of the 150 countries in the Guinness stout empire.

Even back then, with the invention of the term *social media* years away, the Guinness campaign was more a grassroots, word-of-mouth-driven success than a mass advertising play. We used to say, "Better to sip from grassroots than gulp from the mainstream." We learned then that content developed for grassroots advocacy and word of mouth is quite different from conventional advertising. Today, content may involve digitized text, audio, graphics, or video, but the challenge remains. There were different triggers involved in getting people to notice, talk about, and advocate our message. To generate a "bandwagon effect" for wikibrands, you have to create conversation.

You often only get one good chance to make an impression. It is extraordinarily difficult for a manufactured message to infiltrate social networks and create word of mouth. It feels unnatural, and savvy people see it coming from a mile off. You can tell the difference between people who go out of their way and show a passion for something that is helpful or exciting or rare. And with so much more noise out there, your message has to grab them. Unfortunately, in a lot of companies, a gap exists between creating a great user experience and ineffective, insufficient content. Marketers are now publishers—get used to it.

ence of your audience and according to the platforms they're using to communicate with you. Answer the following four questions to create effective content that spreads:

▷ What is it?
▷ Why is it so special/different?
▷ How can I (the customer) use it/see it/purchase it?
▷ Will it improve my (the customer's) life?

Conversational affinity happens when we feel that others understand us and are genuinely trying to help us rather than just trying to profit from us. Trendsetters want to be first in line; experts want to know the facts; opinion leaders want to know the possibilities; tastemakers want to see the big idea; social ringleaders want to know how to share it with others; mainstreamers and laggards want to reduce risk and feel safe. Modulate your communications efforts to appeal to your specific audience. It is human nature to reciprocate when we believe someone is trying to help us.

One Million Acts of Green, but One Incredible Act of Awesome

Cisco had a content issue with the mainstream consumer. While it may have had a strong reputation in the business community, its brand image at-large was shapeless. In late 2008, Cisco wanted to engage consumers, employees, and stakeholders and demonstrate how a "human network" could connect and work collectively to achieve a common goal. The company built a social network of sorts around environmental and green challenges. It included the ability to create user profiles, track challenges, join groups, post photos, and spread the word virally.

With the help of media partner Canadian Broadcasting Corporation, not-for-profit green partners, and a calculator that tabulated members' collective acts of green and amount of greenhouse gases saved, Canadians nearly doubled the company's challenge number and now the program has expanded to the United States. Cisco could have called this the Cisco Green Ambassador Club, but instead by posing it as a "challenge," allowing multiple levels of access and involvement, and providing colorful, human content fed by popular Canadian talk show host George Stroumboulopoulos, the company created a content platform where people, businesses, schools, cities, and celebrities all joined in to make the world a little bit greener.[23]

Key Lessons for Language and Outreach

There are some key lessons to keep in mind when considering your language and outreach strategies.

Awesomeness Trumps Interestingness—Which Trumps Quality

There was a time when just communicating to the "mass middle" at sufficient media volumes was enough to be noticed. In 2006, Flickr introduced an "interestingness" score to help determine its top five hundred photos based on the amount of crowd-based interaction a given submission generated (an algorithm of tags, groups, views, favorites, source of click-throughs, and authority of commenters). But now, with the explosion of content, traffic, platforms, and interactions, even interestingness doesn't guarantee success.

We posit the idea of "awesomeness"—the ability to generate not just interaction but long-lived, cross-platform interaction that taps into some of the basic human instincts described earlier: to survive, connect, make sense of the world, reduce risk, benefit economically, and relieve tension. Your offerings should answer one of these needs. Most great content starts with "Wouldn't it be cool if . . . ?" and ends in "You have to check this out." Capture people's imaginations and find areas of common interest that make them ask open questions:

▷ "Where could you go . . . ?"
▷ "What do you think about . . . ?"
▷ "When was the last time you . . . ?"

Avoid closed questions (such as those beginning with "Are you," "Have you," and "Did you") that require only a yes or no and shut conversations down.

Most great content is fed by organic *and* orchestrated word of mouth. Organic word of mouth grows from a remarkable service, experience, or product. It makes sense that the best content buzz can be linked closely to product and buried inside the product. Orchestrated word of mouth is the proactive encouragement of activity associated with your product.

Provide a Challenge and Pose Questions

Customers do not want to sit back and admire your completed creative work—they'd rather participate in a process. Smart content provides a forum for feedback or participation: a challenge, contest, poll, or question to invite deeper and progressive levels of interaction. We recently drove down the Gardiner Expressway in Toronto and bemoaned the state of outdoor advertising. Of the thirty-five billboards that lined the highway, only one actually asked us to do something, act on something, or engage with something. Shameful.

Even premium brands have started to master the value of posing challenges to their customers. Consider Burberry's Art of the Trench, a campaign that engages key fashion Influencers and fans-at-large in a crowdsourcing photo challenge. Participants submit, rate, and comment on photos of people wearing trench coats. It's a simple but elegant campaign that encourages site visitors to stay a while and explore modern variations on a traditional style. The initiative continues to evolve as an ongoing platform for mixing curated and user-generated content.

Practice the Art of Surprise

People recognize patterns and get jaded really fast. As Just for Laughs festival co-founder Andy Nulman notes, "People have seen it all, and they expect it all. They expect product quality, service, and experience will all be right, and the only way to please these people is to give them something they don't expect. It's the key to all great entertainment, fashion, sports, politics, and the economy." [24]

Occasionally, you can pleasantly surprise your customers by maxing out one feature of the product style, performance, feature, experience, or service. But it's hard to spring a product-based surprise in the corporate world; there are too many chances for the surprise to leak out early.

It is easier to surprise people with high-profile content and entertainment that gets them talking. Broaching controversial subjects, embracing the unusual, stimulating controversy, committing random acts of kindness, seeding secrets, and providing contrary or counterintuitive ideas and information all get customers engaged. Remember the Free Hugs campaign (a social movement involving individuals who offer hugs to strangers in public places) that launched in 2006 and has now been seen by more than sixty million people on YouTube? How about the T-Mobile Dance flash mob,[25] which has been seen by twenty million people and spawned imitations around the world? These campaigns were so unexpected, creative, poignant, or rare that customers paused to find out what they were all about.

Tell Stories

People love to tell stories. When repeated, they reinforce a message; when told really well, they become viral. Stories strike a chord with customers, shareholders, investors, and employees; they humanize brands. The use of social media reduces the number of changes in their retelling, reposting, or retweeting. Being honest doesn't preclude adding some romance and mystery to your brand through stories either.

Lois Kelly, author of *Beyond Buzz: The Next Generation of Word-of-Mouth Marketing*, suggests nine types of stories that people most like to talk about:[26]

▷ **Aspirations and beliefs** help people connect emotionally to a company.
▷ **David versus Goliath** stories allow people to root for the underdog.
▷ **Avalanche about to roll** stories tap into consumers' need to get the inside story of an emerging disruptive trend or event.
▷ **Challenging assumptions** grabs attention and resets assumptions through originality.
▷ **Anxieties** play on people's uncertainty to inspire action.
▷ **Personalities and personal** stories give a face to your organizational culture.
▷ **How-to stories and advice** provide fresh and original twists on solving problems.
▷ **Glitz and glam** link people to celebrities.
▷ **Seasonal/event-related** stories relate content to fixed events and the day's news.

Naked Pizza has a story that taps into many of Kelly's nine types. The company is trying to change the nutritional profile of America by demonstrating that pizza doesn't have to make you fat. From its start in New Orleans, the company has used an instructional brand image and strong social media presence to get the message out about how much healthier its product is than standard take-out pizza. The firm hired a team of biologists and food technologists to create a crust made of twelve whole grains; uses low-fat skim mozzarella; and developed a tomato sauce with "no additives, preservatives, colorants, or weird chemicals or molecules of any kind."[27]

Naked Pizza communicates mostly through social media, which means lower marketing costs. "Social media gives us the opportunity to inform and engage with people," co-founder Robbie Vitrano says. "We're a social media company that happens to sell pizza—pizza is the touchpoint that starts conversations."[28] On a large billboard outside the New Orleans location, the company advertises its Twitter handle rather than a phone number.[29] According to Vitrano, on some days, up to 70 percent of orders are made through Twitter.[30] The LivNaked blog provides lifestyle and health and wellness information.

Naked Pizza has enjoyed rapid growth and healthy coverage in traditional media. Mark Cuban—the owner of the Dallas Mavericks, influential blogger, and one of our favorite Internet billionaires (in no small part because he is *still* a billionaire)—was an early investor through his "Stimulus Plan" investment contest.

Show, Don't Tell: Video Better than Pictures Better than Words

Simple learning theory suggests that the deeper and more intense the experience with content, the more people engage and retain your message. Some training research posits that the average person retains 10 percent of what he reads, 20 percent of what he hears, 30 percent of what he sees, and 50 percent of what he sees and hears.[31] If, however, these forms of passive communication lead to active discussion or experience, the bond grows deeper. This same theory holds true on collaborative spaces on the Web. IDC Research estimates that 124 billion photos will be uploaded to social networks by 2013.[32] Cisco's big bet is that video will become more and more synonymous with Internet use and part of the collaboration/social networking experience. The company's VNI study claims that 91 percent of the world's consumer Internet provider traffic will be video-based by 2014.[33] Never mind the visual medium's ability to transmit story and nuance; the customer is being trained to go visual.

Blendtec's "Will it Blend" is a great example of how video has the potential to go viral in support of a product. Blendtec CEO and video host Tom Dickson's demonstrations of a Blendtec blender shredding items such as an Apple iPhone and iPad, glow sticks, baseballs, and Nike sneakers have become an Internet phenomenon. Cumulatively, more than one hundred million views have registered on the collection of videos, and sales are up 700 percent based on the campaign.[34]

Develop a Content Strategy and Frequency

By incorporating content development into your marketing calendar and production process, you can turn social content marketing into an asset. Consistency of content is essential to maintaining your content promise and search impact. Developing a steady stream of content on your website, community areas, and social media places is tough. Beyond the "how" we discussed in the language section, the requirements for building a smart content strategy revolve around what, where, when, and who:

THE WHAT
▷ What are the key topics to cover or messages to be communicated?
▷ How will your content link to your desired "focus"?
▷ Which content formats will you use (video, audio, photos, posts, updates)?
▷ Has content been developed for search engine and social media optimization?
▷ How will you conduct quality control of content?
▷ How will you measure and audit content performance?

THE WHERE
▷ Does the content already exist?
▷ Can existing content be repurposed?
▷ Does the content need to be created? How much effort and time will be required to deliver new content?
▷ Where will the content be sourced? Will your content be employee-generated, employee-curated, crowdsourced, and/or open sourced?
▷ Does the content naturally lead to a call to action? If so, where are the links?
▷ How will you develop content across all organizational needs?

THE WHEN
▷ When will content be published? Is there a content schedule?
▷ How often will content need to be updated?
▷ Does your content require optimal timing/seasonality?

THE WHO
▷ Who is responsible and accountable for delivering content?
▷ Will your content be developed collectively or individually?
▷ How will it be maintained over time?
▷ Is there third-party involvement?
▷ What are the guidelines for reviewing, editing, and approving content?

You need to consider all these factors at the planning stages, before you find yourself with thousands of adoring fans who come back for more and find a digital "Out to Lunch" sign.

Content Needs to Have a Benefit

In producing content, always ask yourself, "Does anybody care?" and "Does it support our wikibrand focus?" People tend to care about the following things (in order of priority):[35]

> ▷ Exciting or buzzworthy news (32 percent)
> ▷ Real problem solvers or smart ideas (20 percent)
> ▷ Exclusive new content (13 percent)
> ▷ Things they experience/associate with personally (13 percent)
> ▷ Breaking news (9 percent)
> ▷ Innovative, one-of-a-kind stories (9 percent)

Switch your focus from trying to convince people of your merits and instead figure out how to deliver interesting things people will talk about. Here are some rules to remember:

> ▷ **Organize your content.** One of the Internet's marketing traps is the myth of "unlimited content." You are no longer limited by thirty-second TV ads, two-page magazine layouts, or six-foot-high transit posters. You have a never-ending canvas on which to build functions and features. But just because you have room to showcase acres of content doesn't mean you should. Some of the best wikibrand content platforms are simple in layout and features.
> ▷ **Remember that you occasionally get literary or cinematic gold, but you often get dreck.** Your content producers and community managers need to step in regularly and edit community content to highlight what's best for the customer and for the brand. Sometimes you can create a program to determine the most popular content; at other times, human intervention is required.
> ▷ **Respond to feedback.** As you build community, it is most important to recognize member contributions. Make them look and feel good, and you will get that small investment back in spades.
>
>   Dell Ideastorm appeals to people who want to express their ideas to Dell. An icon-driven menu offers four options: View, Vote, Post, and See. The platform also has a submenu option of popular ideas, recent ideas, top ideas, and comments, allowing users to scroll according to their wishes and allowing Dell to curate the better or most topical ideas for others to see. This is minimalistic curated content at its best.
> ▷ **Consider content aggregation and syndication.** Social media does not work without good content, but even the really innovative stuff

still needs to be found. Beyond actual publication, content aggregation and publication helps you discover the best content and ensures that the Googles, Microsofts, Yahoos, popular social networks, bloggers, and other content partners find you.

Job number one is to look at building up your "earned" presence. Content aggregation helps by intelligently gathering and structuring content from the best sources. Its cousin, syndication, delivers that content seamlessly across a number of different Web channels through proper tagging, bookmarking, widgets, content feeds, links, and embeds and by providing an extensive range of content sources and formats for social exposure. The key is to facilitate ease of use and transformation of your content by your end user or customer.

Kraft is a shining example of how to deliver high-quality content in a smart, content-aggregated manner. The company has tapped into the notion that "soccer moms" are one of the most enthusiastic populations on the social Web and have created recipes across a large variety of formats—the iFood assistant iPhone app, a YouTube channel cooking school, a member recipe exchange and rating area, message boards/forums, Kraft mobile content, an RSS feed, recipe widgets, e-mail newsletters, and a downloadable My Recipe Box that is exportable to a shopping list. If you are a busy household cook, Kraft has gone out of its way to make its content available where and how you want it.

▷ **Create action.** Make no mistake, good content needs to have a hard-edged business purpose. The best wikibrand practitioners realize that content needs to promote action without being pushy. Online superstar and wine merchant Gary Vaynerchuk calls this the "lure and lasso." The "lure" is your home game, providing content that encourages people to frequent your Web properties. The "lasso" is your away game, the ways in which you insert yourself into conversations to get people to follow you back to your Web property.

Content should provide the impetus to get customers and prospects to move—in small, easy steps—deeper and deeper into your universe. In an Internet universe littered with spam artists, frauds, and self-promoters, you should always provide an authentic and impassioned reason "when you ask for action."[36]

Amazon is one of our favorite examples of content that creates action. Looking at its pages, you can easily identify up to twenty features that build commitment to action such as purchases: ratings and reviews, Listmania, personalized recommendations, sales rankings, wish lists, and tie-ins ("Customers who bought this also bought . . .").

Should we be surprised that every time we use Amazon's collabora-tive filtering system, we end up leaving the checkout area with more stuff than we originally planned. E-commerce businesses understand the world of action; it's their lifeblood. It's why customer reviews are the most effective social tactic for driving sales[37] and also why 25 percent of the highest ranked search results for the world's top twenty brands are links to user-generated content.[38]

▷ **Harness compelling social objects.** Interest groups and communities rally around relevant objects (not necessarily people) to stimulate social interaction. Etsy is about crafts, Flickr is about photos, Foursquare is about locations, and Threadless is about T-shirts. You need to find an artefact of interest that your audience can play with, claim, co-produce, or mash up.

Sociologist Jyri Engeström is one of the early advocates for the central role of social objects in social networks. He claims that social objects can be either a way of "strengthening self perception or indeed a refreshing way to escape the norms and restrictions of everyday life."[39] He sees a social object as "the centerpiece in a dialogue between two or more people. People don't just talk—they tend to talk 'around' objects. For example, if I'm speaking to my mother about the flowers I sent her, the flowers are the social object."[40] It's more than just people and links between them. One of the key reasons LinkedIn has taken off is that it shifted away from people collecting people and added groups and features that made people collect around professional topics, jobs, and interests. Relevant social objects provide a platform for meaning-ful interaction by uniting participants and giving them something to share.

Consider Frito-Lay and its ability to cultivate enthusiasm and seven million YouTube views around people's passion for new Dorito fla-vor launches.[41] Red Bull created crowdsourced appeal by encouraging people to create art with their cans. For seventeen years, Alberta's Big Rock Beer has been hosting the Eddies—a contest for amateurs trying to create the next great beer commercial. And the granddaddy of com-munities, Lego, creates toy brick–loving zealot interest in new models, buildings, and robots. Even a low-involvement brand like WD-40 has amassed more than 135,000 people as part of its pursuit of new uses for its lubricant. If an industrial lubricant can find a galvanizing social object, can't you?

Language and content are the special ingredients that grease the wiki-brand conveyor belt. As much as the successful examples evidenced in this book rely on all nine factors coming together, language and content may in fact be the most misused and abused. Finding out what you want to say is an intuitively smart thing to wedge into the process between building a wikibrand focus (why and what you're trying to do) and determining incentives, motivation, and outreach (who you will invite to join and how you will motivate them).

Eric Karjaluoto, author of *Speak Human: Outmarket the Big Guys by Getting Personal*, sums up a modern and universal truth about life and wikibrand content engagement: "The habit of making people feel special works as well for companies as it does in personal interaction. It's a secret weapon. Big companies are like the high school prom queen. They don't flirt with anybody because they don't think they have to. This doesn't last forever; the prom ends at some point, as does the reign of any company. Flirting might be the part that eventually turns the tables." [42] As we vaguely recall our younger days, flirting is a great metaphor for the dictionary of engagement. It's pulse-raising, it's human, and it's engineered to impress. Many people are bad at it, but when you do it well, it creates a deeper commitment and willingness to explore. Now the next question: who do you want to flirt with, and how will you get them to say "yes"?

CHAPTER 8

INCENTIVES, MOTIVATIONS, AND OUTREACH

Brand Fans Do It for Themselves, Not for You

If you've ever been to a design event, photographer meet-up, social media conference, or business networking night and had someone slip you a miniature business card, you have probably had a MOO card experience. You would have peered at the shrunken calling card with its heavier-than-average card stock and bright "back of card" design, and you probably glanced back at it again and again. It grabbed your attention. If paper had personality, its face would be a MOO card.

Launched in September 2006, MOO is a London-based, online custom stationery company that has made one of the most prosaic business practices—ordering and giving out (and receiving) business cards—remarkable. The firm has applied new thinking to every part of the process in hopes of taking a small percentage of the petabytes[2] of online content (photographs, designs, cool ideas) and turning it into great print products. MOO now produces more than ten million minicards annually.

People find MOO stationery interesting to create, attractive to look at, fun to collect, and easy to share. Legions of design-centric

> "People don't form and interact with communities in order to support a company. They do it to serve their own emotional needs."[1]
>
> —JAKE McKEE, *partner, Ant Eye's View, and former head of community, Lego*

and small-to-medium-sized businesses have adopted the cards and adore them. Popular blog Boing Boing raves, "It's hard to convey how cool-ass these cards are. They feel like a fetish object, the thick card and soft laminate finish create a great hand feel, and they're visually stunning—playful and intensely personal." MOO has figured out—and mastered—three key customer incentives or motivations:

▷ **Making customers look good:** MOO products are small works of art that attract attention, and they impress colleagues and business partners. People love to be noticed for their creativity; businesses thrive on it. MOO goes out of its way to shine the light back on its most inventive customers by celebrating their creations in competitions, blogs, posts, and Flickr galleries.

▷ **Making customers feel good:** Designing cards is a great creative outlet for MOO customers; it's fun to take your best photos and most interesting designs and turn them into MOO cards. And MOO makes the process easy and personal. From prepurchase to design to giving and receiving cards, customers never feel like MOO is some faceless corporation; it is an engaged partner and ally willing to help, surprise, and delight them.

▷ **Giving customers something valuable:** MOO has made it easy to create and print short runs of distinctive, flexible stationery at a fair price. For more involved customers, MOO offers community events, discounts, and contests.

MOO's return on addressing customer motivation is considerable. The company has triple-digit revenue growth; an extraordinarily high Net Promoter Score (this metric is discussed in more depth in Chapter 14) of 75 percent; and partnership deals with Flickr, Facebook, Etsy, Bebo, and Google. MOO's blog, YouTube efforts, and Flickr engagement are the envy of corporate social media mavens; many posts attract more than a hundred comments. MOO is a wikibrand incentive and outreach all-star.

As social media entered the mainstream from about 2004 to 2009, nearly every business assumed its social media project would attract a massive audience. But sadly, even if you build it, people don't necessarily come. Launch day is thrilling; project teams toast one another, and executives congratulate themselves for betting on this weird social media thing. About a month after launch, enthusiasm turns to concern as response peters out. Three months out, concern turns to worry as content goes largely ignored. Six months postlaunch, disappointed managers request a project review and ask some tough questions about what went wrong. The social Web project is no longer the darling of the corporate suite but a hard lesson learned.

This scenario gets played out all across the global business landscape. Reputations are bruised, high hopes fall, and businesses get cold feet about anything involving social media. What happens? Why isn't success predictable? Let's assume that these are smart companies with an interesting, motivating focus and an understanding of their audiences. Let's also assume that they've chosen the right technology, tools, and content. With the table stakes for success in place, how could these wikibrand-based initiatives possibly fail?

We call it the "wikibrand hangover" effect. After the audience's initial interest fades, there is insufficient motivation to keep people hanging around in these spaces. In a number of launch scenarios, social extensions of brands become merely more content extensions to other media. Beyond the initial joining and broadcasting of your love for the sponsoring product, brand, or famous celebrity, these social media properties usually provide no ongoing value, tangible or otherwise. Nowhere is this more apparent than social network business pages. Even though the average Facebook user joins four pages per month, without careful management, these pages go dormant and most fans do not return.[3]

At some point, prospective fans, followers, or members ask, "What's in it for me?" When the answer isn't clear, online communities, applications, pages, and groups lose followers. When the novelty is gone, they move on.

Other social brand projects use transactional incentives—coupons, contests, and giveaways—to sustain followers' interest. Phrases like "free," "your chance to win," "giveaway," and "limited-time offer" still resonate with customers who want in on the deal. They can be strong supporting elements in large brand and new product or campaign launch efforts.

Do you remember Moonfruit, the U.K.-based Web building and hosting company? We won't fault you if you don't, but in mid-2009, it was all the rage among the Twitter set. Moonfruit was offering ten Apple Macbook Pros on Twitter over the course of ten days. The company had the hashtag #moonfruit, and all you had to do was include the hashtag in as many tweets as you wanted, and you qualified to win. In a week, Moonfruit increased its Twitter following a hundredfold, had 600 percent more traffic to its corporate site, and doubled the sign-ups to its product trial. Success!

Or was it?

As one of the first to use Twitter as an offer channel, Moonfruit created a tsunami of buzz in the press and among online Influencers. For less than $15,000 in Apple hardware, the social media stunt was a smash hit in the short run. But fast-forward a year. Moonfruit's Twitter followers have declined by half (and it's rare for Twitter pages to lose followers). The company could attract new followers, but it has no plan for holding onto them. Moonfruit barely registers its Twitter presence on its front page and tweets less than three times per day. It is the wikibrand equivalent of music's Dexy's Midnight Runners or Vanilla Ice: a one-hit, social media summer wonder.

There are four challenges to basing your wikibrand efforts on "carrot and stick" incentives:

▷ Incentive offers that catch people's attention are usually too expensive to sustain.
▷ Promotional touts tend to appeal to the inherently brand-disloyal, unprofitable deal hunters.
▷ Artificial contest buzz trains people to get involved only when there are deals to be had.
▷ Reward-based enthusiasm doesn't translate into genuine interest in the overall brand proposition.

Beyond the flak you get from online populations that believe promotions pollute the social Web, promotion-based social Web efforts demean the value of your brand.

Dan Pink, author of *Drive: The Surprising Truth of What Motivates Us*, has studied the mismatch between what science knows about incentives and motivations and what businesses do. He argues that monetary rewards have lost their attractiveness in modern culture: "Incentives will increase performance on routine tasks. But for activities that require creativity and problem solving, the bigger the reward, the worse the performance."[4]

Pink makes the case that to feel a sense of commitment, you need to develop a sense of empowerment and ownership. He points out that three factors motivate people to hang around and do more than expected:

▷ Autonomy (the desire to direct their own lives)
▷ Mastery (the urge to get better and better at something that matters)
▷ Purpose (the desire to serve something larger than themselves)

Although Pink's focus is on how contemporary managers lead organizations and motivate employees, his thinking applies—with one caveat—to external communities of ambassadors, fans, and collaborators. We think a healthy balance of incentives is preferable in the social Web. We've identified three categories of wikibrand incentives and motivations:

▷ **Intrinsic motivations:** Community members believe the offering is intrinsically valuable. They may identify with a value inherent in a wikibrand or may simply invest their time for fun, the challenge, or altruism. People make the effort because it makes them feel good.

For example, Livestrong urges people to get involved and help empower and inspire cancer patients to live bravely.

▷ **Extrinsic motivations:** External pressures or influences motivate individuals to embrace the brand. These motivations satisfy some ego drive or need for affiliation with a broader community. People get involved because it makes them look or appear good to others.

For example, in the Nike Plus Challenge, groups or individuals compete in distance or speed challenges against competitors via the Nike Plus website and technology.

▷ **Explicit motivations:** People participate in exchange for tangible rewards; the incentives satisfy some desire for fairness, reciprocity, money, or privilege. People participate because they feel rewarded.

For example, with My Coke Rewards, people win points for entering codes from specially marked packages, which they can then exchange for prizes.

The most successful wikibrand efforts employ a mix of these three types of incentives.

Intrinsic Motivations

Time-starved executives may not understand why a large group of people would spend hundreds of hours on a project without expecting to be paid. Thousands of members of the Lego community, for example, invest countless hours of brick-by-brick effort to create more innovative and advanced buildings and robots for little recognition and no money. Crazy, you say? Think about Canadian retailer The Running Room, whose more than two hundred thousand volunteers, participants, and forum members congregate around jogging in the dead of a northern winter, strapping on layers of technical garments and braving the elements to run twice a week as a group, and then coming back online to share advice and experiences. Ridiculous?

Strange but true: people do things because they like to. Given a forum and a bigger stage on which to express themselves, they get more deeply involved and committed. By investing in online platforms, offline events, and administration and management resources, brands can help bring far-flung people together around their common interest.

Mozilla Firefox is a great example of a brand that intrinsically motivates its community. Half a million volunteers have helped Firefox—up against the much larger and richer Internet Explorer—achieve a 30 percent share of the browser market. Developers, coders, nerds, and geeks love the idea of helping to build the best Internet experience possible. They program, test code, make referrals, build content, translate languages, rise to campaigns and challenges, and refute bad buzz about Mozilla. By codifying their beliefs and genuinely living by them, Mozilla has energized unpaid legions to support an open participatory Web for nothing more than personal interest in the project.

Intrinsic motivations for wikibrand community building include the following:

▷ **Building better lives or supporting a cause:** For example, Mountain Equipment Co-op's The Big Wild community supports saving half of Canada's precious land and water forever.
▷ **Competing in a challenge or competition:** For example, the Audi Design Challenge is an open concept car design competition.
▷ **Enlisting creativity:** For example, Sharpie Uncapped is a user-generated art gallery.
▷ **Creating fun and enjoyment:** For example, Walker's Crisps Flavour Choice was a U.K. contest to determine Walker's next new flavor.
▷ **Celebrating a group effort or achievement:** For example, San Francisco's YouTube Symphony Orchestra is a collaborative effort to determine the best global orchestra.
▷ **Creating a forum for learning:** For example, QuickBooks communities find answers and share advice with QuickBooks users and small business experts.
▷ **Satisfying curiosity:** For example, AMC's "Mad Men" Yourself is a personalized and socialized avatar application.
▷ **Enlisting to make a better product:** For example, Dell Ideastorm is a user-generated idea platform to innovate better Dell products.
▷ **Meeting people of similar interests:** For example, Method's People Against Dirty community rallies for clean in their household products, the environment, and everyday design.

Links to all of these examples are available at **wiki-brands.com**.

Extrinsic Motivations

People need more than intrinsic motivation; customers sometimes participate in exchange for reputation, fame, preferred access, and/or some outward recognition or validation of a job well done. In proper balance and
as a complement to a wikibrand's intrinsic motivations, these are equally
justifiable incentives.

Souplantation, a 110-outlet restaurant chain operating across fifteen
states, features its social media campaign actively in its physical locations. In a year, it has blown through the roof of membership and social
media–driven revenue expectations by leveraging extrinsic motivators. It
regularly offers up opportunities for promotional winners and loyal social
media participants to win Visa gift cards and free meal passes, in addition
to giving out Facebook- and Twitter-only coupons. A "Show Your Pucker
Face" Facebook promotion—recruiting people to share their sour lemon
faces during lemon month—drove a 400 percent increase in Facebook fans.
The community gets to pick contest winners, which also helps members
feel involved and recognized.

Extrinsic motivations for supporting wikibrand community efforts
include the following:

▷ **Ability to join a VIP circle:** For example, Maker's Mark Bourbon
  Ambassador Program
▷ **Access to an exclusive channel or influence:** For example, BMW's
  Ultimate Driving Experience
▷ **Access to exclusive resources:** For example, Google's beta-test invita-
  tions (for Gmail, Google Voice, Google Docs)
▷ **Chance for gaining wider fame:** For example, Jones Soda's personal-
  ized labels
▷ **Reputation building:** For example, Intuit's Love a Local Business
  small business praise and granting program
▷ **Recognition by the company:** For example, the Microsoft Most Valu-
  able Professional (MVP) Program, which recognizes exceptional tech-
  nical community leaders
▷ **Recognition by peers:** For example, the Mountain Dew Dewmocracy
  collective intelligence and package design competition where winners
  are chosen by community members
▷ **Sense of we-ness versus the rest of the population:** For example,
  Harley-Davidson's counterculture HOG community

The key challenge with extrinsic incentives is making sure that they provide enough value to the intended audience to warrant the effort required.

Explicit Motivations

Explicit motivations are tangible; participants get cash or a free product if they join the community. Brands offer these rewards to encourage broad participation and to compensate people for their contributions. According to Razorfish, up to 33 percent of those who enroll in social network brand/business pages do so in exchange for deals and discounts.[5] Too much explicit motivation detracts from the passion behind community participation, but too little—as in a number of crowdsourcing initiatives— can lead to participants feeling exploited. People value customization and exclusivity of incentives much more than strictly cash incentives.

New York–based frozen dessert chain Tasti D-Lite has pioneered a social media rewards program that incentivizes people to link their Twitter page, Facebook profile, and Foursquare accounts to their membership card. Participants accumulate points not only for purchases but also for social media sign-ups, retweets, and visits to product locations.

Beyond product samples, trials, and full use of company products, other explicit motivation triggers that support wikibrand efforts include the following:

▷ **Granting exclusive information or advice:** For example, alerts to U2 fans that an exclusive concert was being held in Second Life
▷ **Providing customized/personalized treatment:** For example, Sea World's advance preview experience for roller coaster enthusiasts
▷ **Compensating with cash rewards:** For example, crowdSPRING, which gives out cash rewards to amateur designers with successful client submissions
▷ **Giving nonmonetary rewards:** For example, digital badges for top Amazon reviewers
▷ **Distributing discounts:** For example, Groupon deals provided to people who participate and recruit others
▷ **Sending invitations to events:** For example, TED event invitations to a limited list of attendees
▷ **Granting points accumulation/loyalty program:** For example, SAP Developer Network points rewards program in return for posts, forum contributions, and online demonstrations

In Table 8.1, on the next page, we've matched a menu of wikibrand community features with twenty-five of the leading engagement motivations.

Outreach: The Influencers and Crowds Are Coming!

At the same time that you are choosing incentives for your wikibrand effort, you also need to understand who will be motivated by these incentives. Across the Web, a cross section of idea people, scouts, leaders, experts, organizers, and charmers are making the marketplace, society, and culture tick. By force of talent, charisma, and enthusiasm, they sway others' decisions about what to buy, think, and do. We call them Influencers. They are much more connected and informed than the mainstream and, depending on how you treat them, can be major allies or pesky foes.

As marketers, Influencers multiply the effect of your advocacy. As media or public relations broadcasters, they spread the word about your brand. As researchers, they are a savvy alchemy of wisdom and untapped imagination. As innovators, they are creative partners and sources of solutions and ideas. As community members, they are an extension of your employee roster.

Sadly, only 14 percent of companies are proactive about creating external brand advocates and leveraging them.[6] These companies are missing out on big opportunities. In a marketplace where more people are listening to their peers rather than advertisers, Marshall McLuhan's "the medium is the message" has become "the people are the message."

With the advent of the social Web, we can now see the impact of Influencers; for example, their Facebook pages and Twitter followings show their connectedness, credibility, and persuasive powers. Jeffrey Hayzlett, author of *Mirror Test: Is Your Business Really Breathing?* and former CMO of Kodak, understands the need to get out there and canvas your audience: "These conversations go on with you or without you. So you want to engage, educate, excite people and they become evangelists, or Kodak ambassadors [as] we call them. . . . It's very important for businesses or individuals, but especially for businesses, to get out there and engage with their communities."[7]

Why Are Influencers So Powerful?

In a 2008 article called "Is the Tipping Point Toast?" *Fast Company* profiled Duncan Watts's provocative study of Influencers. Watts argued that "a rare

TABLE 8.1 COMMUNITY PARTICIPATION MOTIVATIONS

INTRINSIC MOTIVATIONS		EXTRINSIC MOTIVATIONS		EXPLICIT MOTIVATIONS	
TYPE OF MOTIVATION	COMMUNITY FEATURE	TYPE OF MOTIVATION	COMMUNITY FEATURE	TYPE OF MOTIVATION	COMMUNITY FEATURE
Building better life/supporting cause	Affiliated charity	Ability to join VIP circle	Tiered levels of membership	Customer service	Moderated forum
Competing in challenge	User-generated contest	Access to exclusive channels	Secret passcodes	Information/advice	Discussion forum
Enlisting creativity	Photo/video gallery wall	Access to exclusive resources	Direct connection to company employees	Third-party incentives	Giveaways/merchandise
Creating fun/enjoyment	Mashup applications	Chance for wider fame	Featured members	Customized/personalized treatment	Dynamic profile/customizable avatar
Celebrating group effort/achievement	Team wiki	Reputation building	Leaderboard/ranking	Cash rewards	Cash prize for intellectual rights
Learning	Webinars	Recognition by company	Customer advisory panel	Nonmonetary rewards	Test/preview product
Satisfying curiosity	Insider blog	Recognition by peers	Community voting	Discounts	Point system to earn discounts through activity
Wanting to make a better product	Idea submission site			Invitations to events	Restricted-access events
Meeting people with similar interests	Searchable profiles/messaging			Points accumulation	Activity tracker

bunch of cool people just don't have that power. And when you test the way marketers say the world works, it falls apart. There's no *there* there." He suggests that Influencers have no role in propagating trends, ideas, or business.[8]

We agree with Watts that the coolest, youngest, loudest, or top purchasers aren't always the best advocates, but we disagree with his sweeping statement that Influencers have no impact on mainstream behavior. Consider the following statistics:

▷ Ten percent of people on Twitter are posting 90 percent of the tweets, and only 0.7 percent of Tweeters have more than a thousand friends.[9]
▷ Of visitors to Wikipedia, 0.7 percent edit 50 percent of the articles and 1.8 percent author 70 percent of the articles.[10]
▷ High-authority bloggers post three hundred times more frequently than low-authority bloggers.[11]
▷ On social bookmarking site Digg, the top one hundred users control 56 percent of the front-page articles.[12]
▷ Forrester Research claims that 80 percent of online influence comes from 16 percent of the people.[13]

What makes this special tribe of people influential? We've identified four factors:

1. **Reach:** Influencers have a deeper and wider circle of influence because they have:
   ▷ more intimate and close friends
   ▷ more colleagues and associates
   ▷ more affiliations to groups
   ▷ more links to other Influencers
2. **Exposure:** Influencers have more opportunity and motivation to flex their influence because:
   ▷ they adopt earlier
   ▷ they pay more attention to new trends
   ▷ they are exposed to more interests
   ▷ they make sense of the world more easily
   ▷ they receive and pass along more recommendations
3. **Credibility:** Others pay attention to Influencers because they are perceived to be:
   ▷ better informed
   ▷ more authoritative
   ▷ honest

4. **Suasion:** Influencers can convince even the skeptics with their:
   ▷ passion for and commitment to the subject, brand, or topic
   ▷ likability
   ▷ reciprocation and involvement (they practice give and take)
   ▷ expressiveness (they are strong communicators)

Mabel's Labels: An Army of Buzzmamas

Tricia Mumby is co-founder and vice president of Mabel's Labels, based in Hamilton, Ontario. The company makes labels for families and kids. Lots of labels. The kind that will not come off in a dishwasher, dryer, or microwave. Eight years ago, Mabel's was a basement hobby business; now it's a multimillion-dollar business with forty employees, thanks to one of the most powerful forces of social influence: "word of mom."

Mumby originally planned Mabel's Labels as an Amway-style, multilevel marketing, but she decided against this model because she knew her audience—mothers—was really busy. But as it turned out, she started to receive e-mails from women who wanted to spread the word about her product. The light went on. Women loved Mabel's, were talking about it anyway, and wanted their fellow moms to know. So Mabel's Labels set up an unpaid group of power moms called Buzzmamas who spread the word about the products and provide feedback to the company. "I'm one of these moms, so I instinctively know these people," says Mumby. "They have large social groups and are involved in all the activities and mom groups. They research online and ask for opinions before they buy anything. They're passionate about the Web and go out of their way to explain why and what they buy."[14] Of the tens of thousands of applications Mabel's has received, fifteen hundred have qualified as official Buzzmamas. This beachhead of Influencers has now turned into a solid base of moms on Facebook and Twitter.

Buzzmamas have become official representatives for the company in places where it can't have face-to-face relationships. Mumby reports:

We know our Influencer program works. It's one of the top ways people hear about us. When a new Buzzmama starts, as an online business, we can almost feel the conversation and word of mouth happen. Geographic micropockets of sales spring up in towns in Alaska or suburban Houston, and we know it's individual Buzzmamas at work. We were nervous at first, putting so much trust in people we'd never met, but it's been amazing. By personally relating to moms like I would at a trade show and dropping the brand attitude, we've come out ahead. Looking back, it's so simple. Ask your customers for help, and they do it. You just have to ask.[15]

Who Are the Influencers?

To some, Influencers might seem borderline obsessed, while to others they are passionately committed. Either way, they can be your brand's best allies, particularly if you can figure out how to make their passion work for your business. But your first step is to identify them. How can you pick them out of the crowd?

They are typically early adopters, embracing new technologies, behaviors, opinions, and styles weeks or months before the mainstream. They are, for example, twice as likely to have a new mobile device.[16]

They lead cosmopolitan, outgoing lifestyles and are curious about a broad range of subjects, which makes them great fact- and opinion-checkers. Not content to be experts on just one subject, they have a range of interests and are equally comfortable chatting about last year's best vintage, the plight of the homeless, and the latest episode of "Glee." They are twice as likely to read, paint, and engage in technology. Fifty-four percent of them strongly agree that "staying up to speed on trends is very important to me." [17]

Influencers are connected to a lot of people and find it easy to make friends. One mistake businesses make is to believe that friend counts on Facebook and top status on Twitterholic (a tool that measures top Twitter accounts by followers) or becoming a LinkedIn Lion (someone who is open to connecting with anyone) is a straight line to influence. Although digital connection points are a potential indicator of influence, more than 70 percent of word of mouth about brands happens offline.[18] Our research suggests that Influencers have social circles 2.4 times larger than others. They're also not shy about expressing their beliefs and opinions, and they're persuasive advocates for their points of view. Three-quarters of Influencers say they love talking to friends about what they've just discovered.

Researchers like Watts and others overlook the fact that influence is very category-specific. Although there are a number of "natural Influencers" with loud opinions, charisma, and social clout, the most important and credible trait of an Influencer is passion for a topic or interest. The exciting part of the social Web is that you can spot these people much more easily than you could in the past.

Commentators have categorized Influencers in a number of ways:

▷ Malcolm Gladwell distinguished them by talent in *The Tipping Point: How Little Things Can Make a Big Difference*, calling them savvy Mavens, social Connectors, and persuasive Salespeople.

▷ In *Buzz: Harness the Power of Influence and Create Demand*, Marian Salzman and co-authors categorized them by adoption stages, labeling them the Lunatic Fringe, Alphas, and Bees.

▷ In *Citizen Marketers: When People Are the Message*, Ben McConnell and Jackie Huba segmented them by their roles in social media as journalistic Filters, evangelical Fanatics, communal Facilitators, and attention-getting Firecrackers.

▷ Rob Kozinets, co-author of *Consumer Tribes*, defined them by their community involvement—Insiders, Devotees, Minglers, and Tourists.

▷ Charlene Li and Josh Bernoff, in *Groundswell: Winning in a World Transformed by Social Technologies*, studied the issue from the standpoint of participation in technology, coining the term *social technographic ladder* and classifying Influencers as creators, critics, and collectors versus the less-involved joiners, spectators, and inactives.

All these classifications help describe how Influencers support communities and interact with technology. We believe precisely defining the groups and identifying their motivations and timeline for getting involved is essential to wikibrand success. Through years of profiling and interacting with Influencers at Agent Wildfire, we have "thin-sliced" the Influencer prospect universe to create a profiling tool for recruiting new audiences. Each of these audiences plays different roles at different times as new information and products travel to the mainstream. For example, a tastemaker will be very interested in being in on the ground floor of a wikibrand initiative but may have lost interest before a social ringleader gets involved.

Six Classes of Influencer

In this section, we have identified the six classes of Influencer in the order of preferred involvement in wikibrand efforts: tastemakers (who make up 12 percent of Influencers); trendspotters (7 percent); opinion leaders (19

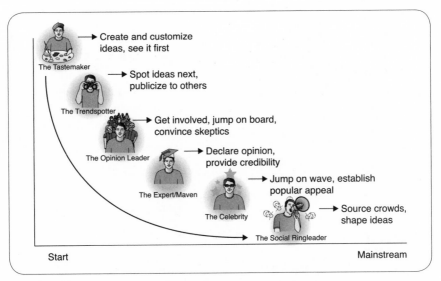

FIGURE 8.1 INFLUENCE ADOPTION CURVE   Source: Agent Wildfire Inc.

percent); experts/mavens (36 percent); grassroots celebrities (8 percent); and social ringleaders (18 percent). (See Figure 8.1.)

The Tastemaker, or Message Starter

Tastemaker motivations: to innovate, to create, to push the envelope, to be different

Tastemaker roles:
- ▷ Prosumption—building new stuff, collaborating on production
- ▷ Innovation sounding board—providing stimulus for innovation
- ▷ User-generated content—creating marketing content

The Trendspotter, or Message Radar

Trendspotter motivations: to be aware; to be first exposed; to have exclusivity, privileged access, and new styles; to participate in change; to be unusual and pioneering

Trendspotter roles:
- ▷ Beta-tester—optimizing the preliminary product
- ▷ Advance previewer—being the first exposed to the new product
- ▷ New trialist—becoming part of a testimonial group for new products

The Opinion Leader, or Message Seller

Opinion leader motivations: to lead, to convince, to be recognized, to debate, to be given the stage, to display passion and enthusiasm

Opinion leader roles:

▷ Testimonial advocate—being a public supporter of ideas

▷ Brand ambassador—converting others to the cause

▷ Seeded adopter—being the first to receive the in-market product

The Expert/Maven, or Message Credibility

Expert motivations: To be right, to be recognized as an expert, to share knowledge, to understand product details, to be asked for recommendations, to know insider information

Expert roles:

▷ Product rater/validator—testing existing products

▷ Key stakeholder—being invited to talk to company staff

▷ Collaborator/advocate—having authentic credibility in building and advocating products

The Grassroots Celebrity, or Message Magnet

Grassroots celebrity motivations: To be known, to be recognized, to get access, to become popular, to be visible, to be a winner, to build an entourage, to stand apart

Grassroots celebrity roles:

▷ VIP insider—getting exclusive access and star treatment

▷ Cause torchbearer—acting as a publicly recognized ambassador

▷ Buzz marketer—attending launch parties and red carpet events

The Social Ringleader, or Message Spreader

Social ringleader motivations: To be social, to share, to gift, to connect, to rally teams and groups, to provide a public service, to organize

Social ringleader roles:

▷ Word-of-mouth influencer—acting as a seeded post-market-launch brand ambassador

▷ Referral network—shaping ideas for popular digestion, inviting others (particularly mainstreamers) to join the cause

▷ Viral marketer—passing along content to others

The World Out There: Prospecting for Your Front Row of Influencers

We have defined the incentives and types of people you should be identifying. The next question to address is, how do you recruit these people and get them involved?

Wikibrand efforts rarely happen in one fell swoop. Instead, you will need to plan progressive recruitment efforts to get the right people involved in whatever small way you need to begin. If you turn your traditional classification of users, customers, and consumers into authors, testers, scouts, or collaborators, they'll naturally become ambassadors, advocates, and evangelists for your business. It's a three-step model of influence:

▷ **The early days:** Recruitment can start up to a year before the formal launch of your wikibrand community. Ensuring that you have a committed core of passionate users before you launch is key to establishing momentum and content when you actually launch. Software and entertainment companies have understood this for decades by providing beta-testing and sneak preview opportunities before wide release of their products. If your members have bought into a product or brand at its development stage, they're much more likely to stay committed to your community when it launches.

▷ **Launch:** You need to be everywhere. Smart communities go where potential members already live and use these extensions as traffic funnels to their community portal. Connections are the new currency: your ability to harness the enthusiasm of "weak ties and distant friends" of members can make or break your growth plans. Even though most people say they have only two or three close friends, the average user has 130 friends on Facebook and 70 followers on Twitter.[19]

▷ **Postlaunch:** To build your online community and help it grow, you need ongoing marketing. Leveraging traditional media and public relations to broadcast successes, using community-developed content to enhance marketing efforts, and serving the community with offline collateral and events are all popular ways to grow a community beyond its hard-core supporters.

Where to Find People: The Wikibrand Front Door and the Outreach Octopus

If you're like most businesses, you've only begun to look at influence as a way to analyze your customer database. Blogger outreach programs are beginning to identify the most valuable prospects. This work is important. Perhaps in the old days of "they told two people, and so on, and so on" it mattered less. In the social Web, where those two people have turned into hundreds of people, it matters a lot more. In a world of unlimited resources, you *could* approach everybody, but in dealing with real people in real conversations, you would get buried under the pile of traffic and interaction.

Scott Monty, head of social media at Ford, understands the need to market to and through Influencers:

> Digital Influencers are becoming part of every program we run for mainstream media. We're creating digital-only events and programs for online Influencers. With our launch of the Ford Fiesta, all we did was approach people with existing large communities, put their activities in one place, and allow for their unscripted, unedited interactions about Ford. We are intertwining owned media, paid media, and earned media together. We can't see this third part of the triumvirate as a broadcast mechanism where we blast information. We've had much better traction and percentage of return when we've become engaged as real people with our key Influencers than as a big behemoth brand. When it comes down to influence and really making people pay attention, it requires repetitive, consistent microinteractions from a human being to the right people.[20]

Word-of-mouth guru and consulting firm GasPedal founder Andy Sernovitz talks about the importance of finding your talkers. These are real people, not Hollywood celebrities. Every product has some talkers, and Sernovitz identifies seven types: happy customers, online talkers, logo lovers (the people who would wear your brand for free), eager employees, listeners, fans and hobbyists, and professionals.[21] Before going into "hunt mode," you should already know these people or have their information. Start with them.

Once you've exhausted your familiar prospects, you can visualize and organize your outreach to brand community members in fifteen social Web areas. We call them the outreach octopus (*quindecipus* not being a common term), which is shown in Figure 8.2. Every year, two to three new categories of social Web appear, so the octopus may have grown some new tentacles by the time you read this.

Although a corporate site and blog are at the heart of the octopus, a wikibrand has multiple community tentacles to broadcast its content, engage its customers, and recruit people to its inner circle. The laws of

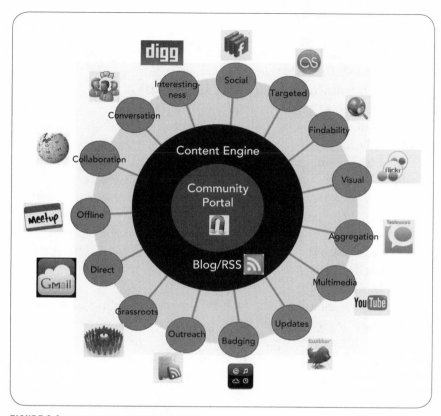

FIGURE 8.2 THE OUTREACH OCTOPUS

FLIRT—an energizing focus, great language and content, the right motivations and incentives, and proper outreach—will bring people to your home base. Following are the fifteen tentacles we identified:

▷ **Social tentacle:** a mainstream social network presence (such as on Facebook)
▷ **Targeted tentacle:** a niche network presence (for instance, Last.fm for music or LinkedIn for business professionals)
▷ **Findability tentacle:** a search engine optimization presence on sites like Google, MSN, and Yahoo SEO (particularly at the start of campaign)
▷ **Visual tentacle:** Flickr-type sharing for photos
▷ **Aggregation tentacle:** an RSS-fed syndication and aggregation of your community's content and news
▷ **Multimedia tentacle:** YouTube-type sharing for videos

▷ **Updates tentacle:** microblogging (as on Twitter) for quick updates and conversations
▷ **Badging tentacle:** widgets and avatars for committed and influential members to broadcast their participation
▷ **Outreach tentacle:** a social media news release (a version specifically meant to support blogger outreach)
▷ **Grassroots tentacle:** an Influencer media presence that niche-targets your audience
▷ **Direct tentacle:** e-mail and other direct-to-consumer communications
▷ **Offline tentacle:** Events and meet-ups for offline connections
▷ **Collaboration tentacle:** wikis and aggregated member-generated content
▷ **Conversation tentacle:** industry discussion forums via external sites
▷ **Interestingness tentacle:** social bookmarking (as on StumbleUpon or Digg) for flagging interesting content

Besides these digital grassroots hubs, leveraging traditional assets can also be extremely effective. Integrate wikibrand efforts with broadcast advertising, mainstream public relations, retail merchandising, search engine marketing, and customer service channels to build a community quickly.

The Community Richter Scale: Membership Is Not Equal

Once you have attracted users from the world out there, the influence meter starts over. Participation is not equal in communities, regardless of influence existing outside of communities. Usually a small group of committed people drive value for the greater good. Charlene Li's Social Technographic Ladder suggests that only about 6 percent of U.S. Internet users actively create content.[22] Community membership breaks down into four strata (from least to most involved):

▷ **Crowds/lurkers** consume, validate, and benefit from content.
▷ **Contributors** scrutinize, add to content, and cooperate.
▷ **Creators** add fresh content and collaborate.
▷ **Evangelists** are passionate, committed, and immersed ambassadors who spread the word about the community.

We have called our breakdown the Richter Scale for Community Member Commitment (see Figure 8.3). It moves from one-time lurkers on the

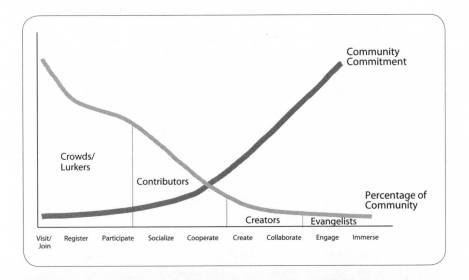

	COMMUNITY IMPACT	LABEL AND TRAIT	APPROX. % OF COMMUNITY MEMBERS
Crowds/Lurkers	Less than 2.0	Visit: people who merely visit and consume content	100
	2.0–2.9	Register: people who have provided some level of personal information	100
	3.0–3.9	Participate: people who perform some minimal level of activity (e.g., provide ratings)	80
Contributors	4.0–4.9	Socialize: people who connect with others (e.g., post full profiles and messages)	40
	5.0–5.9	Cooperate: people who work on group efforts (e.g., participate in a poll)	20
Creators	6.0–6.9	Create: people who develop new content	10
	7.0–7.9	Collaborate: people who work together to achieve goals	5
Evangelists	8.0–8.9	Engage: people who engage, rally, meet up, and visit daily	2.5
	9.0–9.9	Immerse: people who are immersed, pseudoemployees	0.5

FIGURE 8.3 THE RICHTER SCALE FOR COMMUNITY MEMBER COMMITMENT

low end to committed brand ambassadors on the high end, where members are fewer, their commitment stronger, and their value greater. Similar to the seismic scale, the potential impact created at each community level is logarithmically larger than the one before it. Thus, content and incentives that push people from laissez-faire contributors to hyperactive evangelists carry great value.

Even with multiple motivations in play, brand community participation will vary. Be aware of what to expect:[23]

▷ **90-9-1 rule:** Of an average audience, 1 percent will actively answer questions and post, 9 percent will comment and ask questions, and 90 percent will passively read the content on your community. This percentage rule may vary slightly, depending on how well you target your audience, the incentive and motivation involved, and what you're asking people to do. But in most large communities, 1–6 percent of the population drives the majority of content. Smaller, extremely well-recruited communities can get 60 percent of their population to participate actively.

▷ **30-10-10 rule:** During any thirty-day period, about 10 percent of the traffic that sees your community promotion will visit your community area. Of this 10 percent, about 10 percent will register and participate in your forum. This uptake will vary based on several factors, such as the type and placement of your promotion and registration requirements. Also, the percentages tend to be lower for highly trafficked sites, such as major media destinations. Business-to-business communities attract smaller, more targeted audiences.

▷ **Five to ten posts per day:** Members hate visiting ghost towns. You need roughly five to ten posts per day per discussion forum to keep members interested and involved. In the early stages, a core of fans or employees may be needed to help get the community going. For a healthy community, the number of posts per month should grow by 10–20 percent per month for the first year.

CHAPTER 9

RULES, GUIDELINES, AND RITUALS

This Is How We Do Things, and That's OK

When tectonic plates grind and shift beneath the earth's crust, massive amounts of change take place on the earth's surface. Volcanic activity, earthquakes, mudslides, and tsunamis all manifest themselves as a result, and a significant reshaping of the earth's landscape ensues. In fact, the word *tectonic* has become a common term to describe large and unsettling changes in politics, business, and technology. The social Web represents this type of tectonic shift, creating fissures in how corporations have been doing business for hundreds of years. Opening themselves up so transparently to frontline employees and consumers can cause managers to tremor and quake. These shifts in philosophy challenge long-standing beliefs on how business builds management hierarchies, manages its employees, defends its legal rights, and retains its corporate assets.

More than a few companies struggle with finding the right balance. Organizations feel conflicted between the personal, transparent nature of these new tools and technologies and the traditional, closely guarded secrets of corporate strategy. Tension exists between

> "A few strong instincts and a few plain rules suffice us."
>
> —RALPH WALDO EMERSON

an employee's work and personal life. Mashups and social interplay using company trademarks and intellectual property bump up against historical beliefs about what constitutes a company's legal possessions. How much flexibility and encouragement can a company provide to this nascent space while still maintaining a prudent amount of corporate oversight and governance?

With the expansion and importance of new social technologies, what might have been considered pesky distractions are now legitimate concerns and, let us not forget, potential opportunities for established companies. Fifty-four percent of companies impose an outright ban on the use of social networks like Facebook and Twitter at work, and only 19 percent allow for limited work-related or social use of these tools in the workplace.[1] Only one-fifth of these companies have established some type of formal policy for employee use of external social networking sites. The "ostrich-with-its-head-in-the-sand" attitude of managers—thinking if they ignore it, the issue will just go away—disenfranchises employees and companies from their marketplace. With an estimated 1.2 billion global social media participants already, a rise in social media membership heading toward more than 50 percent of many countries' populations, and an extremely high growth percentage of time spent on these sites, it's getting harder and harder to avoid these spaces.[2] One wireless company's ads in Canada recently played on the insight that using your personal wireless device can allow you to interact with social media even if your corporate firewalls do not.

In spite of its potential, the social Web has caused some to consider the potential liabilities. Employee productivity, trademark protection, disclosure of company secrets, harassment and defamation suits, privacy rights, and information security have all been raised as concerns. The top seven areas that IT security professionals see as problematic are oversharing about company activities, mixing business and personal social media use inappropriately, engaging in social network rage, allowing dubious strangers (competitors, trolls) access to information, raising security risks through password sloth, allowing hackers access to servers, and endangering personal information (identity theft and kidnapping).[3]

In practice, some of these concerns have merit; others are red herring issues. For example, in the question of productivity, Workplace Media suggested that 78 percent of at-work Internet users in the United States spend less than half an hour a day on social networking sites when given the option. A separate study suggested that social network participation actually boosts productivity overall.[4]

That said, companies that have a consistent and uniformly enforced policy with regard to customer and employee engagement and the social Web also have a much stronger legal defence, a much more empowered employee base, a much clearer set of principles to guide the member/customer/community experience, and a much more confident and supportive executive team.

Social media gurus bemoan the slow pace of innovation inside companies. With respect to setting up rules of engagement, most are a bit cavalier in their judgments. In fact, these carefree companies may be shooting themselves in the foot.

In our Buzz Report research, when we asked what the biggest hurdles were for companies trying to implement customer collaboration, brand engagement, and social media in practice, five of the top ten reasons related, at least in part, to not having clear rules and guidelines supported by senior management for enabling social business and media use. These reasons were inability for company culture to accept the change (ranked number three), organization adoption issues and silos (number five), real/perceived risk (number six), fear of loss of control to consumers (number eight), and legal/regulatory hurdles (number ten).

Given the widely held belief that the benefits of participating in social media tend to outweigh the associated risks, the common-sense answer to establishing rules is "When you jump, just make sure you have a safety net." It's a reasonable philosophy. Never before have companies been so open to their outside constituents, and never before have more people been involved in the process. Think about how companies have dealt with journalists and traditional media for decades: public relations people needed to be authorized; executives and managers needed to be trained for media interaction and briefed on key messages, context, and the news of the day before speaking to outside parties. Why should social media be held to a lower standard?

As the social Web continues to evolve and become increasingly important, establishing rules and guidelines to encourage thoughtful interaction and scalable conversations will become a necessity. For a company, it means avoiding chaos; building an engaged company culture; and delivering an optimal wikibrand focus, language and content, incentives, motivation, and outreach. Businesses, brands, customers, employees, members, fans, and prospects all stand to benefit. Companies need an engagement code to live by. It is simply smart business to consider what boundaries and encouragement your organization will use to guide its efforts.

The Rules and Guidelines

Obtaining advice and consulting online experts helps to balance legal and practical risks for proposed wikibrand efforts and community experiences. Scott Wilder, formerly general manager for Intuit's online communities and now senior vice president of Edelman Digital, told us that getting chief legal counsel onside early with Intuit's first developmental work in social media was vital. Having counsel involved in building early solutions instead of asking them to play cops in the later planning stages created a feeling of mutual ownership.

Organizations have labeled their rules and guidelines in many different ways—Dell broadly defines it as "online policy," Coca-Cola uses the narrower "online social media principles," and Wal-Mart has developed the even-narrower "Twitter external discussions policy." However they are characterized, the rules need to provide a balance of dos and don'ts. The dos might include a statement such as "Here's what we encourage and the benefits," "Here's how we do it here," or "Here's guidance and support for gray areas."

Adam Christensen, program director of digital strategy and communications for social media communications at IBM, suggests that neither fully top-down policies or completely grassroots development work. Rules and guidelines have to form around company culture and customers, or people will find ways around them.[5] With four hundred thousand employees scattered across 170 countries, this is no small company cultural feat, but somehow IBM makes it work.

Considering the scope of IBM's involvement in social media, there is surprisingly little news of downside issues or problems relating to openness. Once regarded as a staid, conservative company, IBM has embraced vibrant communication. Social media and search marketing manager Todd Watson says that the company's openness has transformed how it does business, improved the speed and accuracy of its communications, and improved competitiveness because it can innovate more precisely to fulfill its clients' needs. IBM encourages its employees to take communication seriously: there are sixteen thousand internal blogs, more than a million daily wiki page views, and sixty thousand staff members linked to each other through social media. Thousands of IBM staffers are tweeting; more than 50,000 are on Facebook; and more than 225,000 have LinkedIn accounts. According to Watson, it is essential that as much of a company's social footprint as possible participate in the communication process;

assigning "social media" to a single twentysomething employee will frustrate people who are trying to engage with real experts.[6]

IBM redefined how it collaborates through some online jams of a colossal scale. Over three days, 150,000 internal and external constituents participated in an online brainstorming session that produced more than forty-six thousand ideas and launched more than ten new businesses, including Real Time Translation Service, The 3D Internet, and Smart Healthcare Payment Systems. IBM followed through with a commitment to invest more than $100 million to develop these new projects.[7]

IBM's own study of CEOs from around the world identified five key drivers of a progressive-minded business:

▷ **Hungry for change.** It continually evolves marketing's approach.
▷ **Innovative beyond customer imagination.** It markets through direct customer collaboration.
▷ **Globally integrated.** It operates as a global marketing organization.
▷ **Disruptive by nature.** It encourages renewed and compelling thinking.
▷ **Genuine, not just generous.** The organization speaks with a genuine voice.

Prudent use of Web-enabled technologies, empowerment of employees, and development of a set of rules and employee self-governance positions IBM for success across all five of these guiding principles.

Much of the social enthusiasm is spawned from an IBM culture that is already employee-driven and collaborative in nature. IBM employee communities have existed for a long time and predate some of the more high-profile efforts. The first Innovation Jam, hosted back in 2003, started IBM's transformation into a collaborative enterprise. While some of these experiments have turned into surprise runaway hits, IBM knows what's going on. The top-rated factors in creating its brand perceptions are experience with company employees, exposure to analysts and professional associations, and friends' opinions. The people are the brand; it's what IBMers do that matters, not what they say they do. News articles, TV, ads, and promotions rank far behind in influencing brand value. For bottom-line business reasons, it only makes sense for IBM to create an engaged employee base that speaks well about the company externally.

In part because of these engagement efforts, the "smell of the place" has also improved. Internal research shows that employees who are more actively engaged in the various networking environments and social collaboration care more about IBM than those who aren't. They are more willing to contribute to the company's success,[8] to meet new people, and to expand their global network. They are also able to access expertise more easily wherever exists.

Christensen remarks, "We represent our brand online the way we always have, which is employees first. Our brand is largely shaped by the interactions they have with customers. We realized we could trust employees to engage. Employees realized, 'If we're within reason, we're going to be trusted.'"[9] To govern the full ecosystem of effort, IBM released a set of employee-built social computing guidelines in the spring of 2005, a set of twelve straightforward rules that have stood up well to time and changing technology.

The question is, if a successful $100 billion Fortune 500 company that is America's largest patent holder and has a conservative reputation and a business-to-business audience can make this work smoothly with little top-down control or direct intervention, might there be hope for other companies to do the same?

Within marketing and communications, social Web practices are maturing, but as times goes by, these same tools are spreading into core areas of the enterprise, including human relations, customer service, research and innovation, and business operations. How do companies support all this activity? How do these conversations scale up? Pages need to be updated, videos generated, communities built, tweets responded to, and blog posts scheduled. The heavy lifting of community building requires some organizational street savvy and sweat. Smart use of content distribution software, monitoring services, moderation tools, and better technology can only go so far. The real hope is getting a broader spectrum of employees, partners, and nonemployee fans and advocates involved.

In a few companies, this type of involvement is expected. More than five hundred employees at Zappos have taken their CEO Tony Hsieh's lead and joined Twitter Nation. More than 60 percent of them have more than a hundred followers. This creates enormous content, word of mouth, and customer service advantages that have helped drive the company's business growth, goodwill, and exposure across one of the world's fastest-growing networks. Given such a tight culture, Zappos's only two policies governing social media are using your best judgment and adhering to the company's ten family core values. We will talk more about Zappos in Chapter 12.

In practice, however, bringing employees and brand fans into the social Web can be challenging. An element of reciprocal trust is missing; management believes bad things will happen, and employees live in fear of an online police state. In one high-profile example, 2010 FIFA World Cup soccer players from Spain, Brazil, Mexico, Holland, Germany, Argentina, and England were forbidden by their management to use social services such as Twitter.[10] Previous bans on sex, alcohol, and late hours were fodder for barroom debate, but these very public restrictions extended themselves to the online sphere of social media, depriving fans of the inside scoop of what was going on during one of the world's top spectacles. Coaches, 1; Fans, Nil.

The biggest hurdle in many companies is establishing a clear set of guidelines and statement of trust to employees about best practices and acceptable behavior. In reviewing some of the top twenty corporate public Web or social media employee policies, we uncovered sixty-five different components to consider when building rules for employee involvement. Including all of them is probably overkill for any organization, but it is interesting to note the considerations they all share (such as code of conduct, privacy, transparency, and treatment of proprietary information) and those that are unique to individual companies (such as Ford's compensation of Influencers, Coca-Cola's global impact on the Web, and Kaiser Permanente's and other health care organizations' concern for patient privacy). Beyond just stating the rules of the playground, some of the smarter companies have also introduced certification processes, employee training, internal collaboration networks, and scenario role-playing.

Wikibrand communities and the social networks on which they operate need to rely on clear, explicit, shared rules to deliver an experience that balances participant and customer interest and still is fun, rewarding, safe, and efficient for everybody to engage in. Investing the time upfront to get these rules right, perhaps learning from other brands' errors or codeveloping with a customer advisory panel, is time well spent.

Fluctuations in policy or introductions of new policy have created community insurrections. Facebook's mercurial philosophy and initiatives that have pushed the boundaries of protection of member privacy—initially expanding member profile information from being shared with just your friends, then to networks, then to all Facebook users, and now to the whole Internet—have been met by stern resistance from its members, leading to negative impact on Facebook's revenue-generation ability, debate about its real motives, and consecutive *mea culpas* by founder Mark Zuckerberg. Proper rules and guidelines direct action in customer collaboration efforts to three audiences. They tell new visitors, "This is what we value"; they say to new or recently joined members, "This is how we do things here"; and they reinforce to existing members, "This is how we live by a code and resolve disputes."[11]

In a legal world, wikibrand activities exist like any other outward-facing company activities such as promotions, investor conferences, packaging, and advertising. Important legal and ethical risks relevant to geography (such as state laws and regulations) need to be considered to ensure that your company isn't liable for damages and lawsuits.

In a user-generated wikibrands universe, the aspect of ownership can also be a contentious one. If you create a work of art using a Campbell's soup can and post it on the company's site, who owns that work of art and image? In a fast-moving environment where profiles, art, photos, film, music, content articles, and literary works are commented on, uploaded, downloaded, mashed up, and contorted freely, there is little precedent to decide where the line is between individual rights and formal brand assets. Ensuring that there are appropriate rules and guidelines to be clear about ownership, licensing and usage rights, and accreditation should also be a consideration in your wikibrand efforts.

The combined list of explicit rules and suggested guidelines fall into four categories:

▷ Employee policies
▷ Experience facilitation
▷ Legal and ethical terms
▷ Ownership

We also propose a fifth category comprising rituals that are not policy-driven but bubble up organically in top-performing wikibrands.

Employee Policies

Jason Falls, principal of Social Media Explorer, uses the "bus rule" when it comes to employee policy: "If you get a hit by a bus, who is going to carry the ball when you're gone?" Falls has a master command of the subject; he has authored and suggested eighteen types of social media policy based on the needs, usage, and type of media.[12] He goes on to mention that many smaller companies seem to know what to do naturally. They use common sense and typically emulate the behaviors of their founder or leader. Falls recognizes that this does not work as well with larger companies, particularly in heavily regulated industries, and that some guidelines are necessary.

He remarks, "The best policies I've seen and developed are not a set of restrictions, but instead allow people to feel more comfortable using their own websites or various social media outposts. Leading companies outline 'Here's what we do, here's what it will take to make you successful, and here are the top things you need to know.'" Although lawyers need some specificity in such documents, a policy is only as strong as what a manager can impart to his or her employees. Falls suggests creating a "top ten important things" cover sheet to attach to the formal policy.

The trickiest legal policy question is, if you are going to have a blog, Facebook page, or LinkedIn profile as a person, can your company have any authority over that? It's a messy issue, Falls admits. In our Buzz Report, executives and managers claimed 38 percent of their time in social media was spent in personal use, 30 percent was business use, and 32 percent was a blend that couldn't be segmented since they had become intertwined.[13] To use a Seinfeld-ism, "worlds are colliding," and some people are feeling the crunch.

Companies have policies on how employees should interact with traditional media, e-mail, phone requests, and other external contacts, and they need policies for employee activity in wikibrand initiatives as well. These policies should govern both work-related and personal online interaction and spell out potential ramifications for policy infringements.

Common sense should prevail here, but given the fact that wikibrand-driven companies allow for the broadest range of employees to participate in social media and communities, you may need to undertake scenario planning and employee training to manage potentially problematic situations. A clear set of employee policies will give your staff the confidence to create or contribute to the company's community without fear of breaking unknown or unarticulated rules.

In reviewing the top industry benchmarks for corporate social media policies and employee handbook additions, we inventoried the language, features, and formats of these guides. Although the policies were comprehensive, they were sorely lacking in one important quality—readability. Many would satisfy their company's legal and communication requirements, but would employees read them, use them as reference tools, or be motivated by them? Not likely.

Kodak deserves special mention. It has produced a colorful sixteen-page guide that provides encouragement from its CMO, an explanation of the social landscape and its relevance to people's jobs, how it all fits in with Kodak's overall strategy, expert tips, examples of Kodak's use of social media in the past, and a web of resources to help employees get started. All of this is published alongside the ten required policies and procedures that support Kodak's official employee business conduct "one-voice" policy. It's a motivating document that contains more carrot than stick, brings the social media effort to life inside Kodak, and likely encourages participation as evidenced by the eleven thousand Kodak mentions every month in the blogosphere.[14]

Smart employee policies dealing with the social Web tend to be grouped into thirteen different sections and answer the following questions:

▷ **Rules of purpose:** Why are we doing this? What is the relevance of the effort? How does it support company policies and goals? How has the customer and business landscape changed to promote this? Why is this policy important?

▷ **Rules of privacy:** How do we deal with proprietary information and trade secrets? How do we protect the privacy of partners and customers? How do we handle financial disclosure? What is the company's official privacy policy?

▷ **Rules of copyright:** How do we treat company and third-party copyrights and trademarks? How do we deal with fair use and user-generated content? How do we handle compensation for partner/member efforts? How do we ensure that credit is given to others?

▷ **Rules of people:** Who gets to speak on the company's behalf? What group of people and partners does this policy govern? Who gets access to administer or jump over the company firewall? Who moderates and approves content? Who can authorize an employee's role as a social media participant? What additional diligence is required by managers and executives?

▷ **Rules of personal responsibility:** Do we understand the potential impact and individual responsibility behind social business behavior and content? How do we ensure that people think before they post? Have we provided an explanation of how the Web has lasting and global impact?

▷ **Rules of effectiveness:** Have we covered the necessity of researching a subject? Are we being human in communications? Are we truly engaging the audience? Are we being responsive and respecting the audience? Are we posting frequently enough or too frequently?

▷ **Rules of transparency:** How do we ensure transparency of identity, role, and intent? Do employees understand that they should speak in the first person and never operate under a false identity?

▷ **Rules of behavior:** Have we made it clear that employees should avoid fights? Are we representing the company prudently? Does our content convey a sense of having fun? Do we adhere to the legal rules of local geography? Do we post only ethically responsible material? Are we respecting the rules of a third-party venue? Are we living up to the employee code of conduct?

▷ **Rules of expertise:** Have we told employees to speak only on subjects about which they are knowledgeable? Do they know they should correct mistakes quickly? Have we encouraged two-way dialogue? Have we covered the proper treatment of official media requests, and do they know how to distinguish opinion from facts?

▷ **Rules of security:** How do we avoid spammers, malicious software, and phishing? Are we protecting passwords? Do we use common sense on personal information?

▷ **Rules of personal spaces:** What are the rules for speaking outside of sanctioned work environments? How do we expect employees to treat the discussion of work matters when they are personal participants in social spaces (such as in personal blogs)? What are possible disclaimers?

▷ **Rules of consequences:** What are the potential repercussions for violating the policy?

▷ **Rules of support:** What is the certification process for representing the brand? What is the step-by-step guide to get started? When in doubt, who can employees contact? Where is training available? What is the list of additional resources employees can turn to? What are supporting Q&As and possible scenarios?

Experience Facilitation

As an experiment, place a number of children in a room, give them some toys, leave them alone to decide what they should do, and let noisy chaos reign. Without some level of suggestion or direction, kids will almost certainly get progressively louder. The initial sense of freedom, novelty, and curiosity might cause small cliques to form that exclude some of the children. Fights break out. Hair gets pulled. Noses get bloodied. The kids may retreat into corners for some alone time. Eventually, even the most excitable child runs out of gas, and even the best behaved become bored, silent, and potentially angry.

It's apt to remember the directionless, bored child metaphor when facilitating and managing customer engagement and customer communities in wikibrand environments. Although strict, corporate-driven rules hinder member engagement and prevent natural communities from forming, having no rules invites the wikibrand equivalent of *Lord of the Flies*. At either pole, brands can single-handedly provoke community suspicion and backlash. Either situation can affect participation across the full range of tools and platforms (see Chapter 10), whether they're built and owned by the company (such as communities, wikis, blogs, and forums) or housed on other networks (social networks, industry forums, Influencer blogs, and so on).

The best customer communities are neither brand dictatorships nor radical experiments in open source development. As Joseph Jaffe, CEO of the consulting firm Crayon, advises, "Don't cede control completely to your consumers. They don't want it. Meet them halfway. Partner with them. Work with them." [15] Prospective community members need to feel that there is a belief system, a structure, a dispute mechanism, and an intelligent method to managing their user experience. Some of this infrastructure can be hard-coded and designed as you build your wikibrand environment.

To be comfortable, participants also need to feel that a real person is accountable for monitoring and shepherding activity, encouraging good behavior, and steering people away from negative actions.

David Armano, senior vice president of Edelman Digital, suggests that great user experiences in social Web environments should be designed to be useful, usable, desirable, sustainable, and social. He notes that it gets progressively more difficult to build user experiences that can evolve, scale well, and support a community.[16] With an infinite number of touchpoints, it's tough to design for every possible avenue, but some can be anticipated. To reach out to a prospective visitor to your community environment, have a simple landing page, provocative graphics, a motto/tagline that states a sense of mission and purpose, and a prominent and easy registration process. For returning members, options for personalization, frequency of new activity, and relevant content are sought-after expectations. For long-standing members, celebrate anniversaries and milestones, highlight their unique and ongoing contributions, and provide a channel for deeper involvement to keep them engaged. A golden rule for any of these audiences is to design function and form that is easy to scan, read, click, understand, and link to, according to their interests.

Other types of experience facilitation need to happen on the fly. Addressing dispute resolutions, new functionality, and changes in technology and features are just some examples. One general rule is to be as consistent and transparent as possible, setting out the rules for your community before you launch, so potential members know what they're getting into. When rules change or are perceived to change midcycle, you can usually expect a backlash. As an example, a Nissan community in Canada caused widespread disappointment among some of its most active participants when the weighting of democratic versus judge-rated evaluations of contest entries changed midcampaign.

Six Additional Rules and Guidelines to Facilitate Wikibrand Experiences

Addressing customer and prospective member wants is paramount in wikibrand universes. Here is some rule-based guidance.

Statements of Purpose or Character

Statements of purpose give the themes and broad guidelines that will govern the community areas and brand activities. Consider them a moral compass for the business soul. They should provide clarity of focus, emphasize meaningful values beyond just making money, and demonstrate the motivating reasons why someone should participate. Hopefully, they provide the wow factor that provokes a reaction from a wikibrand prospect— "Finally, a space for people like me." Support points can include the genesis, history, and story about the effort and your business, profiles of the people who started or are involved with the effort, a list of values or a manifesto about the brand, and testimonials from current participants or the type of participant your community wants to attract.

Even though they sold a majority stake to Coca-Cola, European-based smoothie company Innocent Drinks continues to appeal to customers' casual, humble, ethical nature (and their thirst to the tune of two million drinks per week) with its very human statement of purpose:

We sure aren't perfect, but we're trying to do the right thing.
It might make us sound a bit like a Miss World contestant, but we want to leave things a little bit better than we find them. We strive to do business in a more enlightened way, where we take responsibility for the impact of our business on society and the environment, and move these impacts from negative to neutral, or better still, positive. It's part of our quest to become a truly sustainable business, where we have a net positive effect on the wonderful world around us. Keep reading to find our strategy for . . . keeping things natural, sustainable ingredients, sustainable packaging, sustainable production, and sharing the profits.[17]

Rules of Initiation

The rules of initiation govern initial membership requirements to enter a wikibrand environment:

▷ At what stage is registration required?
▷ How much information must members provide?
▷ How much information and functionality will be provided to visitors and nonmembers before they join?
▷ Is there automatic admission as a member? A judging or peer review process? What are the criteria for entrance?
▷ Will membership profile information be visible to others?

Rules of initiation dictate who gets to participate and how those who do enter the process. Wikibrand efforts are usually kept as open as possible to capitalize on the exponential, social distribution of the Web. Registration should be easy to promote a gradual relationship (open digital identities like OpenId and Facebook Connect make this process even easier). Intelligent wikibrands make the initiation process hurdle-free, providing incentives for greater participation upon user revisits and performance.

In certain cases where a tight community is desired, Influencer recruitment exists, or the potential incentives are large, limiting the number of participants makes sense. Doing so based on some type of qualification criteria adds the potential for delivering aspirational buzz. In wikibrand outreach efforts where the business values the quality of input over quantity, where the hope is to create a network of already-existing fans versus a cross section of everybody, or where resources are stretched to support efforts, it's entirely reasonable to tighten the initiation criteria. Successful communities operate across both low and high initiation standards. H&R Block's Get It Right community provides simple, easy sign-up, whereas the SAP Referral & Influencer Program presents a much tougher entry mechanism and high exclusivity appeal.

Rules of Interaction

The rules of interaction set down guidelines about the types of content, language, content format, and content history that your community allows, encourages, or rejects. Do not be too restrictive; negative comments should not automatically be seen as unacceptable. In many instances, negative comments can either act as catalysts for change within the company or trigger a sense of collective responsibility among community members.

Intel has a smart, even-handed policy with regard to content posted to its forums:

> The Good, the Bad, but not the Ugly. If the content is positive or negative and in context to the conversation, then we approve the content, regardless of whether it's favorable or unfavorable to Intel. However if the content is ugly, offensive, denigrating, and completely out of context, then we reject the content.[18]

In most cases, well-moderated communities can manage what Forrester Research calls the five community detractors—legitimate complainers, engaged critics, competitors, flamers, and troublemakers. Legitimate complainers and engaged critics are perhaps your most valuable participants. Legitimate complainers need help with products or services and want to bring attention to issues, perhaps warning others. Frank Eliason, senior director of Comcast Cares, has built a reputation on solving problems for or explaining policies to legitimate complainers.

Engaged critics think they can make your products and services better, and they may be right. Consider opening up a forum for discussion with this group. Microsoft leans on this type of detractor in its community forums to improve the ongoing development of products and manage quality issues.

More problematic are the other types of detractors. Competitors, flamers, and troublemakers take pride in playing out grudges in public, sometimes using profane language. Not all of them require removal from your communities. Just as you do privately, as a brand owner you need to judge when to engage in a fight and when to learn restraint and leave battles for another day. As long as you are stating facts, rallying around the community focus, and handling exchanges respectfully, few interactions with this group will turn into customer service conflagrations. Addressing concerns privately and, in some cases, banning members for the overall public good may be considered last-resort options. According to Rob Kozinets, professor of marketing at Yorks University in Toronto and co-author of *Consumer Tribes*, one of the positive attributes of mature wikibrand communities is that the community members self-govern inappropriate behavior.[19]

Top companies have established interaction decision trees that diagnose forum and community behavior. The U.S. Air Force has implemented an intuitively smart diagnosis and action grid using transparency, source of best content, speedy response, professional tone, and highlighting influence as response considerations. Based on the nature of the content, the

Air Force has four options of response—share success, final evaluation, restoration, and fixing the facts—and two options of nonresponse—let content stand or monitor only. Consider it a pilot's dashboard for possible social interaction.

Rules of Exchange

The rules of exchange are the most straightforward and help facilitate what we call "the plumbing of your wikibrand initiatives." Frequently found under Help in the FAQs area of a website, these missives outline the required steps that must take place for activities to happen, ensuring that processes can be performed efficiently. They can govern any or all of the following:

▷ Frequency of e-mail/activity/contests
▷ Approved file formats, file types, file sizes, and dimensions of submissions
▷ Method of acceptance or evaluation
▷ Deadlines and requirements for participation
▷ Reward distribution

With the complexity of user-generated content and community interaction, providing an architecture that delineates topics and provides easy access to the most popular types of questions is a rule of exchange best practice.

Rules of Moderation

The rules of moderation determine who is authorized to moderate content and when and how forums and update areas will be posted, displayed, and governed. Resist the temptation to preapprove or screen all potentially offensive or brand-damaging content; members will pick up on the policing and lose interest in the community. In highly sensitive areas, organizations have started to use external moderation companies, particularly in situations where content may be generated globally and therefore requires twenty-four-hour community moderation. In the cases of large or established communities, members may be in a position to police content and educate others on accepted behavior more efficiently and effectively than company staff can. In some wikibrand scenarios, such as Mozilla's or Wikipedia's, these groups of unpaid ambassadors have the authority to moderate content.

Community managers may be called on to play a number of roles as part of moderation. They are the tour guides, sentries, ombudspeople, and cheerleaders for healthy, vibrant communities. Their duties may include asking and answering questions, explaining motives, recognizing regular members, expanding discussions, featuring top-performing members, giving credit for good content, teaching new members, trafficking or fixing technical issues, assessing pain points and frustrations, elevating concerns, identifying opportunities, and communicating status. (See Chapter 13 for more on these roles.)

The golden rule of moderation is you may own the environment and host the community, but you don't own the community. Respect customer needs, apply a human touch, and allow for flexibility wherever possible.

Legal and Ethical Terms

Legal teams need to be well versed in the full range of wikibrand strategies, tactics, tools, and technologies. Whether for personal or professional purposes, attorneys are starting to understand the medium quickly. Half of the top legal firms blog, close to a third of them have company Facebook pages, and three-quarters of them are on LinkedIn.[20] These firms understand that a full range of defamation suits, privacy issues, trademark and copyright concerns, harassment and discrimination business, and contractual issues can arise in a seemingly innocuous social campaign effort. This is compounded by the fact that social networks have added risks from volume, lack of control, and immediacy. A good portion of the growth in social media monitoring tools has actually been driven by a legal need to understand what the environment looks like before taking the first plunge.

Although rules and guidelines will be always specific to local geography, they usually include the following areas:

▷ **Governing law:** What jurisdiction and general code of law will be used to resolve disputes?
▷ **Rules of content:** What types of content will be viewed as inadmissible or grounds for member banishment? (This question is particularly important when children are involved, regulatory issues exist, or the risk of false content is high.)

▷ **Rules of privacy:** How much or how little of members' personal information will be revealed, and to whom?

▷ **Rules of identity:** What types of identity and disclosure are required? Will false identities be accepted? Will multiple identities be allowed? Will false identity information disqualify the member?

▷ **Rules of contests, promotions, and rewards:** What is the deadline for participation? What are members' odds of winning? What specific rewards will be given? What are the evaluation criteria? What are the expected fulfillment and membership criteria (such as age and geography) for community activities?

Even though legal teams can play a key role in mitigating risks, avoid writing your terms of use in legalese. Make the rules clear and explicit to minimize disputes and facilitate a better, safer user experience. When the full legal text is required, some wikibrands have developed a much more "human," shorthand version with a link to the longer form. Ethical boundaries that steer participation in these media can be more challenging and should weigh the principles of freedom, flexibility, and independence on one side with minimizing harm and being accountable on the other.

Ownership

Intellectual property is a sticky issue in an age where many people are personally branded and create their own content and art. When content is used in support of an organizational brand that helps influence and drive company benefits, who ultimately owns that content? Estimates suggest that Facebookers will post 124 billion photos to the platform in 2013.[21] Not an insignificant number, but as an individual participating or a business encouraging submissions, do you really know who owns those photos?

If you ask Facebook, you might not like the answer:

> By posting User Content to any part of the Site, you automatically grant . . . an irrevocable, perpetual, non-exclusive, transferable, fully paid, worldwide license . . . to use, copy, publicly perform, publicly display . . . such User Content for any purpose.[22]

You may need to kiss the ownership of those photos good-bye. This question appears to be a complicated one for both brands posting content on third-party environments and brands providing communities, user-generated platforms, and forums in their own Web environments to their fans.

Articulating two other kinds of rules related to ownership of the community and its assets is necessary:

▷ **Rules of governance.** These rules pertain to the policy and procedures for establishing and changing rules, especially about who actually controls the community. In some situations, a third-party network may have ultimate authority. If you read the bylaws of most social networks, the networks have the ultimate right to shut your page down or will be able to do so at a later date by changing their rules. This is not an insignificant consideration if you have spent years building up thousands of followers only to log in one day and realize you have lost this asset. In some communities, ownership is shared by a collective of people who participate. In other areas, businesses and brands technically own the platforms where content is served but may want to tread reluctantly on enforcing or changing rules. If they are not spelled out clearly, the lack of specificity may impinge on your ability to generate revenue, assert authority when required, and make key decisions within your community.

▷ **Rules of intellectual property exchange.** These rules govern the ownership of creative materials and content submitted in communities. Some believe that historic copyright law is insufficient to support the use and distribution of commercial content online. American writer and online community pioneer Stewart Brand describes the paradox: "On the one hand, information wants to be expensive because it is difficult to create and valuable. On the other hand, information wants to be free because the costs of getting it out to others is getting lower and lower all the time. So you have these two fighting each other." [23] Industries have been put in peril, lawsuits have been won and lost, and government policy has shifted based on the tension between author rights and copyright holders. Our role is not to debate the moral and economic grounds here. Whether it's audio, text, video, or image, Creative Commons—a more flexible copyright model designed for digital use—can act as an effective licensing tool and a complement to copyright law, providing a middle ground for free and legal sharing, use, repurposing, and remixing of content. [24]

The participatory nature of the personal social Web that you experience every day through your favorite social networks, blogs, and e-commerce sites is now expected more and more from the business Web. It is beginning to fulfill some of the visionary promises made by early Web advocates who envisioned a future that the majority wasn't ready for. One guiding opinion on how to operate as a wikibrand comes from Charlene Li, founder of Altimeter Group and coauthor of *Groundswell: Winning in a World Transformed by Social Technologies*: "If you're going to participate as a marketer in the social computing arena, you've got to have thick skin and be ready to engage in the messy world of your customer's opinions." [25]

An appropriate number of rules and guidelines for wikibrands rests somewhere between the beliefs of social Web libertarians, who believe the Internet should be akin to the Wild West of no standards and no rules, and the reactionary establishment types, who believe we can't trust anything outside and sometimes inside the corporate castle walls. When it comes to rules, they should be experimental in spirit and dynamic in nature, designed to build the right behaviors and not lock down mediums. As Seth Godin smartly suggests, company use of social media is a process, not an event. Let your rules be flexible. [26]

The Case for Wikibrand Rituals: A Special Type of Rule

"Welcome to Fight Club. The first rule of Fight Club is you do not talk about Fight Club. The second rule of Fight Club is you DO NOT talk about Fight Club! Third rule of Fight Club: if someone yells, "Stop," goes limp, or taps out, the fight is over. Fourth rule: only two guys to a fight. Fifth rule: one fight at a time, fellas. Sixth rule: the fights are bare knuckle—no shirt, no shoes, no weapons. Seventh rule: fights will go on as long as they have to. And the eighth and final rule: if this is your first time at Fight Club, you have to fight."

—**TYLER DURDEN**, *character from the movie* Fight Club

Rituals have a special place in the *R* of the wikibrand FLIRT model. They are not hard-and-fast statements like rules, nor are they guidelines that provide some sense of the mores that exist in wikibrand spaces. A *ritual* is described as a set of actions performed mainly for their symbolic value. It may be prescribed or follow the traditions of a community. In business-to-consumer environments, rituals can be extraordinarily powerful and allow people to feel a much tighter connection than they normally would.

As loyal Guinness fans, we know that it takes 119.53 seconds to pour the perfect pint. It may not be the fastest way to whet the appetite, but as loyalists, we believe it's the best way. At Starbucks, we instinctively know that depending on our need for caffeine, we will order a Tall, Grande, or Venti. Sure, we could call them small, medium, and large, but where's the fun in that? Prostate cancer charity Movember has tapped into the primitive and uniquely male ritual of wanting to grow facial hair when given the chance. Hockey players grow playoff beards; MoBros grow moustaches in support of a worthy cause. Top-performing eBay PowerSellers are celebrated at annual conventions where they are cheered on by eBay employees; wined and dined; and given highly sought-after pins, collectibles, and swag. Face it: rituals are cool.

As big sports fans, we know that rituals endear fans to teams. As life-long Chicago Cubs fans, we know that we sing "Take Me Out to the Ball-game" in the seventh inning; outfield walls are better with ivy and brick; the best baseball games are played during the day; raised white flags means the Cubs have won; we will never live down the curse of the goat; and you always, always throw back home run balls hit by the opposing team. Despite not winning a World Series since 1908, these rituals and tra-ditions are what keep the faith and bind us closer to the team.

Lebron James does a pregame chalk toss. Detroit Red Wings fans throw octopuses[27] on the ice after home team goals. The New York Yankees take curtain calls after home runs are hit. Winning football coaches should always expect a Gatorade bath. And on the other side of the Atlantic, noth-ing is quite so stirring as watching Liverpool fans sing "You'll Never Walk Alone." The New Zealand "All Blacks" Maori-based haka chant strikes fear in the heart of opponents. Fanship is enhanced by the presence of rituals.

The coiners of the term *brand community*, Albert Muniz and Thomas O'Guinn, defined a structured set of admirers of a brand as having three key markers: a shared consciousness, a sense of moral responsibility, and rituals and traditions. The first two traits suggest a sense of connection and duty to the brand and to the overall community. They described the third trait of rituals and traditions as representing "vital social processes by which the meaning of the community is reproduced and transmitted within and beyond the community. [These] typically center on shared con-sumption experiences with the brand."[28] Further studies have found a posi-tive quantitative correlation between the presence of rituals and traditions and the strength of communities.

When people adopt, abide by, stay loyal to, or master a ritual, it creates emotional connection and social meaning among fans and members, a feeling of being connected to the group. Think about Twitter and the idea of hashtags, Follow Fridays, retweets, tweet up, and fail whale.[29] These activities became a shorthand glossary in the early days for people who knew their Twitter stuff versus the mere enthusiasts or onlookers. They were rituals that allowed members to educate and proudly boast to Twitter newbies.

Rituals can be built into online or offline communities, be direct parts of the product or service itself, and be performed individually or in groups. In some cases, rituals can take the merely average and everyday and turn it into an experience (for example, the art of eating an Oreo cookie); in others, a good experience can become iconic (such as placing the lime in a Corona).

The most successful rituals introduce new people to the brand as a rite of passage. This knowledge is passed on firsthand. Each consumer educates the next in a viral pattern. The very act of performing the ritual gives the consumer ownership. That person learns the ritual and teaches another, who teaches another, and so on. This makes simple, easy rituals more effective. The simpler the ritual, the more likely it will spread. When the act is simple, fun, and easy, the passing of it can become pandemic. Complicated rituals die quickly or are simplified by the people who perform them.

In many cases, rituals bubble up organically within the community, but looking for rituals in the way that consumers experience your brand, formalizing them, and adding wind to their sails is smart wikibranding. If a small group of consumers has built a ritual around your brand, then it may have the potential to become a movement.

In your Web engagement platforms, customer communities, and social media, consider the following questions:

▷ When you are building your community, are there unique ways to welcome your new members? Returning members?

▷ Are there small, distinct ways to say thank you or reward contributions?

▷ Can you create your own brand or community glossary of words and definitions?

▷ Are there silly rules and guidelines that simply exist? Or eccentric ones that improve the experience?

▷ Are there any myths, lingo, or common rites or rituals that suggest somebody has been a part of your wikibrand cult for a while? Can these be shared?

▷ How do you mark member rites of passage and celebrate anniversaries or milestones?

▷ Could a book of brand laws be created for your best advocates?

▷ Could you develop a personality test that members could take to become part of the community?

▷ Can you host periodic fun events to play up a unique facet of your business or brand history?

▷ Can you institute peculiar contests or traditions that people could expect regularly?

▷ Do you have a set of oaths, criteria, or laws for members who want to become true brand fans?

▷ Do you give members or elite members of your community nicknames?

Rules, guidelines, and rituals are only as beneficial as the people who practice them. In defining and codifying them, you need to ensure accountability and establish an audit system to determine whether they are even being practiced. Don't be partisan to the challenges of implementing them. On one hand, a holdover corporate myth of control exists. In a customer-controlled marketplace, people (including your employees) have a lot more control than you think. If your rules are too stringent, people will use tools and filters to find a way around them. Good rules, guidelines, and rituals set boundaries—some important, some fun, some socializing, and some necessary; don't make them handcuffs. On the other hand, there is a myth of democracy. Without good rules, guidelines, and rituals, as well as employees or community managers to enforce them, people—including your most fervent Influencers—will find it too taxing, too unpredictable, too compromising, or too chaotic to promote you through their passions and interests.

One final thought about rules that we have learned as change agents in a fast-moving business world. Question the rules—at least the bad ones. Rules are made to be followed to the extent that they serve their purpose, but they are often put in place to keep the status quo and hamper the types of innovation wikibrands need. In the great majority of organizations, more employees should be asking tough questions:

▷ Why is that rule true?

▷ Does anybody know who wrote that rule?

▷ What happens if we don't follow that rule?

▷ In this century, is that rule still true?

It drives the rule makers crazy. Before asking the tough questions, just be sure to ask one of yourself, "If I don't like their rules, whose would I use?"

CHAPTER 10

*T*OOLS AND PLATFORMS

If You Build It, They May Come

The vernacular and tools of wikibranding will almost certainly change two years after the writing of this book. After all, the term "Web 2.0" has gone from popularization by Web pioneer Tim O'Reilly to everybody's buzzword to agonizingly stale jargon in merely six years.

Consider having a lunchtime conversation a mere half decade ago, when talking about microblogging, tweeting, downloading iPhone apps, watching a YouTube sensation, or Facebook friending and poking would have gotten you quizzical blank stares. In fact, even when a group of digitally experienced managers were recently asked whether Facebook would be the dominant social network three years from now, only 42 percent of them said yes, despite its commanding worldwide success. Steve Chen, co-founder of YouTube, predicted YouTube would go nowhere because "there's just not that many videos I want to watch"; less than two years later it was sold to Google for $1.65 billion.[2] Many digital marketers and Web start-ups might suggest the pace of current Web business cycles can now be measured not in two years but in two months.

"Companies—and the people who comprise them—need to recontextualize how they do business. In a connected world, power shifts with those best able to connect."[1]

—DOV SEIDMAN, *CEO, LRN*

With the accelerated pace of digital time, wikibrand tools may change quickly, but the business goal will always remain the same: how do you engage your customers, prospects, and Influencers across multiple platforms and get people to take action and feel a deeper sense of commitment for your brand? Wikibranding doesn't advocate a complete reset on the motivations and tools for modern-day business. The fundamental idea of getting people to move through the business funnel from mere awareness of your brand, to interest in a trial, to satisfied customers, to happily serviced and listened-to loyalists, to zealously advocating evangelists is a constant. The key differences now are the engagement strategies and tactics that customers value (described in the previous four chapters) and the more pervasive, open, and fragmented tools that are available to get the grapevine growing.

Throughout this book, we have used the descriptive terms of wikibranding interchangeably: customer engagement, grassroots brand experience, the social Web, online community, user collaboration, influence marketing, and new media. They are the seven continents of the wikibrand world. The very use of such a large number of descriptions implies the comprehensive nature of the tools involved; it's a much larger palette than most organizations can even believe. Even though nearly two-thirds of marketers would label the umbrella category of this new generation of tools "social media," Michael Brito, digital strategist for Intel, sums it up best: "Social media is not the messiah; it is one of several tools."[3]

In fact, we can name more than a hundred different tools that play a balanced role in the development of wikibrands across traditional and nontraditional tactics. They can be grouped into four camps: brand/product-based design and attributes, marketing/media communication, customer-brand interaction, and digital/social-enabled technologies. The first two tactics have always been around but need to provide a different resonance; the latter two have become important new tools in the wikibrand arsenal. Across all four camps, the best contemporary businesses recognize that embedding entertainment, sociability, services, and information is important in everything they do, not just in digital media.

Going cold turkey from traditional practices to wikibranding is difficult. Traditional product design and branding still needs to drive good value and differentiation. Customer service still requires a phone cord. Avoiding traditional media that still reach many eyeballs is unthinkable. Instead of doing a complete about-face, present-day businesspeople need to ask three pivotal questions:

▷ How do my traditional tools change in light of a new marketplace?
▷ To what extent do I need to shift to new tools?
▷ Which specific additions do I add?

The Dell Story: Wikibrand Tools as the Ultimate Form of Direct

From the ashes of a customer service crisis labeled "Dell Hell" in 2005, Dell launched its journey as a wikibrand, building a varied nexus of social media tools into its mix. Altimeter's Jeremiah Owyang has characterized Dell as a "honeycomb" social organization that allows a wide set of employees to participate in an organized fashion; more than 40 percent of Dell's employees are on LinkedIn and hundreds participate in the company's forums and in social networks.

Although originally developed to tackle customer service issues, Dell has expanded its social media's mission to include brand reputation, product ideas, and sales. Through its Ideastorm crowdsourcing site, it has waded through thousands of customer ideas to formally implement more than four hundred of the best-ranked into its business and products. The corporation uses the customer rating and review systems on its Dell outlet to establish future product selection, casting serious scrutiny on any product with a customer-based rating lower than 4.5. Customers now flex a considerable amount of muscle in Dell's world.

Richard Binhammer, senior manager of corporate affairs, recalls the early days of Dell's evolution and its current maturation: "Initially pushed by company leadership, we had a rapid expansion of social media involvement. These teams were akin to working in greenhouses on country roads, experimenting and fertilizing plants, then seeding and planting them in distant business units. By early 2009, these teams were organized around business units and had expanded considerably; now we have organized centrally around corporate, business-to-business, and consumer segments to avoid redundancies and inefficiencies. We have also set up an organizational climate and structure that effectively supports being wherever our customers operate; the more places we're available to them, the better it is."[4]

Dell believes it's just as important to go to where the conversations exist. Binhammer likens the company's philosophy to those of Copernicus and Galileo, who saw the Earth's place in the universe differently. The analogy is that if Dell is the Earth, then it competes in the much larger Milky Way of the social Web. As a consequence, woven within its central site is a set of sharing widgets that brings its "owned" content back out to that galaxy. Given a range of blogs, hundreds of official Dell and employee Twitter accounts, more than a hundred Facebook pages, YouTube and Flickr channels, and community ambassadors, Dell was recently ranked the second-most engaged brand.[5] In total, Dell has built an aggregate presence with 3.5 million people across its various communities.[6]

Manish Mehta, vice president of social media and community at Dell, says, "We've learned that social media has transformed the large corporation of the millennium into the mom-and-pop shop of the old days. The emergence of social media simply makes it more possible to connect directly with customers every day. Dell's community goes well beyond our own forums—it now extends to direct contact with millions of followers worldwide."[7]

Binhammer believes this expansiveness in social media is a natural result of his company's core business approach. "Dell was initially founded in 1997 on a direct business model. It's the very fabric of the company," he explains. "People may think it's about manufacturing and customization, but it is really about going direct to the customer, and social media is the ultimate form of going direct. For example, if people are sitting in Starbucks talking about Dell computers, we need to be part of that conversation. With social media and the Web, we can become a part of it, and this is a huge strategic asset for us."[8]

A Generation of Chatterers

If you care about being relevant, no type of business is immune to using these new social tools. Rallying cries for social media and collaboration have historically mentioned how consumers no longer only consume, they now produce. It's true. People don't abjectly sit back, graze, and consume anymore; they blog, provide reviews, edit video, share photos, submit ideas, and mash up tools. Added to all these newfound capabilities, we suggest that the second wave of the social Web is now about chatting.

A Hubspot analysis of social media has pointed to a sea change in social Web behavior over the last two or three years. Back in the old days of 2007, 80 percent of the global social community's engagement happened on an originating website. Whether it was a traditional corporate or media site or a blog, the social activity happened right there in the comments or forums section. Now thanks to Facebook, Twitter, and integrated applications, the social Web itself has been transformed. The source of traffic has reversed; more than 80 percent of engagement now happens away from the originating website.[9]

People are chatting. The average Facebook user shares sixty-two pieces of content every month. In this ever-expanding universe of the social network–engaged, members are retweeting, social bookmarking, sharing, and liking feverishly. If the new generation of prospective customers is no longer visiting islands of owned or paid content, savvy businesspeople are wondering if they should launch boats to the other shores, asking the following essential questions: To whom are these people chatting? Where are they sharing this content? How can we engage them? What tools can we employ?

The Wikibrand Formula

We have talked extensively about how the landscape has changed and how the strategic and tactical elements required to build and maintain a brand have gone through a rinse cycle. As much as we hope you like the journey of exploration and evidence we have provided, we know that people inevitably want shortcuts. What's the magical wikibrand formula?

We have seen a number of algorithms for defining success in a postmodern brand world. Some lean toward participation (among the social media advocates) and others toward scale and traffic (among the e-commerce and search engine optimization, or SEO, groups). We have distilled both sides and added a nod to how traditional business has customarily worked to create a handy formula:

Wikibrand value = (Core product/service + Experience) × (Interestingness + Socialness + Intimacy + Authenticity + Reputation + Incentives) × (Presence + Value Adds + Advocacy)

The elements in this formula can be divided into three categories:

THE ORGANIC FACTORS

Core product/service: The tangible and intangible attributes, value, and differentiation of a product, service, or brand.

Experience: The quality and remarkability of the customer journey across the steps of being aware of, selecting, buying, receiving, using, assisting, maintaining, resolving, and returning to your brand.

THE CONTENT AND TOOL ENGAGEMENT FACTORS

Interestingness: The amount of creativity, relevance, intrigue, and utility of the content your brand produces. This can be an amalgam of entertainment, escapism, information, design savviness, creativity, storytelling, and emotional resonance.

Socialness: A measure of engagement, participation, social connections, and community your brand empowers though your content. This can be ambient (such as downloading a widget), direct (signing up to be a member), or very involved (producing a video).

Intimacy: The level of personal connection, customized treatment, and individualized co-ownership your business produces with customers.

Authenticity: A factor of trust; the real and perceived amount of genuine engagement your brand engenders.

Reputation: The degree of brand affinity; the equity built up by your brand and its social footprint.

Incentives: The magnitude of brand reciprocity; the explicit, intrinsic, and extrinsic rewards your brand provides to visitors and members.

THE AMPLIFICATION AND CONNECTION FACTORS

Presence: A measure of scale. How deep, frequent, and wide-reaching is your brand activity exposure?

Value-adds: A measure of the content, insight, and support your customers produce for other customers.

Advocacy: A measure of word-of-mouth advocacy. How willing and active are your visitors/members in recommending and referring your brand to friends and colleagues?

There you have it. It is about who you are, how and where you speak, and how far your message is positioned to travel. In considering your need for wikibrand tools, you need to audit how well they deliver on your desired wikibrand focus and the elements of our wikibrand formula.

Home and Away Platforms: The Need for Built and Affiliated Communities

"I came to a fork in the road, so I took it."

—YOGI BERRA

According to Jeremiah Owyang, brands have indicated that only 20 percent of their success (in communities) is due to technology; the remaining 80 percent is thanks to a combination of internal roles, processes, organizational models, and support.[10] We have made that same argument about wikibrands, although at some point after the first four letters of FLIRT have been determined, you still need to take on the *T* and make a call on the technologies and tools you are going to employ. And before deciding what programming code will be written, you need to consider where you're going to operate.

A topic of rancorous debate has been the comparative appeal of three very different e-beasts: the corporate website, the online community, and social network extensions. Which do you believe is most important to your organization's success?

In an effort to control costs and complexity, companies that believe they need to consolidate are hunkering down, choosing narrower directions, and sticking to them. This philosophy is being furthered by self-interest groups: boutique agencies that favor gorgeous-looking, stand-alone sites; e-commerce/technology companies that push security-tight, enterprise infrastructures; Silicon Valley, which pushes white-label, company-owned, collaborative environments and ad platforms; and social nets that peddle third-party social network platforms.

On the side of revolution, public relations professional Steve Rubel points out that the future value of the Web will be in Web services, not in building websites. He believes the next great media company will be "all spokes and no hub and will exist as a constellation of connected apps and widgets that live inside other sites and offer a full experience plus access to your social graph and robust community features. Each of these may interconnect too, so that a media company's community on Facebook can talk to the same people on Twitter." [11]

Only 16 percent of professionals agree with Rubel's point that corporately owned websites are no longer relevant and that social networks can adequately house and deliver the required digital business objectives. Companies still do need an arena where they can feel at home and engage their most involved stakeholders.

Rubel's larger point has merit though. Even if they don't give up their home base, the leading marketers on the Web are wisely creating application programming interfaces and plug-ins, turning themselves into embed-and-play services on key portals like Twitter, Facebook, YouTube, iPhone, Amazon, and Microsoft. The mushrooming industry of widgets and social ads is creating an ecosystem of portable content and services on others' sites that can go anywhere and everywhere the consumer wants and helps to overcome the clutter of online choice.

Hopefully, we can put the age-old 2.0 question (Do you build your own online communities or connect on others?) to rest once and for all. We say, "Why choose?" The essential need is to invest in both. Remember the role of the Web in building business value for a wikibrand is to be everywhere for all people with a balance of environments, content, benefit, and control.

Each of these footprints serves a valuable purpose, and if you look at the best engaged brands, they have healthy participation in and integration of the three camps of corporate website, sponsored community, and social media extensions. This is the brain of customer engagement: the corporate website represents the brain stem and cerebellum, controlling a company's vital functions; the online built community represents the limbic brain that controls emotions, value judgments, and positive experiences; and social media extensions represent the neocortex that provides for the infinite abilities of language, imagination, and consciousness.

Table 10.1 suggests how each camp contributes to your organization's wikibranding efforts. Ignoring even one eliminates access to a big part of the digital value chain.

The Hub and Spokes of Community

Think about a bike wheel; the corporate website and built brand community comprise your hub. You control it and host the conversation, inviting the spokes to turn, and it powers what your business does. In many companies, the built community has embedded itself into the corporate site (as with SAP); in others, the two are separate but linked (as with Microsoft and Channel 9).

The affiliated communities are the spokes, extending your good content into the microcosms of the Web and unchaining that content to leave it loose and fancy-free. The most commonly tapped affiliated communities are microblogging channels (such as Twitter), social network pages and groups (such as Facebook), video-sharing channels (such as YouTube), photo-sharing pages (such as Flickr), and external customer forums (such as Get Satisfaction).

Here's the key reason why you need the hub and spokes to your wikibrand wheel: if you look at the six key requirements of building an effective community, built communities and affiliated communities perform differently at each step:

▷ **Outreach:** For most prospective communities, the people you need to find and recruit are "out there," not "in here." Finding enough interested

TABLE 10.1 DISCUSSION LEVELS WITHIN COMMUNITIES

TRAITS	CORPORATE WEBSITE	BRAND COMMUNITY	SOCIAL NETWORK
Ownership	Corporation	Corporation and customers	Customers and network
Tone	Official	Collaborative	Social
Purpose	• Sell • Promote	Engage and incubate participation	• Recruit • Get noticed • Relax/have fun
Audience	• New customers • Users/purchasers • Analysts/partners • Talent/employees	• Business fans • Key Influencers • Engaged employees • Lifestyle advocates	• Savvy networkers • Digital enthusiasts • Prospects • Instant customer service
Content traits	Information	Exchange	• Buzz • Friends • Fun
Content fluidity	Static	Dynamic	Minute-to-minute
Time frame	9 A.M. to 5 P.M.	6 A.M. to 9 P.M.	24 hours
Exposure	Public	Public/private	Public
Ongoing requirements	• Provide official information • Share contact information • Create brand space	• Engage with fans • Create discussions • Show a human face	• Meet a wider audience • Rebroadcast content • Show a corporate pulse
Done well, demonstrates to customers	A well-differentiated business you should buy	A fulfilling, rewarding experience you should immerse yourself in	A personal, fun experience that will take you deeper inside company
Biggest handicaps	• Detachment • Slow pace	• Difficult to scale audience • Need to resource	• Ability to create deep content • Ability to build deep relationships

people among 1.2 billion people in social networks, 500 million Facebookers, 70 million LinkedIn users, and 105 million Tweeters makes building a crowd considerably easier than phoning your best friends. (Advantage: affiliated communities)

▷ **Seeding:** Identifying the right group of users to be your front row of testers, collaborators, users, and ambassadors takes a blend of options. In support of affiliated communities, having a lot of people enter the candidate funnel and already knowing what they are doing and saying in the outside world are important recruitment criteria. In support of built communities, an intimate understanding of the interests and commitment of people who are already linked to your brand makes it easier to identify hard-core fans. (Advantage: neutral)

▷ **Engagement:** Competing in a world of hundreds of thousands of Facebook pages and iPhone apps is way too difficult to create any type of meaningful engagement. The user experience in these arenas is to graze and sip, not to settle into one space and go deep. After initial sign-up and interest, 73 percent of Facebook page signees revisit those pages infrequently.[12] Additionally, all of the meaningful metrics, insights, and opportunity to build a relationship belong to the platform instead of the sponsoring party; you are at the sponsor's whim. Finally, any customization requirements depend completely on what the social network platform or user forum allows you to do. It simply pays to build your own community to engage people on a deeper, more controllable basis. (Advantage: built communities)

▷ **Collaboration:** You may want to break out a discussion, a project, an idea, or a group and get a subset of engaged and informed people to rally around it away from your general mainstream group. Once again, it's tough to create that intimacy and interaction on popular social networks; you're just another subway stop on a user's very long social Web train. Creating a sense of commitment, affinity, and collective interest happens in built communities, which are enhanced by your ability to control and design the environment to address community users' core motivations. (Advantage: built communities)

▷ **Affiliation:** Recall from our incentives discussion in Chapter 8 that people experience extrinsic, intrinsic, and explicit motivations. Affiliated communities allow you to broadcast your reputation to a much larger audience, which drives extrinsic value. Built communities deliver a group of intensely interested people, which is likely to drive intrinsic value. The potential for driving explicit value is up for grabs between built and affiliated communities. (Advantage: neutral)

▷ **Rebroadcast:** When good content goes viral, it infiltrates social networks and user forums away from the confines of the built community itself. Check out the *New York Times* as well as most established media; the majority of their Web traffic now comes through links from affiliated communities rather than specific destination visitors. Their good content gets marginalized if not for the eyes of these extended networks. In addition, these rebroadcast extensions support stronger search engine rankings to create a second level of rebroadcast appeal. (Advantage: affiliated communities)

The short argument is that affiliated communities help build scale and built communities help build engagement. One without the other will hobble your brand bike, no matter how hard you pedal.

Built Community Tools

Built communities operate under many names and have different levels of exclusivity, depth of interaction, touchpoints of connection (online, offline, integrated), and motives. By polling organizations, we found that the top ten types of built communities (in order of priority) are: word-of-mouth referral and Influencer programs, customer challenges and testimonial programs, brand ambassador programs, Influencer seeding, customer advisory panels, community outreach, employee referral programs, online brand communities, fan clubs, and crowdsourced networks.

Choosing the appropriate platform to house the online activities of your company-sponsored efforts is a significant factor in the success of your online communities. There are four basic approaches:

▷ **Basic portal:** This is a preferred approach for small organizations. Your company owns a basic central page that links out to brand spaces on third-party platforms. Naked Pizza provides an example of a simple website with an accompanying LIVNAKED blog and key brand extensions on Twitter, Facebook, Flickr, and Foursquare.

▷ **White-label platforms:** The community is built on a hosted software platform that delivers custom branded networks. Companies like Ning have built more than one million of these types of networks for small business, not-for-profits, and trade organizations. This approach has appeal given the low cost, simplicity of creating a community, self-supporting content management and moderation tools, and no requirements for deep technical knowledge. The downside of these sites can include limited customization, support, and security.

▷ **Made-to-order platforms:** This approach capitalizes on open developer support (Drupal and Joomla), commercial software (such as Sharepoint or Lotus Connections), or software as a service (such as Jive, Kickapps, Lithium, or Liveworld). Your business has complete ownership of the site (or site subscription) and data but often not the software code. Companies find this option interesting because of the ability to outsource the building, integration, and maintenance of feature-rich community sites to seasoned experienced professionals. However, customization, integration, and cost creep can be challenges.

▷ **Customized platforms:** In build-your-own scenarios, your business builds a community from scratch with its own content, data, and code. Companies find this appealing because they can create fully customized designs and incorporate innovative functionality. But benefits may be mitigated by the costs of development, support, user experience testing, and the lack of applications and a stable set of internal technical skills to maintain upkeep.

James Cherkoff of Collaborate Marketing says that staying in front of consumers on the technology front is a much bigger challenge than it used to be:

> Consumers now effectively have the cutting edge when it comes to technology, which is new because previously corporations had all the expensive, efficient, powerful enterprise technology. But enterprise technology is moving very slowly in comparison to the tools and applications available on the Web. So I think in some degree, the consumers have the edge for the first time when it comes to the technology they're using.[13]

In recent years, the technology options available for built communities have multiplied to catch up to customer technology empowerment. There are a core set of popular platforms and vendors, all with their own pros and cons, as well as literally hundreds of less-prominent platforms, many tailored to particular functional or industry niches. In considering viable options, a number of questions need to be asked: How sophisticated does your community's technology and activity need to be? To what extent should you build your site yourself? What are the branding, cost, and security implications? If your community expands, will you be able to add functionality and support easily?

We believe there are fifteen core considerations in choosing or building a technology platform:

TYPE OF SOFTWARE/LANGUAGE

▷ **Language:** The building blocks of community (PHP, .net, AJAX, .asp, Ruby on Rails, Java, and so on) all have varying traits that may help determine your choice.

▷ **On-premise software versus software as a service (SaaS):** You need to balance the licensing, cost, and speed benefits of SaaS with the deeper functional requirements achieved by on-premise software installation.

▷ **Open source versus proprietary software:** There are appearance, cost, support, security, functionality, and switching cost considerations on both sides of software choices.

COST AND TIME

▷ **Sunk costs:** If you have already bought a license or made structural or training investments to work on one type of community software, this may steer your decision.

▷ **Deployment time and process:** How long will it take and how difficult will it be to deploy or transition to a community platform?

CUSTOMIZATION

▷ **Customization:** Brands have design needs that often go beyond the cookie-cutter templates offered by some of the white-label services. How much brand look and feel can you create?

▷ **Integration:** Ease of use and the ability to work with other social networking sites, programming languages, other media (such as mobile), an internal database, and customer relationship management programs are all considerations.

▷ **Skills:** What skills will employees need to work with the chosen software and platform?

▷ **Support:** The extent of service that will be needed before, during, and after implementation is an important consideration.

SCALABILITY AND USABILITY

▷ **Scalability:** The functionality needs of a community of one thousand are much different than those of a community that will support millions of people.

▷ **Features and APIs:** Can the platform integrate all key community features and also third-party applications that may need to be added in the future?

▷ **Availability of plug-ins/modules:** Can the platform provide a ready-made set of additional functionalities and developer extras?

▷ **Management:** Your company's technical and nontechnical staff must be able to administer the community requirements.

SECURITY AND OWNERSHIP

▷ **Security and data integrity:** Larger companies and regulated industries tend to set higher standards for protecting member and company information and databases.

▷ **Ownership of assets:** You need to determine who will own the data, content, software, code, and hosting.

The platform choice may be one of the most important decisions you make in building your community. Today's online community platforms come with an impressive combination of features, add-ons, and capabilities that support connections between you and your customers. Like selecting between cough and cold medicines and toothpaste, they almost defy comparison. Do you want the medicine for a hacking cough or the tooth-whitening toothpaste? Avoid the full laundry list of concerns and focus on the essential issues you want to solve.

The Eleven Cs of Built Communities

Online-based brand communities are not just elaborate websites. They are more member-driven, they have more open contribution, they are more personalized, they are more dynamic and interactive, and they're certainly more participation-driven and engagement-inducing when done right. You also have to plan for all the potential permutations of user-driven activity, so they require more tools and features than a garden-variety website.

Members of brand communities want to connect, play, react, reach out, create, and collaborate. One study estimates that the one-third of users on e-retailing sites who take advantage of community features generate two-thirds of sales.[14] You need to empower that one-third.

We have categorized brand community features into the Eleven Cs chart in Table 10.2 to explain the range of possible features in order from the simplest engagement to the deepest.

The community 101 tools are what most mainstream brands understand. Frequent and compelling communication/content and competitions are as strongly received in community arenas as they are in traditional arenas. Dogfish Head Ales provides a strong example of how even a small, craft-brewed company delivers interesting content across a variety of forums, blog posts, and frequently updated Twitter and Facebook pages. San Diego–based Souplantation provides a simple menu of blog-, Twitter-, and Facebook-based promotions that have deepened brand engagement and real-life action and purchases.

The community 201 tools build sociability into community. Customization, conversation, connection, and community tools allow members to not only dialogue with the brand but broadcast and connect themselves to other community members with similar interests. Method Home's People Against Dirty provides a great example of simple customization of profiles of community members who share a love of Method's products and values. The Cisco Learning Network facilitates conversations among 230,000 members who are entering IT careers, through blogs, discussion forums,

TABLE 10.2 THE ELEVEN CS OF BUILT COMMUNITIES

COMMUNITY TOOL	DEFINITION	GREAT FOR	FEATURES
Communication/ content	Members receive motivating information, media, and entertainment vehicles.	Brands with content-rich, extendable, or steady streams of activity	• Feature content • Search content • Corporate blog • Podcast • Photo gallery/blog • Video galley/blog • Recent updates/news • Opinion stream • Music list
Competition	Members have opportunities for payoffs, reputation building, and special status as top performers.	Brands with motivating rewards and merit-based performance criteria	• Rewards • Contests • Status levels • Leader boards • Points acquisition • Challenges
Customization	Members can personalize the appearance of their online presence.	Brands that like to mine the creativity and fun, personal tastes of users	• User profiles • Avatars • Widgets • Activity tracker
Conversation	Members can contribute to conversation threads.	Brands that want to support customers and benefit from expert users	• Blogs/updates • Forums/message boards • Commenting • Poking/social presence • Live chats
Connection	Members can connect with other members seamlessly on and off the community site.	Brands that have passionate, involved, and/or social evangelists	• Messaging • Integration with other sites • Feeds • Relationship/social graph
Community	Members have a forum where they can socialize and join specific tribes within the overall community.	Brands that have many target groups, local cells, or top performers	• Friend search/friending • Groups (interest/locality) • Teams • Mapping • Social network integration • Advisory panel
Categorization	Members can demark and aggregate community content.	Brands that have a lot of variety of products, content, or discussion	• Tagging • Social bookmarking • Sectioning/grouping • Levels • List building

(continued)

TABLE 10.2 THE ELEVEN CS OF BUILT COMMUNITIES *(continued)*

COMMUNITY TOOL	DEFINITION	GREAT FOR	FEATURES
Collective wisdom	Members can contribute to and mine collective crowd insights and solutions.	Brands that can deliver better solutions through predictive feedback tools	• Rating • Ranking • Voting • Polls • Reviews • Favorites
Co-creation/ collaboration	Members can work closely with the community owner or with other members as a group for a common goal.	Brands that can rally users around a central goal	• User-generated content • Idea generation • Problem solving • Recommendation engines • Wikis • Shared ownership
Contextual extensions	Community extensions/forums let members participate beyond the community portal.	Brands that have many touchpoints and opportunities for offline engagement	• Mobile • Instant messaging • Online events (webinars) • Live events • Member direct mail/ID cards • Member merchandise/ badges • Offline media
Culture building	Members can build their commitment to the community.	Brands that have a shared consciousness and a strong commitment or code	• Recruitment • Gifting to others • Milestone hitting • Community performance • Engagement/ commitment building (petition signing) • Causes

community, and groups. American Express creates connections and proactively seeks out relationships between business owners through their Open Forum collaborative business-to-business network. Harley-Davidson builds authentic community and local chapter support among a million-plus owners who identify with the values of the HOG (Harley's Owner Group).

The community 301 tools build a sense of intimacy between company and community and confers true empowerment to members. Categorization, collective wisdom, and co-creation/collaboration tools are less frequently used by companies that fear losing control of their brand or message, but ironically these are the tools that often raise commitment to the brand the most.

The community 401 tools are the rarest of community tools; they expand the role of community to become more immersive and pervasive inside a company. Contextual extensions and culture building put the community at the center of a company's operations. Camp Jeep and Jeep Jamborees are an example of contextually extending online Jeep fans into offline, off-road community experiences, and such communities have a pronounced effect on brand loyalty and provide intimate feedback to company staff. eBay's PowerSellers, those in its highest tier of top-performing sellers and customer satisfaction vendors, are a potent example of how a preferred and motivated online community of power users can build and influence company culture and significantly drive its bottom line, by not only higher levels of activity and volume of sales but by intimate collaboration with company employees in future developments.

As you consider employing these features to build your community, here are a few guiding principles to consider:

▷ **Registration:** Allow for easy sign-up and consider identity portability tools like Facebook Connect and Open Social to make initiation painless.

▷ **Flexibility:** People want to choose their own paths on communities. Allow users to influence the taxonomies of community content and features.

▷ **Me and we:** Balance the need for personal, group, and community-level participation; each has a role to play in gluing members to a community.

▷ **Newbies and veterans:** Provide enough attractive features for newcomers to join and for repeat visitors to stay engaged. This gives you a compelling argument for providing progressively more information, participation, and contribution with return visits.

▷ **Directions:** Make it easy to navigate, simple, and intuitive; use graphics and icons to steer interest and action.

▷ **Tiering:** Provide levels of membership and access to increase the motivation and longevity of top-performing community members and to address their need for rewards.

▷ **The public square:** Allow users to choose personal privacy settings, but leave defaults as public unless privacy or brand integrity is impacted.

▷ **Dynamic:** Highlight social presence and make sure people know that there is a pulse to the site by letting top-rated and/or recent content bubble up.

▷ **Progressive inclusion:** Get people intrigued so they will participate as early and as often as possible in building the community; incorporate their feedback into the ongoing design of the environment.

▷ **Utility:** Make it personally useful. Do not count on brand strength or altruism; satisfy member needs and make it worth their time.

▷ **Hosting:** Facilitate and moderate the discussion; don't drive it. Provide good directions, but give users the keys to the car; allow members to start conversations and content areas.

▷ **Minitasks:** Design for bite-sized participation and not burdensome tasks, especially early in the community's life.

▷ **Integration:** Embed activities with the external social Web and internal CRM systems, ensuring that disparate parts build off each other.

▷ **Upfront content investment:** Invest heavily in content up front and allow users to self-govern and take a leading role over time.

Affiliated Community Tools

Scan through an online service called Namechk and you will find no fewer than 149 different social networks and bookmarking sites that will check the availability of desired usernames. Nearly half of these sites have at least one million members each. You can be swamped trying to manage all of these possible brand outposts.

With 32 percent of all organizations' community-building efforts having no full-time employees assigned to them and the most common resourcing of larger business community efforts having just two to five full-time people, where time gets deployed in affiliated communities is of some consequence.[15] When in doubt, revert back to your wikibrands focus of what you're trying to achieve and the preferences of your target audience.

As a corporate representative, what do you need to do in these areas? Monitoring content about subjects of interest, your brands, and competitors' brands is a first step. Free tools provided by Google, Technorati, and Twitter and paid services such as Radian6, Visible Technologies, and Nielsen Buzzmetrics offer cross–social media monitoring services so you can easily track what's going on in these spaces.

Participating voraciously with relevant affiliated communities of content and people is your next step. Earn your engagement stripes by joining relevant pages, groups, and subscriptions; interacting with blog comments and personal profiles; and following, friending, and linking to target Influencers. When you're comfortable doing so, approach potential advocates and Influencers in each of these spaces about future collaboration.

When you're properly ensconced in the world of affiliated communities and have developed brand or brand-sponsored spaces that can act as a funnel for interested people, establishing a dialogue tool with advocates and a rebroadcast tool for content is your coming-out party. Applications and tools such as Tweetdeck, Friendfeed, Hootsuite, or Seesmic can improve your efficiency in updating and tracking these areas. Ensure that activities cross-pollinate through links with your built communities.

The top tools of affiliated communities are discussed here in declining order of business use.

Microblogging

Twitter, Plurk, Tumblr, and Jaiku are the best microblogging examples, with Twitter being the dominant platform. In a brief period of time, businesses have become most comfortable with tapping this medium. Pear Analytics evaluated the content on Twitter as follows: pointless babble, 40 percent; conversation, 37 percent; pass-along value/news, 13 percent; and self-promotion/spam, 10 percent.[16] So you can imagine that monitoring of the good content is a must. Microblogging's strengths for brands are rooted in identifying key Influencers efficiently, tracking relevant content, producing potential viral effects, building a loose-knit community for receiving a stream of brand content, and providing a responsive customer service and promotional outlet. Members of Twitter believe themselves to be much more responsive to brands than members of other social nets. Frequency of content, responsiveness, and shining the light on others' content are seen as the most successful attributes of top-performing brands in Twitterville. Airliner JetBlue has amassed more than a million followers by providing customer service, grabbing insights, and humanizing the brand through constant interaction.

Social Networks

Social networks constitute a blend of social interactions, relationships, and self-expression traits in the same space. Updates, walls, applications, messages, chats, and various applications all bake in sociability as the core social network focus. Brands and users can easily express themselves through group and personal profile pages. Let's distinguish between the big and targeted social networks.

Facebook, MySpace, Orkut, Hi-5, Friendster, Badoo, and Bebo are the world's top social networks (varying by geography), with Facebook having global significance and use. Google Buzz is a competitive foray to tap into social networking and combine it with e-mail, messaging, and other Google tools. Based on their size and range of features, these networks have become as much platforms for sociability as they have been databases of users. Social networkers tend to go deeper with content but click less frequently, given the array of content available to them in these networks. Social networks' key strengths for brands are the abilities to scale conversations through a user's social graph, establish rich media impact across a range of activities, and provide a more casual face to a corporate brand. H&R Block provides a great example of a brand that aggregates and socializes its key content into one page.

LinkedIn (professionals), last.fm (music), Flixster (movies), CaféMom (moms), Etsy (crafters), TripAdvisor (travelers), and BabyCenter (new parents) are just a few of the more targeted niche social networks. Although smaller in absolute number of members, they provide strongly engaged and Influencer target opportunities. SAP effectively integrated business professionals and technical experts who are members of either LinkedIn or its own community by prominently highlighting sought-after SAP skills and experience in their profiles and by interacting with clients trying to meet the ongoing demand for SAP professionals.

Blogger Outreach

By targeting and building relationships with influential bloggers who are relevant to your audience, you can garner effective, unbiased reviews of your products and third-party credibility. High-authority bloggers are potential loudspeakers for your message. Identifying high-quality blogs, approaching them with enough background and advance time, and creating social currency and easy embedding of creative assets are characteristics of strong blogger outreach programs. Ubisoft and Wii have teamed up to use blogger reach as an asset in launching new game titles. Netflix has involved one of its most passionate bloggers at Hacking Netflix as a key conduit of information from the company to the blogger's many readers and Netflix fans.

Discussion Boards, Forums, and Rating Sites

As one of the earliest forms of social media, forums and discussion boards may be considered old school, but they really can point to candid product feedback and important customer service feedback. Tracking public general-discussion forums like Epinions and Get Satisfaction and industry-specific forums can provide tangible insights to your business, but beware of using forum marketing as a tool for promotion. This practice is riddled with issues and may cause negative reactions.

Video-Sharing Channels

YouTube is the dominant player here, with a more than 40 percent share of Web video, but Hulu, Veoh, Metacafe, Revver, and Vimeo also compete. In any given month, four out of five online users have browsed a video. Given the increasing ease of producing, editing, and saving video, video sharing has a bright future, and plenty of brands have used it to drive traffic quickly, go viral, and build immersive exposure and brand impact. As evidence, try searching Volkswagen "Piano Stairs" or John West's "Salmon" ad, with more than hundreds of millions of views collectively.

There are success factors in video sharing beyond content interest, brevity, experimentation, context, collectability, and rebroadcasting across a wide berth of channels. Traditional brands are in the unique position of being able to create this type of provocative content more effectively than amateurs, given the production costs involved. The European launch of the Nissan Qashqai was an enormously successful use of video sharing to seed car interest in the absence of car availability by leveraging creativity and slick production.

One caveat is that only a very small percentage of videos that are expected to go viral actually do. There is little predictability about what works and what doesn't, so be prepared to hear crickets before you hear wolf howls.

Photo-Sharing Channels

Flickr, Picasa, and Photobucket are the key players in photo sharing; Facebook also plays a role as the world's biggest photo site. Well-tagged photos on photo-sharing sites provide great search engine optimization for brands and are effective in embracing creative tastemakers, trendspotters, and distributors. Graco has implemented a popular photo-sharing contest every Wednesday on its Heart to Heart blog. Photo sites will never be large traffic or interaction generators, but they do provide brand aesthetic appeal with an early adopter audience.

In-Depth Content Sharing

Content wants to be free, at least that's what content providers like Slideshare (presentations) and Scribed (documents) would like you to believe.

Very effective for business-to-business firms, these in-depth content-sharing tools provide a stage for thought leadership and exhibiting business transparency. They can be added to a suite of publicly available white papers, research papers, e-books, audiobooks, livecasts, and webinars. As a prime example, Adobe has launched its own inventive use of Slideshare, building a corporate channel devoted to exposing the creative portfolios of its users.

Mobile Applications and Marketing

Mobile applications are viewed as being the top growth area for future wikibrands. Despite their potential for creating highly customized, contextually specific benefits and a novelty channel for tech lead users (who download ten or more iPhone apps per month), mobile still remains the great unrealized hope for brands. The potential is limitless but has historically been prone to lack of standards, poor usability, and low level of smartphone usage. With the growth and availability of iPhones, Androids, and other APIs now available, the potential might be here. As one example, Pizza Hut has developed an effective iPhone app that allows you to create a mobile virtual pizza and automatically send an order to a local restaurant for a live pizza purchase.

Wikis

Wikis have tended to get more attention inside companies than outside. However, Wikipedia and Wikia (an extension of Wikipedia) provide the best example of a broad set of external users collaborating for a common goal. Unlike the corporate blog, which is really a broadcast communication with some level of interaction, a wiki is interactive, collaborative, and simple for nontechnical employees to use. Consider contributing to other industry wikis and leveraging your own to facilitate deep collaboration with your audience. This practice is used by many authors to encourage greater, more-dispersed contributions and a feeling of co-ownership among contributors when the content is published.

Podcasts

As the audio form of blogs, podcasts provide a very targeted and immersed group of advocates around key topics. The pluses are that podcasts provide convenient listening formats for their audiences, can offer a wide variety of communication, and lend a personal tone of voice to one concentrated area. The challenges are to create high-quality content that adds value and to ensure that production and editing don't become big time wasters. CBC Radio, Canada's public radio broadcaster, has repurposed hundreds of its shows as podcasts to extend fanship of its personalities and shows.

Location-Specific Networks

Location-specific social networks have become the chant of early adopters, with Foursquare and Gowalla coming to the fore and other larger networks getting involved. Geolocation awareness and GPS-enabled wireless devices increase the relevance of brands and venues within social networking spheres and provide merchandising and promotion opportunities for local businesses and restaurants. Starbucks, Intercontinental Hotels, *Financial Times*, and Chipotle have all experimented with the medium. North Face developed a geofencing promotion that sends location-based promotional texts to registrants when they are within a certain range of its stores.

Social Bookmarking Sites

Tools such as Digg, Stumble Upon, Reddit, and Delicious serve as search engine accelerators for your good content. When big announcements or interesting news happen for your brands, these tools can provide deep spikes in traffic. Bookmarking provides simple ways of sharing content, and unlike social networks, users don't upload photos, updates, or profiles; they share, organize, search, and manage bookmarks. Done well, you can provide a network of tightly concentrated social content around the interests of your brand versus the chaos of the Internet. Building up a reputation bank, however, takes considerable time and resources and may not be worth the effort.

The Greater World Out There

People who live on the Internet 24/7 are sometimes blinded to the fact that people do other things than just surf; they have a first life as well. Other elements of your business can play a key role in amplifying your social wikibrand effects.

E-Mail

Nielsen recently suggested that people spend more time on social networks than reading e-mail. E-mail may have lost the time battle to social media, but don't let anybody tell you that e-mail is an old, outmoded medium. Social media use actually makes some people consume *more*, not less, e-mail; this is particularly true for those with the highest frequency of social media use. The two mediums shouldn't be as much competitive as partners. E-mail marketing messages with a social sharing option generate 30 percent higher clickthrough rates than e-mails without these features. And e-mail still remains the most active medium for creating action. Today, you can add links, audio, graphics, video, and other functionality to make your e-mail more interactive. Having a content strategy that includes a regular schedule of e-mail communication is an effective practice for wikibrands.

Search Engine Optimization

On a par with microblogging use, companies are at their mature phase of adopting search engine optimization. It's a $16 billion industry in North America, stealing more and more dollars away from print advertising, direct mail, and conferences. Businesses realize that sometimes people need to stumble over you in order to fall in love with you. It's the reason why SEO is predicted to be the third-highest online growth spend (after social media and online video). Keyword ownership, optimized website architecture, new content, and link building are the success drivers of effective search engine optimization.

Live Experiential/Buzz

Although a princely amount of word of mouth exists online, always remind yourself that more than 75 percent of buzz and brand conversations travel offline and are usually considered more credible, more positive, and more action-driving than when they happen online.[17] A paradox exists in that a lot of buzzable content starts online, but the wealth of it finishes offline. Brand experience events, guerrilla marketing, teaser promotions/media, live stunts, and lifestyle product placement all play a role in accelerating these naturally occurring, live referral networks. Red Bull has been the benchmark for creating inventive live brand experiences such as Flugtag, Crashed Ice, Air Races, and X-Fighters that make people chatter both online and off.

Grassroots and Social Responsibility Efforts

With authenticity being a key business value that is embraced and talked about by customers, cause/charity sponsorship and corporate social responsibility are high priorities for businesses. Cone Research found that 88 percent of millennial consumers (aged eighteen to twenty-four) and 79 percent of all consumers would switch from one brand to another (all else being more or less equal in quality and price) if the other brand were associated with a good cause.[18] An Edelman study found that six out of ten consumers have bought a brand that supports a good cause even if it wasn't the cheapest brand.[19]

Good cause association also carries topspin with employee engagement. Häagen-Dazs's recent employee and customer embrace of the decline of the honeybee cause, which included social Web activation, produced an 18 percent increase in sales.[20]

Partners and Affiliate Programs

As a wikibrand, you are in the business of meeting customer needs. Finding solutions for customers often can't be done by companies themselves, so wikibrands are increasingly turning to partners and affiliates to further their causes. The sponsorship industry is growing faster than traditional forms of communication based on its ability to link values and engage a captive audience via partners. The types of sponsorships being pursued are event sponsorships, branded entertainment, tours and attractions, arts support, festivals, fairs and events, and associations. Some of the best partnerships are happening between like-minded companies with similar audiences. Nike and Apple's collaboration on the Nike Plus project is a perfect example of one company working with another to produce something more than the sum of its parts. John Fluevog shoes recently partnered with Vancouver-based hotel Opus to produce a signature-hotel concept shoe to reinforce both brands' embrace of "cool" and innovation.

Traditional Communication

The world's advertising budget is well over half a trillion dollars, with traditional forms of communication flat to even and with some segments still experiencing small levels of growth during the economic recovery. Even though the trend is digital, the traditional mediums of TV, radio, print, and outdoor aren't going anywhere soon. Companies can, however, provide an enormous awareness boost to their social Web efforts by including the promotion and results of their customer engagement and social Web efforts, even in the form of small tags in traditional advertising.

Exposure to wikibrand programs can also be boosted by inclusion on packaging and within retail merchandising environments. With the strategy of befriending every person who walks by, there is nothing more constant, commerce-driving, and personal than the offline purchase environment. The mere perception of being in innovative social platforms creates affinity with shoppers. Piers Fawkes of PSFK talks about the future of cities and how walls and retail environments will actually talk to shoppers through digital signage, QR codes, and wi-fi–based social networks in the near future.[21]

Alan Moore, founder of consulting firm SMLXL, sums it up this way: "Human beings are a We species; we have an innate need to connect and communicate, and today we have been given the tools to take back control of that fundamental need."[22] To be relevant in a customer-controlled marketplace, businesses and marketers need to be in their game, publishing everything they have everywhere they can. Follow the trail—more brand content across more tools means more connections resulting in a bigger footprint and larger business influence.

The same factors that make this objective a hurdle are the very things that make them work if you can overcome them. Manpower constraints and fear of losing control are the top two concerns of companies toward this strategy. Eighty-four percent of CMOs spend less than 10 percent of marketing budgets experimenting through digital, collaborative media, and nontraditional channels.[23] This needs to change—new resources, accountability, and tools need to be applied.

To truly empower a "customer knows best" philosophy and achieve scale in their wikibrand efforts, businesses need to embrace a broad set of new tools and refocus the tools they are already using. Successful brands will be the ones that let their best content spread across their community and to customers wherever they exist. Over the last decade, CRM and internal collaboration have become the focus for building intelligent business growth. Moving forward, firms must redirect their focus outward and look externally to customers, Influencers, fans, stakeholders, and partners to advance their wikibrands. Once they have established a beachhead there, the next challenge will be to maintain their efforts.

PART 4

INCUBATING YOUR WIKIBRAND COMMUNITY

CHAPTER 11

COMMUNITY DEVELOPMENT

The Life Stages of a Wikibrand Community

Customers are no longer faceless targets who have homogenous tastes according to their age, gender, ethnicity, income, or postal code. They are vibrant pools of individuals who aggregate around interests, aspirations, and hobbies. The sophistication of the connected Web allows brands to see and act on these customer motivations and build communities around their niche interests.

What Is a Brand Community?

A brand community is more than a Facebook application, a corporate blog, or a Twitter initiative. It's more than just creating a new media channel. And it often rests outside of most CRM and promotional practices because it focuses as much on the community members' needs as on the company's. According to a 2008 Nielsen study, member communities showed twice the growth rate of any of the other mentioned sectors (including general-interest portals and searches).[2]

Typically, a brand community has five characteristics:[3]

> "Tribes matter. They always have. Now, though, they matter even more. This is a primal human need, but the Internet has joined together previously fragmented groups. We need to start embracing this phenomenon and start deciding whether it's worth the effort. I think it is."[1]
>
> —SETH GODIN, *author of* Tribes

▷ It revolves around a shared interest in a company, product, or brand.
▷ It connects companies or brands with customers, Influencers, or other community members.
▷ It connects members with each other.
▷ It connects companies and members with nonmembers and prospective members.
▷ It upholds rituals and traditions that involve public greetings to recognize fellow brand/community lovers.

Most communities are built to support top-line revenue and communication objectives by leveraging the passion and commitment of their members. François Gossieaux, Partner at Beeline Labs, says the main reason that brands build communities is to help generate word of mouth.[4] Some of these communities engage in immersive brand evangelism strategies or overt call-to-action referral programs; others are less explicit in stoking the lead-generation grapevine, instead providing ways for members to build buzz for the community.

A Deloitte study of one hundred brand-sponsored online communities showed that most of them fail to achieve their business performance goals. In addition, only 25 percent achieved a membership of a thousand or more.[5] The study pointed to a number of reasons for such disappointing results:

▷ Putting the needs of the brand ahead of those of the audience it's trying to attract
▷ Being overly interested in technology at the expense of the community's social infrastructure
▷ Having understaffed and underskilled custodianship of the community
▷ Focusing on metrics that are unconnected to objectives
▷ Devoting too small a portion of the brand's marketing budget to the community

Does this mean that you should give up entirely on building wikibrands because there is such a slim chance of success? No. It does, however, mean the people, culture, funds, and strategies that many companies have put in place to support these efforts have been woefully ineffective. And this is a result of not planning for success.

A well-developed brand community is a better tool for brand advocacy than conventional promotion efforts, because community members feel a high degree of affiliation with the brand and the community:

▷ Community members are 82 percent more likely to recommend the company to others.[6]
▷ Fifty-six percent of online community members log in at least once a day.[7]
▷ Community members are three times more likely to trust their peers' opinions over advertising when making purchase decisions.[8]
▷ Customers report good experiences with community forums more than twice as often as they do with calls or e-mail.[9]

Sean O'Driscoll, owner of Seattle-based Ant's Eye View and former general manager for Microsoft's communities, characterizes three types of communities by the level of discussion that takes place:[10]

▷ **911—Emergency questions:** Something is broken. The community exists to solve problems and troubleshoot.
▷ **411—Education questions and discussion:** Community members come to learn from each other.
▷ **511—Advanced user discussion:** Community members explore, share, and evangelize about the product.

A community can evolve from 911 to 511, but generally, it needs to fulfill the first two levels before it can reach the third (see Figure 11.1).

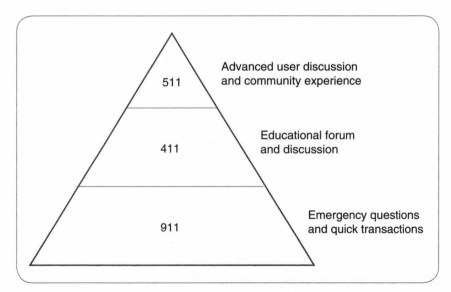

FIGURE 11.1 THE HIERARCHY OF DISCUSSION LEVELS WITHIN COMMUNITIES

The following sections describe some of the more innovative brand communities we found during our research. We'll also discuss the stages through which communities evolve:

1. **Conception:** The company seeds the audience and builds the goals of the community. Key factors at this stage are a consistent, motivating focus; seeding Influencer audience relationships and validation; smart user experience development; strong, simple, and social design and technology; and adoption of rules and guidelines.
2. **Birth:** The company ensures that content is fresh and encourages conversation from the community. Key factors at this stage are freshly produced content; publicity and expanded outreach; highlighted member contributions; social network extensions; and the availability of member incentives.
3. **Adolescence:** The company highlights the contributions of community members and demonstrates how its culture has changed. Key factors at this stage are milestone achievements; user-generated content; incentives and internal change materialization; a regular and expected cycle of activity; and expansion of audience.
4. **Adulthood:** Members of the community adopt leadership positions. The company broadens the focus of the community and begins to segment the audience. Key factors at this stage are broadened focus and community extensions; tangible evidence of company culture change; creation of tiers of membership by influence and longevity; self-governance by members; and potential expansion of target audience.

Feedback should be gathered and reviewed at regular intervals throughout a community's stages of growth. However, the full maturation of a community from conception to adulthood may take three to four years before requiring radically new functionality, technology, or expansion. When considering investment and payback from brand community efforts, a mid- to long-term commitment and payback cycle is required to optimize results.

Lunapads

Lunapads is a Canadian company that sells feminine hygiene products with an environmental and woman-friendly bent. Its products include the

DivaCup, a reusable silicon cup tampon alternative, and Lunapads, washable inserts.

We spoke to founders Suzanne Siemens and Madeleine Shaw about their success (sales continue to grow at 20 percent annually). They spoke glowingly about the power of community. According to Shaw, they were initially surprised at the impact of their forays into social media.[11] The community is very active, and many of its members are vocal advocates of the company's goal to "help women have healthier and more positive experiences of their menstrual cycles, and by extension, their bodies overall." This comment from the Lunapads Facebook page is representative:

> Between your fun patterned pads and my Diva Cup, I have greatly reduced my environmental impact and don't have to shell out $10 every month to some mega corporation. Lunapads help me feel like a feminist-ecowarrior every month, and I freaking love them!

Reusable menstrual products have been available for a long time, often sold through the classifieds in Birkenstock motif magazines like *Mother Jones* and *Utne Reader*. A technology-enabled community (Siemens and Shaw report that 90 percent of their sales are through the website) enables education, discussion, and advocacy. Shaw touts education as a very important aspect of their community, as many of their customers were happy to relearn how they looked at menstruation, as well as how to use, wash, and transport their new reusable supplies. They were pleased to learn from other women (rather than a faceless corporation) using online communication as a facilitator of private discussions. Some of their clients have said that they did not have a real-life confidante with whom they could discuss menstruation openly and were pleased to meet one via the website.

Roger Smith Hotel

The very nature of social media suggests that most communication occurs electronically—and remotely. In *Grown Up Digital: How The Net Generation Is Changing the World*, Don Tapscott describes how the Net Generation views trust differently. He reports that one young interviewee said, "Of course you can do business with someone you haven't met. After all, you can fall in love with someone you've never met."[12] There remains, however, much to be said about meeting in person. Keith Ferrazzi, author of *Never*

Eat Alone and *Who's Got Your Back* advises people that the vigor of a relationship is accelerated by a "long, slow dinner." Afterward, a remote relationship can thrive.[13] By the way, Ferrazzi throws a wicked dinner party; we were lucky enough to be invited to one at a cool boutique hotel in Chicago. If you follow him closely (he is very active on Facebook), you can sometimes snag a last-minute invitation.

In any case, social media enthusiasts sometimes need a real-life (as of 2002, we were officially not allowed to use "bricks-and-mortar") clubhouse. In New York City, said clubhouse is the Roger Smith Hotel (RSH). This midtown boutique became the hub for tweet-ups and unconferences, including the Social Media Club NYC, leading social media news site Mashable, and Social Change for Social Good. Social media A-listers such as Chris Brogan and Sarah Prevette of Sprouter blogged about their stays. CEO James Knowles explains, "Our connection to a community of people is based on storytelling, offline connections, and relationships built on passion."[14]

1000 Awesome Things

Neil Pasricha is one of the best bloggers in the business. 1000 Awesome Things (1000awesomethings.com) is a bright, positive light among millions of angst-filled rants littering the blogosphere. Monday through Friday, Pasricha blogs about an everyday phenomenon that he considers awesome, such as wearing underwear right out of the dryer, old dangerous playground equipment, or the smell of bakery air.

Zen Habits, one of the site's fans, summarizes the project nicely:

> There's something riveting about 1000 Awesome Things that makes you want to keep coming back. Aside from the great humor, it reminds you of the little things in life, and how awesome they can be.[15]

The *Vancouver Sun* called it, "Sunny without being saccharine, it's a countdown of life's little joys that reads like a snappy Jerry Seinfeld monologue by way of Maria Von Trapp."[16]

The blog is a sensation. The vibrant community receives more than forty thousand hits per day. The community members voted online to help the site win three Webby awards and provided an eager market for a bestselling book. A typical entry will generate more than fifty comments, many of them sincerely thanking Neil for being a consistently bright spot in their lives.

Stumpjumper Trail Crew

Specialized Bicycles is a high-end manufacturer that sponsors and services professional cyclists (including the Tour de France competitors), as well as serious hobbyists; many of its bikes retail for more than $3,000. The company attracts bicycle aficionados as employees. In fact, we had to schedule our interview with Chris Matthews, global marketing integrations manager, around the office's noontime ride.

Not unexpectedly, Specialized also attracts passionate bicycle fans as customers. The company leveraged this passion through the Stumpjumper Trail Crew, a group of fans who became ambassadors for the launch of a new, versatile, high-end bike, the Stumpjumper FSR. Crew members auditioned via video and were evaluated on their passion for cycling as well as their standing and influence within the cycling community. The final team included an IT professional, a professor, a bike shop owner, and Ross Powers (an Olympic Gold Medal–winning snowboarder).[17] Matthews explained that they were looking for a group of riders with the right mix of ride leadership, trial advocacy, and diplomacy.[18] Each ambassador received the use of the bike for one year and the option to buy it at dealer cost minus discounts earned through ambassador activities such as writing blog entries or posting videos featuring the Stumpjumper.

Squad 6

Teams in the National Basketball Association compete not only with other teams but also with any number of events from ballet to boxing for entertainment dollars in major cities. Disposable income for basketball tickets could be spent on other sports events, concerts, or even a nifty home theater system. Professional sports teams serve more than just those who attend games in person. Pat Gillick, while general manager of the Toronto Blue Jays, said that he had a duty to all fans, even those who just read the box scores or listened to games on the radio. The passion of sports fans naturally lends itself to community development like online clubs and detailed statistical analysis (volunteer sabermetricians who diligently record and calculate baseball statistics have actually altered long-standing baseball strategic wisdom).[19] Through fantasy sports leagues, fans can become more closely involved with the game. Some of the most active celebrities on Twitter are sports figures, among them Shaquille O'Neal (@the_real_shaq has almost three million followers).

Andrew Bogut, a basketball player for the Milwaukee Bucks, was surprised that home crowds were not as boisterous and passionate as those he was used to in his sports-mad native Australia. Bogut personally purchased one hundred lower-level tickets for each game for an initiative he called Squad 6 (named for his jersey number). To qualify for the squad, fans had to persevere through three rounds of auditions (see **wiki-brands .com** for a link to video of the tryouts) and risk losing their seats if they are too sedate or fail to attend games.[20] He reported to ESPN columnist Chris Sheridan, "On a Tuesday night in winter and it is 10 degrees outside and the kids have school the next day, we're not fortunate like L.A. or New York who have tourists who will come. We don't have that, so I thought let's get some people in that building that'll keep it rocking whether there's 10,000 people there or 18,000 people. They're going to be there every game and provide a great atmosphere."[21] Squad 6 adds a fantastically lively dimension to Bucks games; members wear crazy costumes, scream inventive cheers, and raise the intensity of the whole experience. Technically, they don't even really use the seats that Bogut buys because they stand during the whole game. The community extends off the court as well: Squad 6 shares its spirit via Facebook and the Bucks' team website.

Entertainment Industry Examples

Similar to sports teams, entertainment franchises benefit greatly from brand communities. They provide an opportunity for more intimate connections for dedicated fans. For example, U2 fans who were able to decipher a puzzle uncovered an invitation to a concert in Second Life. Henry Jenkins, in his book *Convergence Culture: Where Old and New Media Collide*, describes how the creators of the movie *The Matrix* combined "multiple texts to create a narrative so large that it cannot be contained within a single medium." Characters in the third installment, *The Matrix Revolutions*, were introduced in an online short film. He describes the Matrix franchise this way:

> A transmedia story unfolds across multiple media platforms, with each new text making a distinctive and valuable contribution to the whole. In the ideal form of transmedia storytelling, each medium does what it does best—so that a story might be introduced in a film, expanded through television, novels, and comics; its world might be explored through game play or experienced as an amusement park attraction. Each franchise

entry needs to be self-contained so you don't need to have seen the film to enjoy the game, and vice versa. Any given product is a point of entry into the franchise as a whole. Reading across the media sustains a depth of experience that motivates more consumption.[22]

Fan fiction allows amateurs to create story extensions based on existing characters. In some cases, dedicated sites provide an audience for their works. J. K. Rowling endorses Harry Potter fan fiction. She believes that just as her books encourage kids to read, they can also encourage them to write. She does, however, become litigious when people try to commercialize the end product.

"The Daily Show" with Jon Stewart runs for half an hour, the last third of which typically features a discussion with a guest. Often, when a conversation gets intense (typically when the guest's philosophy differs from Jon's and his social commentator side comes out), the interview is artificially truncated for television and posted in its entirety on the Comedy Central website.

Weird Al Yankovic has been on top of his game for a quarter century— seriously, who is the world's second-best pop music parodist? He actively engages his audience by releasing songs one at a time online rather than waiting for an album to be completed, creating an opportunity for attentive fans to engage in what Chris Brogan, coauthor of *Trust Agents,* calls "gatejumping."[23] Yankovic recruited the extras for the video for "White and Nerdy," his best-selling single, via his MySpace profile.

When NBC announced that Jay Leno was moving back to the "Tonight Show"'s traditional 11:30 P.M. time slot and uprooting Conan O'Brien, O'Brien's fans leapt to his defense. Social media was their chief weapon. Team Coco set up multiple Facebook groups, the largest, "I'm with Coco," had almost a million members. Featured on the site are more than five thousand photos, including some remarkable pieces of original Photoshopped art showing likenesses of Conan as Queen Elizabeth II, Superman, and Neil Armstrong alongside unflattering pictures of Leno. Team Coco also disseminated multiple petitions, including one imploring fans in the studio audience to join their fight and cry, "Captain, my captain," when O'Brien appeared onstage. A fan infiltrated Leno's "Jaywalking" routine with a Team Coco message scrawled on his hand. Other tomfoolery included enough vandalism to Leno's Wikipedia page to justify a semiprotection tag. Interestingly, the Wikipedia entry for "Indian giver" included Leno under the "see also" section for a long time.[24] We feature our favorites of the Team Coco artwork on **wiki-brands.com**.

Since O'Brien's audience skews more toward younger, more technolog-ically savvy viewers than Leno's, not only are they more likely to deploy social media to champion their host, they are also more likely to view Conan's show on YouTube or other nontraditional means. Ironically, if his audience had actually watched his show on television, the ratings would have been high enough to avoid the entire situation.

Museum of Modern Art

Victor Samra is the digital media marketing manager at the Museum of Modern Art (MoMA) in New York City. When tasked with building the museum's digital marketing presence, he investigated the usual suspects. However, the museum did not want to stampede toward a corporate Face-book page "just because everyone else was doing it," and the psychedelic presentation given to MoMA by a representative from MySpace didn't res-onate with the museum's marketing department.[25] Instead, Samra devel-oped a consistent voice and personality wherever he felt people in the art community hung out, careful that communication was focused on conver-sation and education rather than museum branding.

Monitoring Facebook and Twitter allowed Samra to find out what people were saying about MoMA, whether it was a complaint about how long the coat check took or how a particular exhibition resonated with the community. In what is a common problem for social media managers, he needed to determine which of MoMA's Twitter followers should be fol-lowed in turn. He says that he has been chastised by a couple of artists for not immediately following them back, claiming he "wasn't supporting the local artist community."[26] Samra wasn't trying to be elitist; it is a struggle for busy Twitter accounts to keep up with requests (and setting up auto-matic follows leads to a lot of spam accounts—or at least a lot of lonely, beautiful women apparently eager to chat).

A real concern for Samra was the view that following local artists could be considered a de facto MoMA endorsement of their work. MoMA sup-ports an important constituency of stakeholders who may never actually set foot in the museum. Eight months after launching MoMA's Facebook page, Samra looked at Facebook's analytics tool and found that more people from Milan were fans of the page than people from New York. In fact, Italy and France were both sources of frequent online visitors, even though Facebook is less popular in those countries than in North America. MoMA's board, which happens to be among the wealthiest in New York

City, felt that it was vital that the museum share its art with as many people and in as compelling a manner as possible.

Cisco

LaSandra Brill is the senior manager of global social media for Cisco Systems and a respected thought leader in the field (many of her insightful presentations are available on Slideshare.com/lasandra5). Like many of the people we interviewed, she tells us that Cisco first became involved in social media with the goal of "actively listening to what the market was saying about it and deliberately moving to where the conversation was happening."[27] Due to the technical nature of the company's products, both employees and customers in the Cisco ecosystem were early adopters of social media technology.

Conversation in the business-to-business milieu is different than in the consumer space. Brill reports that "it is typically more serious and purpose-based, and privacy is much more important. While people want to share and collaborate to solve problems, since proprietary information is more likely to be shared, security walls and identity authentication need to be in place."[28]

To ensure that its voice remains authentic, the company encourages all employees to participate and offers a social media certificate that employees can earn after taking six hours of live or online courses. Cisco is developing an advanced course that will be affiliated with a university; a nuance that Brill believes will increase its credibility.[29]

In 2009, someone lost an opportunity after tweeting "Cisco just offered me a job! Now I have to weigh the utility of a fatty paycheck against the daily commute to San Jose and hating the work."[30] A Cisco employee noticed the tweet and publicly responded to the candidate, "Who is the hiring manager? I'm sure they would love to know that you will hate the work. We here at Cisco are versed in the Web." Brill thinks the situation could have been handled better if the employee had responded privately to the candidate, since the hoopla would not have occurred if it were not for the retweet. The general sentiment (at least among the blogging community) was that the job seeker, not Cisco, looked ridiculous and unsympathetic.

Cisco was able to see real results from engaging the online community through its successful, completely digital launch of its ASR[31] 1000 series, which combines all of the necessary service features into a single router platform. Compared to the launch for the CSR-1, a product launch that was similar in market impact, ASR scored better in virtually every metric. Since the CSR-1 launch required attendees to travel physically to San Jose, it was expensive (more than $20,000 was spent on travel costs alone) and created a great deal of carbon emissions (Brill estimates 199 tons of coal or 42,000 gallons of gas).[32] While the CSR-1 launch attracted 135 members of the press who went on to write 87 articles, the ASR counterpart generated 245 articles, thousands of blog posts, and more than forty million impressions.

Brill was thrilled with the overall results but would not choose to include Second Life in future launches. This part of the campaign was expensive and time-consuming and, in the end, only attracted sixty visitors, including one who displayed some unfortunate behavior (if he were one of James Cameron's Avatars, you would have seen a little too much blue).

The Four Stages of Brand Community Development

Successful brand communities evolve their strategy as the cooperative nature becomes more sophisticated.

Conception

In some cases, brand communities start as an experiment. When Neil Pasricha started 1000 Awesome Things and his mom forwarded it to his dad, the traffic doubled. Lunapads, Specialized Bikes, and MoMA started their respective communities without a lot of expectations but began to spend more resources on them as they started to gain traction. SAP and Cisco made a concerted effort to harness the attention of their technologically deft clientele. Team Coco mostly gained momentum from the grassroots spirit of its fan base but received plenty of support and on-air recognition from Conan himself.

In any case, it is important at the early stage of a community to build a welcoming environment that provides a platform for communication among members.

Birth

At this stage of the community's development, the leaders still need to pay close attention to participant behavior, particularly if it is a corporate brand. If community forums are not refreshed with content or, even worse, are overloaded with spam, participants will not return. Neil Pasricha's attitude toward reader comments to his blog posts at the outset was diplomatic. He allowed all comments that were not profane, obviously spam, or an off-topic personal message to him.

The team at Roger Smith Hotel are not just hosts of New York's social media party; they are enthusiastic participants. There is an active blog (the hotel offers a special discount for blog readers); three active Facebook pages; one official and fifteen staff Twitter accounts; two YouTube sites (including the very interesting Roger Smith News Channel); and a community website that tells the story of RSH ambassadors, often illustrated with compelling videos. The hotel also encourages guests and fans to join the community and makes it easy by providing links to easily add photos to Flickr and videos to 12 Seconds, and to post reviews on TripAdvisor and Yelp.

The impact of RSH's social media efforts goes beyond the actual participants. Adam Wallace, new media manager at the hotel, reports that the employees, including housekeepers and janitors, take greater pride in their work because they believe that "the social media attention compels them to act like they are onstage."[33] Wallace includes photographs of the employees and all staff in the social media campaign, reinforcing that they are all a part of the community.

Adolescence

At this point, the community should be creating real value, and the organization should be using the information created to accelerate innovation and improve business processes company-wide.

1000 Awesome Things was enjoying modest growth until the entry "Old Dangerous Playground Equipment" was featured on the news aggregator Fark (from which it was picked up by Wired.com). A few weeks later, the post "Ordering off the menu from fast food restaurants" was featured on the Digg front page. For a nascent blog, a nice feature on a site like Digg provides an enormous boost that is sometimes fleeting, but in this case, many of the visitors were so impressed by Pasricha's terrific content that they became regulars. He was also able to attract visitors via mentions on popular blogs like Cake Wrecks and PostSecret and through recommendation engines such as StumbleUpon.

We asked Adam Wallace at RSH what he expected would happen when the staff who maintained the active Twitter accounts departed; after all, the hospitality industry typically experiences a high turnover rate. He seemed a little puzzled by the question, then responded, "We actually have pretty low turnover, and because of the relationships we build, we expect that our people will stay close to the community after they leave." [34] For example, a former intern returned home to Europe after his work term and subsequently created an online presence for the Roger Smith Hotel in Barcelona.

At MoMA, one of the challenges Victor Samra faces is how to balance exposure of the art with legal and copyright restrictions (digital cameras are not even allowed within the featured exhibition areas), especially since only a handful of the displayed pieces are in the public domain. [35] Also, since the type of art that MoMA displays is often avant-garde, it is more challenging to present via digital means.

At Specialized Bikes, Chris Matthews believes that "the self-selected, diehard fans are the most important people to have on board, especially for a sport like cycling that generates so much passion." [36] Local support is also crucial; Matthews states that he would much rather have a hundred bike shops with a thousand fans each than a hundred thousand followers of a global corporate site. [37]

Adulthood

Once a successful community reaches adulthood, it usually polices itself. On 1000 Awesome Things, Pasricha rarely comments and never defends himself against negative posts (he is well loved by the community and has an almost impossibly high positive-negative comment ratio). In the event that someone does post a complaint or squeezes some spam past the filter, the community jumps to its defense. Freddo is the unofficial sheriff (by day, he is a San Diego banker). He gently shames anyone who makes a complaint and chides those who get too commercial; for example. "We don't post spam on your Colon Health site about bakery air."

Like most good communities, Lunapads sets up the infrastructure, provides leadership, and lets the members do the work. There are two active Facebook pages (one focused on discussions), a YouTube network (with instructional videos, some of them cheeky in nature), and a Twitter page. Community members are invited to donate products to girls and women in developing nations. They are also polled on name choices for new products.

Adam Wallace believes that the social media focus reflects and reinforces the leitmotif of Roger Smith Hotel. He believes in the power of relationship and community: "It's not about the number of Facebook fans you have; it's how active they are in the community."[38] Fans of RSH go out of their way to spread the word about the hotel and defend it when a negative review is posted on a site like TripAdvisor. Brian Simpson, director of social hospitality, describes the authenticity of word-of-mouth marketing: "If we put a sign in Lily's that says, 'We make the best Bloody Marys in New York City,' some people may read it, they may believe it, they may come in and try one. If you call your buddy who says he's going to brunch tomorrow and says, 'Where's the best Bloody Mary?', and you say, 'Go to Lily's at the Roger Smith Hotel, they make the best'; they're going to believe that, because they're going to trust you."[39] Wallace estimates that event revenue has doubled year by year, and he attributes the bulk of that increase to the hotel's status as the social media hub of New York City.

As with many of the active communities we studied, the members of Roger Smith Hotel's are its greatest advocates, as well as a great source of ideas on how to grow the business. During the "Roger's Room" giveaway promotion, one hotel room was awarded via Twitter for each day in January. Wallace and his team experimented with various methods of granting the room, including "retweet a number between one and one thousand." He also allowed the community to come up with other novel approaches to determine winners.

MoMA encourages its members to participate in building the museum's community. For example, it encourages amateur travelogues delivered via podcasts. These are an interesting phenomenon; rather than hearing an "official" tour of the Louvre on one those rented yellow handsets, you can download and enjoy a *Da Vinci Code*–themed version. While these productions may cause history purists to shudder, they offer a whimsical new look at an 800-year-old building. MoMA encourages amateur podcasters; Samra says he was impressed with the quality of those produced by Marymount College students as part of their class work.[40] Similarly, he was so impressed with the images posted by visitors on photo-sharing site Flickr that he used them in the museum's official user guides.

CHAPTER 12

INTERNALIZING COMMUNITY AND CHANNELING TOM SAWYER

The Graying Line Between Employee and Enthusiast Champions

In order to provide a great brand community, it is important for organizations to internalize the spirit of the community. Organizational commitment must be built, and internal advocates (including some from executive row) need to be empowered. Some of the best examples from our research are discussed in the following sections.

Zappos: A Super-Engaged Workforce

Zappos is bolstered by a passionate community. The online retailer originated when one of its founders had trouble finding the exact pair of shoes he wanted and realized that navigating through the vast array of unique shoes (think of all the permutations of length, width, style, color, and so on) was perfectly suited for the Internet. Shoes could be held in a central inventory or sourced from around the world rather than limited to the frustrat-

"We have people in our forums who spend more time there than we do. Not only do they answer more questions than we do, but they answer questions that we couldn't. Some members even turn to the community for help with non-Freshbooks products, demonstrating a high level of trust in the forums." [1]

—MIKE McDERMENT,
CEO, Freshbooks

ingly puny collection that could be housed in even the largest physical store.

We were fans of Zappos before it was cool.[2] As early advocates, we were often met with puzzled looks at the very suggestion that we would buy shoes, especially luxury shoes, without trying them on. This is, as it turns out, the whole point. Zappos offers an absolutely effortless return policy without even a whisper of guilt. It goes so far as to send the return paperwork, including return shipping labels, with the original order. Its original motto, "We are a service company that happens to sell shoes," is obsolete only because it now sells handbags, clothing, watches, and accessories (and coming soon, much more).

The company's whimsical nature is apparent on a visit to its website; the senior executives are introduced as "monkeys." They publish an annual "culture book" that describes what makes Zappos employees tick and display it proudly at the head office. The company blogs show employees who truly seem to love their jobs. But having happy employees isn't enough; attention to customer service is also taken seriously. Since it takes the right attitude to succeed at Zappos, new employees are offered $2,000 to quit after their training period, under the rationale that anyone who takes the money does not have the proper Zappos attitude.

The company's enthusiasm for social media encourages its community. Tony Hsieh himself is a Twitter superstar, influencing more than 1.7 million followers[3] with messages covering a wide range of topics that meanders well beyond haberdashery. Hsieh isn't alone. Visit twitter.zappos.com and you will see all public mentions of the company, along with links to Zappos employees who tweet (more than five hundred, including some with more than ten thousand followers) and the tweets themselves.

Zappos has an impressive Facebook presence as well. More than seventy thousand users like Zappos, and their comments flood the company's page each day. More than 140 videos have been posted along with many photos of Zappos fans showing off their purchases. The YouTube site is packed with videos of consumers telling their Zappos stories, such as a nervous bride whom the company helped find perfect shoes at the last minute.

Zappos makes it easy for shoppers to ask a friend's opinion on a handbag or blog about a fabulous pair of shoes by clicking on a link. A widget then automatically sends the information to the friend or uploads the graphic of the shoes directly to the blog editor. The company also provides an effective rating and comment section.

Sean O'Driscoll, the CEO of social media strategy firm Ant's Eye View, believes, "It is important to compare your customer service to best practices outside your industry, or you will suffer from incrementalism. The world has changed, and customer expectations have changed with it. You could have the best customer service in your industry, but if you're not comparative with Zappos, you're not going to impress your customer base."[4]

Zappos is eager to share its best practices with the world. You can visit its office in suburban Las Vegas for a free forty-five-minute tour and a crash course in Zappos culture. The company also offers extended tours and two-day boot camps for those who really want to delve into how Zappos works.

We decided to take the tour. The experience started with a pristinely detailed Zappos SUV picking us up at our hotel on the Strip and shuttling us to the Henderson, Nevada, office. We waited for the other guests to arrive in a brightly lit lobby complete with Zappos memorabilia, press clippings, a library of business books, and a retro pinball machine. Jonathan, our tour guide (employees all have day jobs and take turns giving the tours), gave a quick history of the company before leading us through the building.

As we wound our way through the marketing department, call center, and warehouse, we were greeted by employee cheers and creatively decorated workspaces. Although it wasn't occupied at the time, we were impressed with the fact that the CEO had a standard-size workspace located in a row of call-center employees and that it was decorated with the same nutty accoutrements as in other spaces. The tour ended with a photo opportunity for us each to pose with a throne and a crown (representing the promise that the customer is king). We obliged but took a pass on using said photos for the inside jacket cover of this book.

Zappos has done such a good job at becoming a poster child for effectively using social media that its mention generates some fatigue among close followers of the space. Critics dismiss the company's success with such generalizations as "They are small and a start-up; it's easy to build such a culture when you start from scratch," or "Shoes and accessories are a simple transaction; their lessons don't apply to an enterprise as sophisticated as mine."

Even O'Driscoll agrees the problem with using Zappos as an example is that "it is only five years old and had the luxury of starting from scratch with a customer focus. It is a lot harder to accomplish that with a company that is ten, fifteen, twenty, or a hundred years old."[5]

We think some of the criticism is unimaginative. While developing a Zappos-like atmosphere and engaged workforce in a legacy organization is challenging, emulating elements of the company's strategy is not rocket science. Performance metrics for call-center employees that are based on customer satisfaction rather than call length are more likely to turn your clients into advocates. Setting high expectations for employees and hiring passionate team players just makes sense. So does encouraging pride in your organization and recognizing the motivations of individual employees. All of these fundamentals make Zappos innovative and successful. Its social media campaign would not be effective if company's behavior did not back it up.

Some of its fans were concerned that the firm would lose its mojo when it was acquired by Amazon for a rumored $1.2 billion in 2009. So far, it seems like the promises made by Hsieh in his e-mail to employees have been kept:

> Although we'll have access to many of Amazon's resources, we need to continue to build our brand and our culture just as we always have. Our mission remains the same: delivering happiness to all of our stakeholders, including our employees, our customers, and our vendors.[6]

Amazon: A Perfectly Curated Universe

Amazon knows a thing or two about building community. It was one of the first Web companies to truly embrace customer-created content. Reader reviews do more than help consumers evaluate their purchases; the reviews (and the follow-up debates) are entertaining. Great prestige goes with a high ranking (those anointed may identify themselves with tags such as "top 100 reviewer").

Amazon provides a lot of value through its community section, including discussion sessions on everything from science fiction movies to gardening techniques. One thread that caught our eye was titled "Gift ideas for an obnoxious teenager." Some forum participants made suggestions that the obnoxious nephew who is "about fifteen years old" might be interested in a video game or TV box seats. Others suggested ways to address the obnoxiousness, including sitting down and really listening to the lad.

The discussions and review sections are well moderated. Amazon investigates if an author is suspected of posting a fake review, and decorum is maintained in the discussion areas. In fact, in one well-publicized case, a Russian scholar confessed to anonymously posting negative reviews about books penned by rival historians.[7] Generally, if the community thinks a

DON MITCHELL: AMAZON REVIEWER EXTRAORDINAIRE

Don Mitchell is one of the top Amazon reviewers, at times holding the number-two spot. By the middle of 2010, he had reviewed almost 4,000 books and received more than 97,000 "helpful votes" (Mitchell estimates that if all review sites were counted, he would have more than 120,000). When he evaluates other people's reviews, he looks for how much they tell him about the book, how clear the basis for their views is, how well they write, and what expertise they appear to have in the subject (for nonfiction books).[8] Mitchell has achieved celebrity status in the book community. Authors consider his reviews a badge of honor. A bestselling author once phoned him to discuss one of his critiques and made changes to the next edition based on his suggestions. About 80 percent of the books he receives come directly from the authors.[9] He reports that the time he spends on each review varies greatly:

> My style changes all the time. Some days I'm writing short reviews, ten minutes tops. Other days I'll write thousand-word reviews—at least forty-five minutes. The length of the review largely reflects how much of my interest the author caught. But in other cases, what the author did was so transparent that it only takes a few ideas and words to get the point across. I strive for brevity. I often do these at 2:00 A.M., and bed is calling at that hour.[10]

Mitchell asks authors whose books he wouldn't typically review for a donation of $1,000 to Habitat for Humanity (he makes it clear that the donation does not ensure a positive review, and the author receives the tax benefit for the donation); he estimates that he has raised more than $40,000 for this charitable organization. He also receives other perks, such as dinner invitations. When he included in a review the fact that he had never golfed at the Yale course, he received in short order an invitation to play.[11]

post has not added anything to the discussion, it is removed but can still be viewed after clicking through a disclaimer.

Amazon founder Jeff Bezos takes community very seriously, crediting the Amazon community for contributing much to the success of the firm. In 2009, Kindle users found that the works of fiction they had downloaded had been surreptitiously removed from their devices after Amazon discovered that it did not have proper copyright. Outrage spread quickly through the blogosphere, because users felt violated and subject to Big Brother–style thought invasion (and yes, *1984* was one of the affected titles). The problem was quickly fixed, and Bezos delivered one of the best CEO apologies ever:

This is an apology for the way we previously handled illegally sold copies of *1984* and other novels on Kindle. Our "solution" to the problem was stupid, thoughtless, and painfully out of line with our principles. It is wholly self-inflicted, and we deserve the criticism we've received. We will use the scar tissue from this painful mistake to help make better decisions going forward, ones that match our mission.

With deep apology to our customers,

Jeff Bezos

Doesn't that look great to you? By the way, it was first posted in the Amazon Kindle community.

Best Buy: A Safe Haven for Answers

Best Buy is a fantastic example of a company that has internalized the benefits of wikibrands. Tracy Benson, senior director of Best Buy's U.S. marketing, digital, and interactive, tells us that "using technology to build community came easy to us, because people who choose to work here do so because they like technology. We all use social media in our personal lives, even our senior executives, such as CMO Barry Judge."[12]

Two successful Best Buy initiatives are the company's Facebook presence and its Twitter support channel called Twelpforce. The Facebook page has more than one million fans, many of whom are actively engaged. Best Buy does not use the page for promotions or giveaways, but rather for product education, response to customer service issues, and advice—including the occasional reminder that the Facebook group giving away company gift cards is not affiliated with the company (along with a gentle warning against providing personal information to the group). Customer service issues are handled in a transparent, efficient, and nonconfrontational manner. The voices of the Best Buy employees are authentic. Their responses are not scripted; they receive communication training and follow the policies in the company's social media guidebook. Benson realizes that authenticity is paramount: "If communication isn't authentic, or companies try to use ghostwriters, customers can smell that in about twenty seconds."[13]

Twelpforce is a rapid-response team of thirty-five hundred Best Buy employees (known as blue shirts) that responds to customer questions on Twitter. These "twelpers" are rated on metrics such as activity level and trouble-shooting efficacy. The top-rated twelpers remain consistent over time. They are effective ambassadors for the company because they love to solve problems, are adept with technology, and speak their customers' language (geek code is well suited for Twitter's 140-character limit).

More than twenty-five thousand people follow conversations even though the content (generally discussions of technical electronics issues) does not sound like electrifying material. In fact, many followers (who have no affiliation to Best Buy) like to jump in and help customers with technical issues. Since Twitter isn't particularly good at archiving, a searchable database of past responses is posted at BBYfeed.com.

In 2009, Best Buy won the Marketer of the Year award from the U.S. Direct Marketing Association.[14] When Benson and her team accepted the award, she brought the top ten twelpers to the ceremony, all of whom had day jobs as blue shirts.

The Best Buy forum solicits input from the general public about all aspects of the company's operation (although the conversation typically focuses on product mix). The most active users (*superusers* in the company's vernacular) are held in special esteem; three of them were invited to the Consumer Electronics Show as Best Buy's VIP guests. Community manager Gina Debogovich explained, "Best Buy decided to invite a few customers to CES. It made total sense to invite three of our superusers from the Best Buy Community. They each contribute a huge amount for us, and it's great to be able to say thank you by treating them to the full Best Buy CES experience!"[15]

Engaging External Communities

Once an internal community has been created, a firm can recruit external participants. If governed correctly, it is incredible how much value volunteer contributors will provide. Think Tom Sawyer convincing the other kids that painting Aunt Polly's fence is actually fun instead of a chore.

Krista Thomas, vice president of marketing and communications at Reuters Thomson, says, "The ego of the contributor is important; people like to show how smart they are and how skilled they are at solving problems. Another common motivation is entrepreneurs interested in building their own brand. I want people to know how freaking cool my business is."[16]

Sean O'Driscoll identified four types of community members, along with how to address their core motivations for participation:[17]

▷ **Critics:** Make sure you listen to their concerns and close the loop on their complaints and suggestions.

▷ **Connectors:** They want special access. Have them sign a nondisclosure agreement, and then provide them with sneak previews to operations, updates, and so on.

▷ **Creators:** Stroke their egos; give them the tools they need to create new offerings.

▷ **Collectors:** Provide them with proof of their contributions, such as digital badges.

In this section, we discuss some of the best examples of using external contributors effectively.

Intuit: A Safe Haven for Answers

Intuit, maker of the popular QuickBooks and TurboTax software, launched its online community in 2005. It operates with the goal of enabling users to get efficient, high-quality answers fast. According to Scott Wilder, group manager of Intuit's online communities, "We're kind of like the plumbers just building the environment and setting up the infrastructure." [18] But instead of charging staff members with answering user questions, Intuit has created a community in which members themselves can help one another. In the words of Christine Morrison, Intuit's social media marketing manager, the community "helps customers find the right answer quickly but also provides a subtle undercurrent of confidence." [19]

Since the average consumer perceives tax preparation as complicated, receiving helpful, near-real-time help shows users that they are actually making progress and that it is not so difficult.

One challenge for Intuit, according to Wilder, is that its community encompasses a broad variety of users who speak different languages and have different needs. The entry-level end user is different from the IT specialist who is different from the CFO, yet they all use Intuit products— albeit it for a wide range of purposes. Given this complexity, Wilder notes, "It's better to let people who are doing the same type of work answer the specific questions." [20]

So how does Intuit maintain its base of half a million members? Wilder says his team focuses on those who best serve the community. Forums and discussion threads account for more than 70 percent of content; the rest consists of wikis, webinars, podcasts, and articles. Morrison says it is important to know your audience; people are serious when they do their taxes, so a professional forum discussion is a lot more appropriate than zany YouTube content.[21]

Intuit differentiates members by experience, level of collaboration, and expertise with its products. The community's more advanced collaborators are flagged as All-Stars, and those who complete QuickBooks certification programs are given advanced titles such as Certified Pro Advisor or Advanced Certified Pro Advisor, to bestow some recognition on and perks to top contributors. For instance, Wilder explains that All-Stars "go to our private forum so they can talk to us and share their ideas privately. They get recognized on the site as All-Stars, and we take a lot of direction from them." However, he cautions that special treatment for the top performers cannot come at the expense of less-experienced members: "The caveat is that we can't forget the novice user. We reach out to [them] and garner their input as well."[22]

Another key to the Intuit community is that it's not used for sales. "We do have a section on the site for people who are considering buying our products, with information to help differentiate between features," says Wilder. But the absence of any explicit sales pitch means that the community provides a "safe haven where users can go and know that they won't be sold to."[23]

With the rapidity of the community's growth over four years, Intuit has had to find ways to update and scale their model. One development has been the integration of community into desktop products. Wilder explains, "As a worker, when you're in your workflow and at a certain screen, you can, from that screen, ask questions and get answers tied directly to the community."[24] By building this functionality into the Quicken software as a widget, Intuit has found a way to bridge the user workspace and the community, allowing members to enjoy the support features without having to break work flow to visit the online site.

One of the TurboTax superusers, a retired CPA who asked us to refer to him only as Howard, has made more than forty thousand contributions to the community (mostly answers to tax questions) that have been viewed more than seven million times.

While using TurboTax in 2006, Howard was puzzled with a query he received. When he went into the Live Community to ask about it, he was impressed with how professional and knowledgeable the other users were. It occurred to him that becoming a superuser himself was an excellent way to put his years of experience to use while really helping people through a difficult yearly process. Beyond altruism, participating in the forum required him not only to keep up with the tax code and Internal Revenue code regulations, but also to learn about unfamiliar areas. For example, during his career, his clients were mostly wealthy and did not qualify for the earned income credit, yet many of the people he helps in the community have questions about it.

When asked what surprised him most, Howard quickly points to how seemingly simple tax questions seem to baffle users. Upon reflection, he adds that he sometimes finds it difficult to comprehend the computer shorthand prevalent in the forums (such as "4" instead of *for* and "ur" instead of *your*), saying that he had to "read questions five times to understand the problem."[25] This issue reminds him that one of the reasons he thinks the TurboTax Live community is successful is that it contains a healthy combination of tax experts such as himself and technology experts who are adept at solving software issues.

SAP Labs: Selfless and Collaborative Geekdom

Marilyn Pratt is the community evangelist for SAP Labs. She gave us an enthusiastic tour of the SAP Developer Network, an active community where developers meet, conduct discussions, learn about upcoming releases, and work collaboratively to solve problems (the tagline of the community is "Feed Your Inner Geek"). The community boasts more than 1.3 million members who produce more than six thousand posts per day. It receives more than half a million unique visitors monthly and supports more than a million topic threads.[26]

Pratt understands her constituency: people from varied backgrounds and different companies who want to solve problems collaboratively. When asked what impressed her most about contributors, she replies, "How enthusiastic they were; they make a commitment to follow a project through to completion and selflessly transfer knowledge to each other without being concerned with personal fame or glory."[27]

Pratt describes the governance system within the SAP community as liberal: "We set some 'rules of engagement,' but generally, users are allowed to blast the product."[28] Since software companies typically generate a lot of improvements and new features from forum discussions (sometimes the complaints lead to gold), it does not make sense to stifle the discussion through heavy-handed corporate moderation. Besides, according to Pratt, "The contributors themselves are typically the harshest defenders of the product, and they jealously guard the community against attack."[29]

Salesforce.com: A Sporting Developer Rivalry

Matt Brown and Steve Molis are customer heroes within the salesforce
.com developer community. They are not on the company payroll: Brown
is a salesforce administration assistant at Blackboard, an e-learning company, and Molis works in Boston as a management information systems
application developer at Epsilon, a marketing services firm. But both add a
great deal of value to the community by answering questions, participating in discussions, and solving customer problems.

Although they have never met in person, they know each other well;
each speaks highly of the other's technical ability, problem-solving skills,
and sense of humor. Well aware that the other is highly ranked in the community, Brown and Molis have developed a friendly rivalry. After Molis
responded more quickly to a discussion thread that Brown started, banter
went back and forth in the thread long after the original problem had been
solved. Molis followed up by sending Brown a YouTube video of Larry Bird
smugly walking away from his winning shot in an NBA three-point contest
before the ball had begun its descent toward the hoop.

Motivations of Volunteer Community Experts

Volunteer community experts offer the following as their motivations for
participating in the community:

▷ **They have a genuine need to help people.** All the dedicated forum
participants we spoke with really enjoy helping people solve their problems and, by doing so, gain an authentic sense of satisfaction. Molis
empathizes with a beleaguered IT department that is instructed to use
salesforce.com in a way that doesn't seem to make logical sense. He tells
us that he offers a cautionary tale: "If you really have to use it that way
because of your business processes, please be aware of A, B, and C."[30]
Howard, the Intuit community CPA, enjoys helping people with the
yearly anguish of figuring out their taxes and was particularly satisfied
by drafting a letter that a community member sent to the IRS explaining why a questioned deduction was actually legitimate.

▷ **They get a thrill from solving problems.** Active participants in customer groups are predisposed to solving problems. When Molis was left
at home alone as a child, he would take appliances like the toaster apart
and try to put them back together before his parents came home (if he
had to abort the mission, he'd throw the parts into the casing and hope
that he could finish the project before anyone needed to make break-

fast). According to Molis, people like him do not "solve the *New York Times* crossword or play Soduku, they answer people's salesforce.com questions." [31]

▷ **It makes them better at their jobs.** To solve customer problems, experts need to know the product intimately, and the logic and solutions involved in their salesforce.com activity is directly applicable to their day jobs. Also, since they are given sneak previews of new features, they are better equipped to forecast how their company's needs can be met by the product in the future.

▷ **It builds their personal brands.** Not only are they celebrities in an (admittedly niche) community, but volunteer experts also have the opportunity to impress people with their problem-solving and professional communication skills. Molis tells us how after he solved a particular tricky problem for a community member, she sent him a thank-you gift from her brother's winery. [32] We think she would be thrilled to help him if he decided to send her a résumé.

▷ **Helping gives them a sense of ownership in the product.** For people like Brown and Molis, seeing their ideas come to life as a feature in a new salesforce.com release is exciting. It also amplifies their dedication and engagement in the community. Brown says that seeing his ideas become part of the product "makes me feel like a stakeholder and increases my emotional connection to the company." [33] Howard enjoys finding an error in TurboTax software, although he rarely does so and is impressed by how quickly it gets corrected. [34]

CHAPTER 13

COMMUNITY MANAGEMENT

How to Build a Brand Garden, Not a Ghost Town

Community management goals and requirements change as a community matures. For initial members, individual contact is important, as Stewart Butterfield, co-founder of Flickr, describes:

> We very carefully built the community on Flickr, person by person. The team and I greeted every single person who arrived, introduced them around, hung out in the chat rooms. It was a very hands-on process, building the community. And in the beginning Flickr was built side-by-side with feedback from the community. We were posting over 50 times a day in the forums. After you hit, say 10,000 members or so, hopefully you've created a strong enough culture that people are greeting each other. It really is kind of like building a civilization. You need to have a culture and mores and a sense of this is "what people do here."[2]

At some point, a successful community hits its stride—features are added, the community is integrated with other brand and

"A community manager is one part collaboration guide, whose job it is to pose the provocative questions, manage the discussion, identify content to generate ideas; and one part community coordinator, whose role it is to make sure that community questions/problems are triaged, conventions are followed, updated content is posted, etc."[1]

—STEVE GUENGERICH,
managing director,
BroadBrush Ventures

225

company activities, events are organized, members earn recognition and feel a sense of purpose, and supercontributors are identified and become champions. The community begins to govern itself and grows organically.

In mature communities, members need to be given fresh value at regular intervals to shake off doldrums. Joseph Jaffe, CEO of the consulting firm Crayon, emphasizes that a brand community should experiment with its deliverables, "We distill this into a very real and workable number: four. Four experiments over a calendar year. Is one experiment per quarter (for a community) that unrealistic or irrationally exuberant? I think not."[3]

The community approach at Canadian wireless provider WIND Mobile increased customer motivation and ownership behind the brand. Customer experience manager Kasi Bruno experienced this phenomenon when she worked with a research partner on a customer survey. The research firm was surprised by how willing and eager WIND Mobile customers were to help. They were happy to provide opinions without receiving any incentive and had the unusual patience to stick with an online survey that lasted for twenty minutes.[4]

Obstacles and Challenges

A report published by Deloitte Consulting and the Society for New Communications Research, in an investigation of 140 companies (including Fortune 100 firms), identified the following challenges with respect to building an effective community.[5] The community leaders were allowed to identify multiple answers:

▷ Getting people engaged in the community (51 percent of respondents)
▷ Finding enough time to manage the community (45 percent)
▷ Attracting people to the community (34 percent)
▷ Getting people to come back (26 percent)
▷ Getting people to join the community (22 percent)

Common Mistakes

Once a community is established, new challenges present themselves. This section explains some of the key mistakes businesses make while managing their communities.

Focusing Too Much Attention on Technology

According to Amber Naslund, the director of community for Radian6, just because many of the most successful communities occur via online forums, that shouldn't necessarily be the starting point. A successful community happens by gathering members and fostering communication between them. Many of the examples that we have already discussed succeeded in online forums because the members spend their days typing on their keyboards. However, Naslund talks about a community of emergency room triage nurses that doesn't fit this profile: "They want to share information and best practices, but near-real-time discussions on an online forum doesn't make sense for their jobs. They may share information in a manner that would seem bizarre to a developer, such as printing out a blog post and handing out hard copies to colleagues."[6]

She continues, "Too many companies think that technology is the key; just building a community site with all the bells and whistles will encourage people to show up and participate. There needs to be compelling conversation or interesting, regularly refreshed information for them to return between purchase cycles."[7] Susan Fournier and Lara Lee point out that "unfortunately, most company-sponsored online 'communities' are nothing more than far-flung focus groups established in the hope that consumers will bond around the virtual suggestion box."[8]

Misaligned Goals

Firms need to resist measuring the success of communities solely by the number of members or even the amount of interaction. Naslund reminds us that "the goal is not to attract a million people to your site. It's to figure out what to do with them when they get there. How do you encourage conversation between them and mobilize them?"[9] Social media expert Euan Semple believes that terms like *collaborative community* are often used as "weasel words." If behavior and the overall spirit of an organization do not truly change, then the wikibrand strategy will fail. In his experience, too many companies try to replicate traditional communication processes online rather than encouraging edgy, innovative discussions.[10]

Inadequate Investment

Brand communities are driven by members, but to grow beyond the first spark of interest, they need benevolent leadership. Unfortunately, one study found that 30 percent of online communities are managed by only part-time employees, and many of even the most sophisticated communities have fewer than five employees involved.[11]

Customer Fatigue

Mathew Ingram of GigaOM stresses that "customer expectations are higher than ever, but at the same time, there is customer fatigue. People are not interested in having a relationship with every company with whom they do business."[12] An unsolicited, aggressive community invitation will soon be regarded with the same favor as early-morning, door-to-door proselytizers.

Community Management Strategies

It is important to integrate the entire business into the community. Early and deep involvement by both members and as many departments as possible from the organization can create critical mass and momentum. This effort may require cultural and organizational change. Patience is also important; communities often take two years or more to mature. Managers need to anticipate the evolution of the brand community and develop ongoing twelve-month plans.

Brand communities can embed customer centricity deeper in an organization. Community interactions begin to look less like marketing and more like cooperation, mutual brainstorming, and co-development of ideas and outcomes—which, of course, they are.

Companies must recognize why people join brand communities. There are many reasons, but generating improved financial results for the host company is certainly not at the top of the list. People join to generate a social connection, express their opinions, develop a hobby or interest, develop new skills and talents, or simply make a contribution. Sometimes they participate for a chance to win a contest or achieve a monetary reward, although that is uncommon. In some cases, people will join because the company (or an associated cause) resonates with them.

There is a community benefit cycle for companies that achieve traction: with content and incentives come members, with more members come more interactions, then more repeat visits and referrals, then more impact in the form of a better site. And the cycle continues.

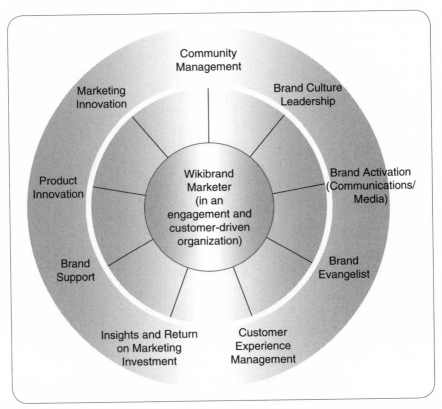

FIGURE 13.1 THE ENGAGED WIKIBRAND ORGANIZATION

Figure 13.1 illustrates how the wikibrand marketer deploys customer information to many different aspects of the organization. Within the wikibrand organization, the following transformations need to occur:

▷ The arbiter of brand strategy and positioning moves from the classic, externally focused brand management function to a more internally focused role: brand culture leadership. Having significantly more interaction with human resources, operations, and sales channels, the brand culture manager becomes the custodian of how the brand operates and exists within the company.

▷ Instead of parceling outbound communications to a number of functions (advertising, promotions, digital, and so on), broadcast messaging is integrated in one place through brand activation and support groups.

▷ The traditional public relations function expands and rises in importance to become a publicly identifiable brand evangelist who works closely with the CEO and channels key strategy imperatives and customer directions from and back to the executive suite. This function embraces all forms of stakeholders, including broad outreach to social media, traditional media, and industry partners.

▷ An insights and return on marketing investment department operates throughout the entire sales process to create real value. Establishing constant streams of contact with customers, brokering across-the-board customer engagement by all departments, and managing a dashboard of new customer-driven marketing measures aimed at evaluating marketing investment are this group's core tasks.

▷ Product and marketing innovation departments are established to provide a consistent spectrum of improvement options and ongoing contact with lead users and beta-testers. They can also help to integrate community information into product and marketing processes.

▷ Finally, a community management function is developed to create interaction with and governance of a private brand group of fans and key Influencers.

This drive to brand collaboration expands the role of the marketing function, providing more opportunities to service line functions and to exert a positive impact on innovation, sales, product management, corporate reputation, employee recruitment, and brand insight. In so doing, the marketing department is better positioned to be the voice of the customer across the enterprise—building a congregation, creating forums for dialogue with and between customer audiences, and being the filter for the organization's and its customer base's thinking.

The Role of the Community Manager

Community managers require an eclectic set of skills: part corporate journalist, part public relations, part customer service, part likable host, part sociable and enthusiastic face, part technologist, and part brand fanatic.

Amber Naslund believes that basics such as strong interpersonal and communication skills are crucial in a community manager. She clarifies that a diverse portfolio of skills is required: "An effective manager must be able to speak well; debate diplomatically in comments and forums; and write effectively, whether it is in a blog post or a 140-character burst on

Twitter." [13] Likewise, the manager needs to have an engaging personality both online and off. In the event that community members (or even different internal departments) are not communicating properly, the community manager needs to act as translator and perhaps an empathetic diplomat.

This person also needs to be curious, constantly learning, and hungry for knowledge. Adroitness with social media is a requirement of the job (Naslund says she would not hire someone without some previous experience—at least a personal blog). Plus, the manager needs to stay abreast of new developments, platforms, and technologies.

Jennifer Evans, chief strategist for Sequentia Environics, believes that community managers also need to be able to determine the true voice of the membership and manage the "vocal minority" without spending an inordinate amount of time on this group. [14]

Scott Monty, head of social media at Ford, tells us that one of the most important skills community managers need is the ability to take off a public relations or marketing hat and think like, speak like, and speak to a customer. In addition, they need to be naturally curious and eager to experiment. [15] Since Ford operates in 127 countries on six continents, Monty needs to ensure that his team respects cultural sensitivities and cultural norms. Regional managers on his team need to be able to take the global infrastructure and overall message and adapt them to their local marketplace. [16]

Juliana Crispo, who blogs at The Social Capitalist about social media optimization, believes that it's also important to have soft skills such as diplomacy—the ability to take negativity out of a conversation and to deal compassionately with community members who are frustrated or disgruntled. [17]

Responsibilities of the Community Manager

Community managers play a balancing act between being the voice and conscience of the customer, the passionate champion and cheerleader of the company, and the ombudsperson between the two. As a result, the community manager serves many bosses and wears many hats. The fifteen essential roles that community managers perform in successful companies are listed in Table 13.1.

Obviously, as communities become more advanced, the responsibilities of the community manager become more complex—moving from product educator and administrator, facilitating external innovation, and catering

TABLE 13.1 THE COMMUNITY MANAGER ROLES

	INTERNAL/COMPANY	BRIDGE	EXTERNAL/COMMUNITY
Expert Level	*Client Agitator* "Bringing about change inside"	*Strategist* "Delivering community innovation"	*Personal Concierge* "Catering to the Influencers/VIPs"
401	*Internal Trainer* "Galvanizing employee interest"	*Events Host* "Being the face online/ offline"	*Expert Listener* "Having an ear to the ground"
301	*Research Filter* "Getting to insights"	*Responder/Liaison* "Brokering connections/ managing flow"	*Social Networker* "Being the magnet for recruitment"
201	*Brand Ambassador* "Living/evangelizing the brand"	*Content Developer* "Keeping the community fresh"	*Moderator* "Building effective engagement"
The Basics	*Product Educator* "Being the expert"	*Program Manager/ Administrator* "Ensuring stuff works daily"	*Problem Solver* "Fixing the frustration"

Source: Agent Wildfire, Inc.

to valuable members. A community manager needs to develop a team that can perform all of the following functions:

INTERNAL ROLES

▷ The *product educator* is the guru, expert, historian, and details person who intimately knows the portfolio of brands/products the community supports.

▷ The *brand ambassador* exudes passion for the brand and is a role model for the type of people the company wants to attract. This person recruits and engages community members.

▷ The *research filter* synthesizes community feedback information and analytics and then creates actionable insights to which a company executive can react.

▷ The *internal trainer* becomes a missionary inside the company and promotes employee involvement, demonstrates success, communicates value, and demystifies the world of technology and social media underlying the community.

▷ The *client agitator* provides the internal rallying cry and the conscience of the community/customer inside the company, frequently at executive levels. This team member spearheads change management and revises processes that hinder community success.

BRIDGE ROLES (BETWEEN THE COMPANY AND THE COMMUNITY)

▷ The *program manager/administrator* manages the day-to-day details of running the community, including staffing, activity tracking, overseeing communications, and providing feedback.

▷ The *content developer* creates a fresh supply of interesting news from the company and about the community using video, pictures, forums, updates, or blog posts.

▷ The *responder/liaison* plays the intermediary role between company and community, whether the communication is planned or given spontaneously to highlight emerging issues.

▷ The *events host* of both online and offline events creates a sense of presence and leadership at all community occasions.

▷ The *strategist* develops new applications, platforms, and course corrections for community engagement that benefit the sponsoring company.

EXTERNAL, COMMUNITY-MINDED ROLES

▷ The *problem solver* addresses member/customer problems directly or provides a forum and process to solve ingrained issues with the company, product, or community.

▷ The *moderator* acts as the ombudsperson, rule maker, conversation starter, and referee in user-generated forums and community debate inside and outside the community.

▷ The *social networker* recruits new members into the community, where they are engaged by the brand ambassador.

▷ The *expert listener* tracks conversations about the company inside and outside the community and responds intelligently. See the sidebar on the next page for a more detailed description of the required listening skills for this role.

▷ The *personal concierge* serves top-performing community members, highlights key member contributions, and provides VIP treatment to key industry and community stakeholders.

Examples of Effectively Managed Brand Communities

The following examples represent a cross section of three well-managed customer communities.

LISTENING SKILLS REQUIRED FOR COMMUNITY MANAGERS

▷ **Customer monitoring:** Knowing what people are saying about you involves making sure you get as much information as possible from the time you spend listening. Be it for marketing, customer service, or research, companies need to have a system in place to perform this listening function. Whether it's done manually with data drawn from applications like Technorati, Twitter search, Hootsuite, or a social media monitoring vendor such as Radian6, you need to understand how your brand is being discussed.

▷ **Customer culture:** To know what your customers and Influencers are doing, you need to meet your customers on their own turf. Listening can no longer be limited to messages through the key traditional media channels (TV, radio, outdoor, print ads, newspaper, direct); it needs to be everywhere. Engaged businesses should devote resources to tracking the culture of their marketplace.

▷ **Customer centricity:** Community members will know if you are actively listening. It is not enough just to know the social environment of the product and customer universe; you need to participate actively. The majority of Whole Foods's social media activity is responding to customers nationally, on an interest- and geographic-specific basis. It is no surprise that Whole Foods is the seventy-fourth most popular Twitter page.[18]

▷ **Customer driven:** Community members will recognize if your company responds to feedback. Any community, no matter how solidly entrenched, will get bored over time. Members will disengage or leave if they don't feel their contributions to the community are inspiring change. You need to improve your community-based customer feedback, preferably giving credit to the audience.

GovLoop

When Steve Ressler started his career as a third-generation public servant, he was puzzled that, although different departments and branches shared similar challenges, technology was not being used to share knowledge. He started GovLoop, a community designed to solve government problems, find and contribute best practices, research trends, and connect with peers. The mission of the GovLoop community is to "connect government to improve government."

He was quickly humbled by his success; he was soon spending forty hours per week managing the community on top of the forty to fifty hours at his day job. He eventually resigned to run GovLoop full-time, as the community grew to more than thirty thousand participants, including more than 30 federal chief information officers (CIOs) and chief technology officers (CTOs), more than 60 state and local CIOs, and more than 125 city mayors. Local chapters sprang up in Brazil, Canada, Australia, and the Netherlands.

Ressler credits the members with the success of the GovLoop community. Since they self-select, the community is "filled with people who are passionate about their jobs and are eager to find better ways of serving their constituents."[19] He was surprised with how easy internal governance was; he had to gently coach some members who were pitching their services a little too actively, but in general the community itself did a good job of policing itself. Although he is too humble to characterize himself as such, Ressler believes that a charismatic leader is important in running a community. Members will participate more often and behave better if they know that someone is providing leadership as well as taking responsibility when a mistake is made.

The Globe & Mail

When Mathew Ingram was community manager of the Canadian newspaper *The Globe & Mail*, he was faced with the challenge of managing online comments. Although he encouraged journalists to actively participate in conversations with readers, some were not interested. Ingram described one elder statesman of the newsroom as "kryptonite to Captain Community. He felt that his role was to think of smart things, write them down, then cash his check."[20] Part of the plan was behavior modeling: if readers realize that they are dialoguing with the author rather than a faceless moderator, they are more likely to be civil.

The level of control required to monitor comments properly is not inconsequential. On Ingram's watch, the *Globe* was receiving seven thousand to eight thousand comments per day, which made it challenging to find the resources to address them, especially with the severe economic pressure affecting the newspaper industry. Ingram compares how two other newspapers, the *New York Times* and *USA Today* handle reader comments. The *Times* only opens up a few stories at a time to comments and edits them closely, while *USA Today* is more of a free-for-all. Not surprisingly, the quality of comments differs widely. Those in the *Times* are well written and on topic, while *USA Today*'s frequently turn into off-topic rants filled with spelling and grammatical errors—a typical comment said, "A bridge washes out in Tennessee. What do you expect in Obama's America?" According to Ingram, one of the trickier challenges for community managers is how to adjust the dials between the democratization of participants' input and the control and quality of the host's brand.[21]

One of the most interesting aspects of community within the newspaper space is that it takes the guesswork out of readers' interests. By tracking where readers click, you can see a heat map of what stories they read, how long they are on the page, and in the case of longer articles, whether they read through the entire article. Similarly, the Kindle and other electronic book readers provide insightful data into how books are consumed. For example, which sections are skipped or read multiple times? At what point is a book abandoned?

WIND Mobile

WIND Mobile is a voice and data provider that began building its brand before it even received a license to compete in the Canadian market. Will Novosedlik, vice president of brand and communications, says that it was critical to build the company's image as an underdog and a more customer-friendly option than the incumbents. WIND Mobile actively communicated with its market and incorporated respondents' suggestions, not only with respect to product offerings, but as actual copy in the advertising campaign. In addition, the company maintains active conversations with its customers through its customer forum and Facebook page.

Novosedlik believes that the keys to building a successful brand community are to know your customers, communicate with them in an authentic manner, acknowledge their power, and be prepared to respond to and act on their input. On the other hand, he believes that the biggest mistakes companies make while building their brand are trying to control the conversation and treating the social media interactions as an isolated channel.

It turns out that WIND Mobile's built-up goodwill was crucial, because the network was, by all accounts, too weak to handle the traffic generated at launch. Suddenly Bell and Rogers, the two main incumbents, responded with advertisements targeted at WIND Mobile customers, proffering the reliability of their own networks. Novosedlik believes that, even though the growing pains hurt, the community approach proved useful; the company's image of freedom was reinforced when dissatisfied customers were able to shut down their contracts without the punitive consequences imposed by most wireless providers.[22] Also, he believes that by not censoring discussions about service trouble on the community forum and Facebook page, WIND Mobile reinforces its belief in the importance of communication.

MEASUREMENT AND METRICS

The Imperfect Science of Monitoring Wikibrand Performance

Traditionally, marketers have measured effectiveness based on how much activity was generated, how efficient the inputs were, and other fluctuations in awareness and brand equity. The full impact of customer involvement provided by an influential consumer (such as advocacy, improved insights, user-generated content, and product development) were discounted—mostly because they were difficult to determine quantitatively.

Traditional brand metrics only provide a measure of passive interest in a brand. For example, a function of a person's brand loyalty may be based on decision inertia, low involvement, lack of autonomy, or consumption of products from a virtual monopoly. Mercurial shifts in customer expectations or quick-moving industry standards can cause these ratings to swing quickly, which is especially important for products with long purchase cycles. Finally, using brand awareness as a key metric becomes less relevant in a world where upstart businesses can rally hordes of people overnight.

"ROI is a campaign metric; social media is a commitment. What's the ROI of your telephone? What's the ROI of putting your pants on in the morning? You know there's value to it, and you're in trouble if you don't do it, but it's hard to quantify."[1]

—SCOTT MONTY,
head of social media, Ford

The more we learn about the measurement of brand power in the digital age, the more we recognize the degree to which engaged customers hold the key to brand success. The investment in these users has led to a new definition of ROI—return on influence. With the rise of social media, engaged users with large networks of friends are becoming much more valuable than traditional single media impressions. Amber Naslund, director of community for Radian6, believes that "pure ROI of online communities is only one metric, and not necessarily the right one, especially if it's being used as a way to really say 'we don't know how to justify this project.' An effective campaign will build trust and impact many different areas of the business and increase the likelihood of a purchase at multiple touchpoints, most of which are not directly at the point of sale." [2]

The quotation from Scott Monty at the beginning of this chapter is clever, but it does not account for the opportunity cost of reallocating resources from other activities to wikibranding, and the attitude it represents certainly would not satisfy a critical chief financial officer. In an era in which marketing budgets are usually in the top three line items of an organization's budget and peer executive teams are demanding more marketing rigor and less "trust me it will work" attitudes, proper brand metrics are essential. Only 7 percent of senior-level financial executives are satisfied with their marketing function's ability to measure ROI. [3]

Three main types of questions arise with respect to the ROI debate: [4]

▷ **Resistance questions:** These questions are generally framed as reasons not to engage in a social-driven, wikibrand initiative. For example, "What direct financial return will we receive from this activity?"
▷ **Business questions:** These questions ask what the business result of the initiative will be. For example, "What cost reductions will we realize by moving customer service from the phone to an online forum?"
▷ **Analysis questions:** These questions focus on what greater insight will come from the initiative. For example, "How many questions will be answered via the support forum?"

In a wikibrand universe, greater accountability for marketing performance and greater accuracy in measuring the totality of it are required. At a minimum, three critical questions must be answered:

1. How can we more effectively measure our customer-facing/marketing spending?

2. Are we measuring the right things?
3. What are the measures telling us over time?

On this point, a majority of senior marketers agree with the CFOs. In an excellent white paper titled "Social Marketing Analytics: A New Framework for Measuring Results in Social Media," Jeremiah Owyang and John Lovett posit that "existing social marketing measures and metrics fail to deliver actionable insights and offer little more than digital trivia."[5]

Of course, it is important to measure the success of your wikibrands strategy. In some cases, the return on investment is very clear; by the end of 2009, Dell reported selling more than $6.5 million of product through its Twitter channel.[6] In other cases, the benefits of the strategy require more investigation. Since an effective wikibrands strategy will affect all touchpoints of the sales funnel (including after-sales service), a prospect may become aware of a product through the blogosphere, research it on the Internet, and then customize it in a virtual store before purchasing it through a traditional retail channel. Anytime a wikibrands strategy advances a consumer along the purchase cycle or improves the after-purchase experience, there is return on investment; it gets tricky, however, when you try to parse out precisely where to attribute percentages, since wikibrand strategy and traditional marketing work in concert.

Sanjay Dholakia, former CMO for Lithium Technologies, points out:

> If you can identify a benefit you're seeking to get out of the community—reduced support costs, lead generation, increased loyalty—you can tie activities and metrics within the community directly to those benefits. That takes the community from being a toy of some backroom techie to a real business tool. It helps people start to understand that a community provides you with a transparent look into your customer base.[7]

Not only is wikibranding providing viable approaches for measuring consumer engagement, consumers are providing cheaper, quicker, and more accurate evidence of their engagement. Perfecting a way to measure engagement accurately will go a long way toward establishing the importance of brand value and rekindling executive interest in the role of wikibrand activity. As Jim Sterne states in *Social Media Metrics: How to Measure and Optimize Your Marketing Investment*, a marketer using social media can "tell you whether our digital visitors [as compared to consumers reached by TV ads costing hundreds of millions of dollars per year] are more engaged with our brand, come back more often, buy from us and discuss our products with their friends."[8]

The rest of the chapter highlights some of the key measures in five categories: customer engagement, brand differentiation, community participation, customer influence, and organizational capacity.

Customer Engagement

Measuring how excited customers are about the brand becomes easier with social media technology. Google Analytics and other tools can easily be set to create an instructive dashboard. More sophisticated results are achieved when social metrics are matched with Web analytics. Marcel Lebrun, CEO of Radian6, explains, "Social mentions on their own need to be combined with the degree of influence of the speaker, both in the number of people reached and in the propensity of those people to buy (or whatever other activity matches your business goal)."[9]

Brandon Murphy, chief strategy director at advertising agency 22Squared, conducted a study that quantified how socially involved customers spend more and drive higher spending among people they influence. The study showed that a group engaged in simple social activity, such as reading a company blog or providing feedback on a company's website, spent a 26 percent premium over a control group. A group with a greater level of participation (there were ten ways to judge this level, including writing about the company in a personal blog or mentioning it in a Facebook status update or Twitter post) spent a 147 percent premium.[10]

It is important to consider context when evaluating standard measures like number of followers. An entertainment property such as an action movie would be disappointed with a fan base that would make most consumer products ecstatic. We have a client that manufactures specialty construction products; not many people in the world buy such products, so share of attention and the growth of that share are more meaningful metrics than pure numbers.

The key metrics for evaluating customer engagement are as follows:

▷ Corporate Web presence/traffic macromeasurements
    Number of page views
    Number of unique visits
    Percentage of return visits

   Click-through rates (the percentage of individuals viewing a Web
      page who click on a specific link—traditionally a banner ad—
      appearing on the page)
▷ Website navigation/presence
   Time spent on the site (website, community, blog, other)
   Pages viewed (website, community, blog, other)
   Bounce rate (percentage of visitors who "bounce" to another site
      without traveling deeper into your website)
   Navigation path (the order in which visitors move through your site
      and what pages they view)
   Next clicks (where visitors go next)
   Exit pages (the last page visitors see)
   Navigation (where visitors arrive from—Google, blog posting, com-
      petitive site, and so on)
▷ Impact of your corporate website/blog
   Number of RSS feeds
   Number of backlinks
   Technorati rating (a measure of a blog's impact)
   Page rank
   Amount of ad revenue
   Number of Digg links
   Search engine optimization (SEO) rankings
   Conversion rate of search terms
▷ Impact of your built community
   Number of members
   Number of active members
   Number of evangelists (super-participatory people)
   Amount of original contributions
   Percentage of activity participation (response/total pool of invitees)
▷ Popularity of corporate social media identities (top five networks)
   Number of "likes" on Facebook
   Number of blog readers
   Number of webinar attendees
   Number of YouTube viewers (on channel and embedded on others)
   Number of Twitter followers (on base, affiliate, and/or employee
      profiles)
   Adjusted number of followers (removing spammers and "Twit-
      ter celebrities" who follow anyone who asks but do not actually
      engage with their content)

▷ Influence of followers
    Reach of followers (how many people follow those who follow you and how many of them are influenced by your followers)
    Activity level of followers (how often they post)
    Share of conversation (what percentage of their posts relate to your company)
    Hit rate/blogger outreach (percentage who get involved)
▷ Growth and activity trends
    Speed of follower growth
    Spike of conversation/brand mentions/links
    Mentions in hashtags
    Mentions on aggregator sites such as Digg
▷ Revenue attributable to social brand activity
    Increased yield
    Number of new business leads
    Increased conversion rates of prospects
    Reduced purchase cycle time
    Increased geographical diversity of clients
    Seasonality of buzz/activity
    Improved intent to buy (likelihood of purchase)
    Sales resulting from webinars
    Number of touchpoints along purchase chain
    Short-term versus long-term impact on revenue
    Acceleration of purchase process
    Frequency of purchase
    Conversion rate from visitor to consumer
    Attendance at in-person events attributable to social media
▷ Improved customer service attributable to social network activity
    Reduction in burn rate
    Increased customer retention rate
    Improved customer satisfaction
    Faster response time to customer complaints
    Speed of identifying problems via social networks
    Customer engagement score

Be careful with metrics such as the number of followers. Unless Facebook "likes," Twitter followers, and LinkedIn connections are actively engaged in your brand, merely collecting them is ineffective and likely to be misleading. Look at your own profiles: how many Facebook or LinkedIn groups have you joined that subsequently turned into a wasteland? Your

EXTREME CONSUMERS

Extreme consumers may have always existed, but the ability for these corporate keeners to influence others through technologies such as social media, fan sites, and YouTube videos have made them more relevant. A team led by a professor, a think tank leader, and a chemical industry product manager studied the phenomenon, describing these fans as "people who are so infatuated with the brand that they spend more than 10 percent of their lifetime income on it." [11]

Examples of such behavior are quirky (one person lived exclusively on food that contained Arm & Hammer baking soda for more than twenty years); obsessive (one person had purchased more than 150 Canon cameras since 2006); and gastronomically repulsive (one person had drunk nothing but Coca-Cola for twenty years, and another had consumed twelve Krispy Kreme doughnuts per day for more than four years).

Don Gorske doesn't spend 10 percent of his salary on Big Macs, but he does receive 90 percent of his solid food intake from them. He has consumed more than twenty-three thousand Big Macs since 1972, at least one daily with the exception of eight days (including the day his mother died, fulfilling a promise to her). Gorske, by the way, has a healthy body mass index and cholesterol level, primarily due to the fact that he consumes fewer overall calories than most Americans.

Each of the two thousand consumers studied say they personally identify with and gain meaning from a favorite brand, 98 percent have defended their favorite brands against perceived attacks in the media or from other firms or individuals, and 96 percent consider the brands part of the family. Yet the same study shows that 65 percent of managers are "wary" of extreme consumers, and 10 percent actively avoid them. [12]

customers will not engage with you (so their "like" status provides no real value) unless there is a compelling reason to do so, such as fresh content or lively conversation.

Brand Differentiation

There have always been avid fans of brands (see the preceding sidebar for some examples of people who take their fandom to an extreme). Social media make it easier for people to build a community around these brands and truly make that community part of their lives.

The key metrics for evaluating customer differentiation are as follows:

▷ Brand premium development
　　Degree to which customers identify with your brand
　　Momentum of the product's prelaunch
▷ Brand reputation improvement
　　Degree to which customers trust your brand
　　Increase in customer satisfaction
▷ Brand affinity enhancement
　　Percentage of customers who share information (such as their e-mail
　　　address) with you
　　Increase in loyalty
　　Increase in share of wallet
　　Degree of content engagement
　　Degree of customer identification with your brand
▷ Brand awareness increase
　　Message recall and retention
　　Percentage of customers/prospects reached by media
　　Breakdown by segment
　　Media penetration
　　Mentions in the trade press
　　Mentions in academic journals
　　Purchase consideration

Community Participation

Many of the firms we studied declared that traditional Web measures such as page views or even raw counts of fans or followers were no longer important. Recently, we asked a panel on Digital Media, "What term, concept, or technology will be so obsolete in five years that it will be considered quaint, even adorable?" Without hesitation, Brent Lowe-Bernie, president of Comscore Media Metrix Canada, spat out, "Click-throughs!" The trouble with that key dot-com metric is that it collects people who are bored, rewards poorly constructed websites, and counts nonhumans. Jim Sterne references the Turing test[13] when making measurements online. He writes, "Be certain that you can tell whether you are measuring human activity or bot activity. This is not to say that robots are bad, it's just important that you know the difference."[14]

Edward Terpening, vice president of social media for Wells Fargo, agrees. He advises his staff to think of social media as event marketing rather than interactive marketing. He says that he is "not interested in member counts or viewership, but rather in the quality of dialogue and depth of conversations, as well as the frequency and quality of conversations that take place after the event is over."[15] Sentiment is important. Terpening obviously prefers positive comments but understands that great discussions can come out of negative comments, especially during events like the stock market tumble during the autumn of 2008.

Krista Thomas, vice president of marketing and communications at Thomson Reuters, shares that "based on comments, our community is not as interactive as it was a year ago. Even our Facebook page, which used to be loaded with comments, has slowed down. Almost all of the conversation has moved to Twitter; on some days, it is wildly active."[16] Twitter is where Thomson Reuters now sees requests for new features, new languages, and so forth.

Social media expert Euan Semple notes that one of the key metrics he uses to evaluate the health of communities is the sense of fun and tolerance in the conversation. In his experience, formality or smug behavior is often typical early on in communities. When members are comfortable enough with each other to engage in friendly banter and develop inside jokes, the overall quality of conversation improves. While robustness of humor is obviously difficult to quantify, he believes that savvy community members "know it when they see it."[17]

Sentiment analysis refers to the degree to which an entity is viewed as positive, negative, or neutral by its audience. It is a difficult nut to crack because of the vagaries of language and the prevalence of sarcasm in online discussions, especially when comments are penned by a disgruntled consumer. When one company demonstrated its product to us, it characterized two blogs with identical content but opposite results—one positive and the other negative. Compare "The movie was a bomb" and "The movie was da bomb"; they are almost identical statements with opposite meanings. Faint praise ("My experience with my cellular provider's call center met my expectations") or sarcastic language ("Dinner at the new bistro is highly recommended, especially if you enjoy late-night visits to the emergency room") throw another wrench into the sentiment analysis machine. Software companies are now employing linguistics experts to work with their programs to develop algorithms for improving the sentiment analysis, but true mechanical understanding is still years away. Perfection in sentiment analysis is not the goal; even humans frequently disagree on whether a statement is positive, neutral, or negative due to context, cultural norms, and the ambiguity of the message itself.

In 2008, Motrin set off a minicontroversy when one of its advertisements (the video is posted at **wiki-brands.com**) suggested that if mothers carry their babies in a sling rather than push them in a stroller, they may improve the baby's well-being and boost the mother's social standing. By doing so, the mothers will provoke "good pain," which Motrin could then relieve. The ad set off a firestorm within the baby-carrying community that felt the advertisement was demeaning, condescending, and factually inaccurate (community members believe that if a sling is tied correctly, the mother won't suffer *any* pain). Bloggers demanded boycotts of Motrin; the controversy became the most discussed topic on Twitter; and within forty-eight hours, a nine-minute video composed mostly of screenshots of social media messages decrying the advertisement and encouraging others to purchase generic ibuprofen instead of Motrin was distributed widely around the blogosphere.[18]

The Motrin incident was a good example of a community making a difference. The community gained strength from a common cause, it was able to educate others about an important issue, and it was able to influence the company to act. Kathy Widmar, a marketing vice president at Motrin's parent company, McNeil Consumer Healthcare, responded with a sincere apology, "We certainly did not mean to offend moms through our advertising. Instead, we had intended to demonstrate genuine sympathy and appreciation for all that parents do for their babies. We believe deeply that moms know best, and we sincerely apologize for disappointing you. Please know that we take your feedback seriously and will take swift action with regard to this ad. We are in the process of removing it from our website. It will take longer, unfortunately, for it to be removed from magazine print, as it is currently on newsstands and in distribution."[19]

Jennifer Evans, chief strategist for Sequentia Environics, believes that stories like Motrin's often represent a "false spike"; although the level of conversation is briefly high when a story goes viral, there is little long-term impact on a brand, especially if it is handled as deftly and sincerely as Widmar's apology was. Evans believes that if a company has a built-in, engaged community, it will provide risk mitigation by coming to the company's defense in a time of crisis. She often quotes the Arab proverb "The dogs may bark, but the caravan moves on" to her clients.[20]

Relevance and depth of comments are important. If a comment is used as a thinly disguised (or obvious) promotion for another blog or service, or it adds little more than a thumbs-up, it does not count as a thoughtful comment that adds insight or furthers the discussion.

The key measures for social media activity are as follows:

▷ Social media activity
  Comments and uploads (documents, photos, videos) to a Facebook
    site
  Retweets and mentions on Twitter
  Number of appearances in hashtag discussions, views, ratings, com-
    ments on YouTube, and mentions in blogs
  Audience engagement (comments + shares + trackbacks ÷ total
    views)[21]
  Frequency of social media page embedded in blogs
  Duration of engagement (such as how long users stay on your web-
    site and how many pages and features they view during the visit)
  Number of documents or applications downloaded
  Deviance from the 90-9-1 rule (90 percent visit as lurkers, 9 percent
    participate, and 1 percent actively participate)
  Transition rate from lurker to participant
  Frequency of blog comments
  Intensity of blog comments (a spike means something's up)
  Percentage of blog comments on topic
  Number of comments
  Word count of comments
  Number of social bookmarks
  Share of discussion (comments about your company divided by total
    comments)
  Percentage of page views from members versus nonmembers
▷ Contribution to business intelligence
  Number of trial downloads
  Depth of insight (discounting comments like "agreed" or "LOL")
  Reduction in research and development expense
  Quality of sensing (timeliness and accuracy of information)
  Improvement in forecasting accuracy
  Accuracy of price forecasts
  Speed of response to competitive offerings
  Degree of understanding of marketplace and competition
  Accuracy of attributes in tags
▷ Customer advocacy
  Increase in positive word of mouth
  Decrease in negative word of mouth
  Association with key attributes
  Size of user groups
  Activity level of user groups

▷ Contest participation
  Value of ideas/feedback collected during contests
  Increase in overall engagement of contest participants
  Percentage of contest participants who become advocates
  Percentage of contest participants who become customers
▷ Survey responses
  Percentage of visitors who respond
  Number of responses
▷ Customer-co-created products
  Percentage of products developed externally (crowdsourced ideas)
  Quality of offerings developed externally
  Time to market for new offerings
  Margins on co-created products
  Reduction in product flaws
  Sales volume of new products
  Margin generated by new products
  Reduction in inventory (if customers are given precisely what they
    want, they are less likely to make a return)
  Reduction in distressed goods

Customer Value/Influence

With wikibrands, brand metrics that quantify the intensity of a consumer's engagement, potential for deep involvement, and word-of-mouth advocacy need to be applied. In an environment where purchasing decisions are often most influenced by peers, the tendency of consumers to recommend a brand to somebody has primacy. Such essential facts must be measured.

Frederick Reichheld, a Fellow at Bain & Co., has pioneered the Net Promoter Score as the ultimate organizational question and most important marketing measure. It asks, "Would you recommend this brand or product to a friend or colleague?" and uses a simple, ten-point scale to reflect the resulting interest in a brand.

This system implies that customer word-of-mouth participation has greater importance in today's marketplace. In twenty-four different industries tracked, the Net Promoter brand leader is growing at 2.5 times the rate of the industry. Intuit, Enterprise, and General Electric are all using this measurement tracking system.[22] In fact, GE has not only incorporated the system across its organization, but it also ties part of its executive bonuses to the measure.

The use of Net Promoter Score tracking is a great start, but marketers should also consider an expanded set of measures that adequately tracks their wikibrand efforts on four key criteria: brand engagement, differentiation, participation, and customer value and influence.

Marcel Lebrun, chief executive officer of Radian6, appreciates the Net Promoter Score metric but reinforces that survey methods in general measure what people *say* they would do, where with social media you can measure what they *actually* did or said. Net Promoted Score, although not an officially recognized metric, is a term he uses to emphasize the point that, through social media, you can measure if people actually *did* recommend your brand (actual advocacy) versus a survey method that measures their propensity toward advocacy (potential advocacy).[23]

The key metrics in this area are as follows:

▷ Revenue from community
   Sales from referrals
   Margin on referral sales
   Peer-to-peer conversions
   New customers created
   Size of referrers' network
   Influence of referrers' network
▷ Peer support
   Reduction in customer service calls
   Increase in problem resolution
   Improvement in response time
   Percentage of calls moved to lower cost channels (telephone to chat to forum)
   Percentage of forum requests that receive responses
   Average time of response to question in forum
▷ Overall cost reductions
   Reduction in marketing costs
   Percentage of media transfer from traditional to social media
   Reduction in travel costs
   Reduction in IT costs (hardware, software, personnel, telecom)

Organizational Capacity

The principles of wikinomics—openness, increased collaboration, peering, and sharing—can provide great benefits beyond the marketing department. The insights garnered from social media should be distributed throughout the organization. Not only do sales, customer service, finance, and the C-suite need to find out about important information, they to make the intelligence actionable. Also, just as many of the implemented initiatives from MyStarbucksIdea came from employees, the wikibrand philosophy needs to be closely attuned to voices inside the organization.

Some of the key metrics are as follows:

▷ Corporate buy-in to wikibrand concepts
    Percentage of activity moved to collaborative process
    Participation rates (by level, department, and function)
▷ Human capital benefits of wikibrand concepts
    Reduction in recruiting costs
    Lower training costs
    Reduction in turnover
    Higher level of employee satisfaction
    Improved employee engagement
▷ Collaboration beyond the enterprise
    Percentage of offerings developed by suppliers
    Number of touchpoints in the supply chain that are improved by
        collaboration
    Improved investor engagement enabled by social media
    Increase in investor participation

PART 5

APPLYING WIKIBRANDS BEYOND THE CORPORATION

CHAPTER 15

THE PERSONAL WIKIBRAND

Your Brand Is What They Say About You When You're Not in the Room

As technology continues to make it easier for people to build their personal brand, the bar for a quality profile continues to rise. To stand out, an individual's brand needs the help of a community. A LinkedIn profile with few contacts or recommendations, a blog or Twitter account without followers, do little to enhance a brand. On the other hand, once a personal brand gains momentum, it can quickly accelerate, provided the substance behind it is compelling to its audience.

In fact, personal branding is what brought us, the authors of this book, together—a partnership and friendship spawned on LinkedIn. During 2004, New Paradigm was working on a syndicated research program called Information Technology and Competitive Advantage that would form the basis for *Wikinomics* and wanted to study how technology was changing word-of-mouth marketing. The program operated with a small core team of researchers, and Mike would search the world for the best experts on various subjects to form the faculty. Sean's LinkedIn profile immediately suggested that he was a great candidate; he was obviously an expert in the field, techni-

> "If you want to build a successful personal brand, then you have to focus on one particular niche; otherwise, you'll be lost in the online zoo. Decide how you want to be positioned in the marketplace, then craft your social profiles. Brand yourself before someone else does it for you!"[1]
>
> —**DAN SCHAWBEL,**
> *author of* Me 2.0:
> Build a Powerful Brand to
> Achieve Career Success

cally savvy, and located in Toronto. Even though we had a lot in common, including growing up in Western Toronto, attending undergraduate programs at rival universities where our friends knew each others' classmates, and even overlapping at the Toronto office of Procter & Gamble, we hadn't met. Without a well-designed LinkedIn profile and an effective search function, this project would not have happened.

"Search engines and social media sites now play a central role in building one's identity online," says Mary Madden, lead author of "Reputation Management and Social Media," a Pew Internet report. "Many users are learning and refining their approach as they go—changing privacy settings on profiles, customizing who can see certain updates, and deleting unwanted information about them that appears online."[2] The report explains that 57 percent of adult Internet users searched for information about themselves online, up from 47 percent in 2006.[3]

Building a personal brand has become vital in today's economy. Consider the wrath most baby boomers and even Gen-Xers would suffer by accidentally leaving a copy of their résumé in the office photocopier. Arguably, maintaining and updating a LinkedIn profile is a similar activity. In fact, due to the search function and the Internet, it is much more likely to attract attention from a prospective new employer than its bond-paper ancestor or even a soft-copy curriculum vitae. Yet because having a well-organized and active online profile helps a knowledge worker do his or her job, an employer should expect it to be kept up-to-date. That being said, as an employer, if you notice a lot of updates on your employees' pages, it might be a good time to invite them for coffee. They'll probably enjoy the attention.

Building a personal brand is easier than it has ever been due to the availability of online tools. For most people, LinkedIn and Facebook profiles are the most important social networking platforms. We advise professionals to have both but adopt different strategies for each. Consider LinkedIn to be a gray flannel suit and Facebook to be a Hawaiian shirt. Both can play important but different roles in your wardrobe. If someone appeared in a boardroom wearing a Hawaiian shirt, they would look flippant. On the other hand, showing up at a party on a boathouse roof wearing a gray flannel suit would make you look arrogant.

One of the benefits of LinkedIn is the ability to "marry up," especially for those who are in the early or midcareer stages. Having connections with senior, well-respected people really helps to build personal gravitas. But just like marrying up in real life, it only works on LinkedIn up to a certain level in the organization, because very senior people tend not to participate. Barack Obama has a mighty LinkedIn profile, but it probably wouldn't surprise you that he isn't a very active participant.

John Campagnino, head of global recruiting for Accenture, a firm that planned to hire fifty thousand people in 2010, estimates that at least 40 percent of the candidates will be hired through social media. He states, "This is the future of recruiting for our company."[4]

LinkedIn

A thorough, thoughtful LinkedIn profile can provide the following benefits:

▷ Connection with many people (especially those in senior positions) builds credibility. It is important to build your profile and network diligently over time; it is obvious if you're slapping a profile together because you are desperate to start a job search. Our friend Rob Cottingham (follow him on Twitter, @RobCottingham) made a whimsical but insightful comment: "Facebook is where you hear from your high school girlfriend; LinkedIn is where you hear from your college buddy who just lost his job."

▷ A strong recommendations section is superior to the traditional "references available upon request," because an inquisitive party can look for patterns without the necessity of contacting referees. In addition, the public nature of a LinkedIn recommendation encourages a referee to provide an honest assessment of a candidate. A set of recommendations is much more valuable if they are collected over time rather than entered in a batch. Ideally, each job description has at least one recommendation (understandably, it is trickier to hunt down clients and colleagues from jobs you held a decade ago or more). On the other hand, like most activities in social media, quality is better than quantity; having too many LinkedIn recommendations looks a little needy and may overwhelm a prospective employer. Remember that the recommendations you provide for others are visible on your profiles; make sure to provide them only for people you believe in and that the message is well written.

▷ Without the space limitations of a résumé, a LinkedIn profile can include multiple terms that will highlight a candidate based on a detailed Boolean search. If you are a forensic accountant with a degree in game theory and a working knowledge of Spanish who was on the junior varsity archery team in college, all that information could identify you as a uniquely qualified candidate for an opportunity. Whereas that information is tricky to squeeze into a one-page CV, the mechanics of LinkedIn allows for much more depth of personal information.

▷ Joining LinkedIn groups helps you to build your network and to connect with other important people whom you would not otherwise have
an opportunity to contact. These groups also allow access to interesting articles and conversations. It is worth noting, however, that your
LinkedIn goal should not be to build as large a network as possible, but
rather to judiciously generate a powerful network. Good candidates are
either people with whom you have had a business relationship or share
a common business or research goal or people who would build your
business profile. Simply adding people for the sake of building a large
network or—even worse—pleadingly advertising on your profile page
that you accept all invitations reminds people of the kid who gathered
friends simply because he had a really nifty ping pong table.

▷ Participating in the answer section increases your attractiveness as
a candidate or subject matter expert. In fact, we advise colleagues
who are starting a consulting business or accelerating a job search
to spend at least an hour per week participating in the answers section. Similar to creating a blog, demonstrating your writing skills on
LinkedIn is superior than simply claiming to have those skills on a
CV. Answers are rated, so a thoughtful response becomes highlighted,
giving you an opportunity to illustrate your expertise for free. Let your
content speak for itself. The LinkedIn community responds swiftly
and severely to spammers and hucksterism. Your LinkedIn connections can also use the "recommend an expert" feature; make sure to
let your network know your areas of expertise and your openness to
introductions.

▷ LinkedIn enables users to do reverse reference checks. (We credit Guy
Kawasaki for this idea, which he presents in his article "How to Use
LinkedIn" posted in the FAQ section of the site. More on Kawasaki later
in this chapter.) Disable the "current job only" feature and find out who
in your network has previously worked at your target company. A little
more digging can illuminate the health of the target company. Is there
a lot of turnover? What is the average tenure at positions similar to the
one you are seeking?

LinkedIn is, of course, much more than just a vehicle for building your
profile. It is a rich resource for research in preparing for a job interview
or meeting. Keep in mind that breaking the ice with information from a
LinkedIn profile should be done in a diplomatic manner. Some good conversation starters might follow these lines, "I noticed on LinkedIn that you
completed your undergraduate degree at Stanford; my niece is enrolled
there in September," or "You were at 3M engineering at the same time as

my colleague. Did you work together?" LinkedIn also makes it easy to stay abreast of the main industry news, since various groups already do a great job of aggregating white papers and relevant news items. When building your network, it is important to create a personal distance. If people do not accept your invitation quickly (or at all), it is more likely that they are not active on that platform or have specific guidelines about whom to accept than that they harbor any negative feelings toward you.

Facebook

In its infancy, Facebook was a social networking platform exclusively for college students. In fact, you needed a .edu e-mail extension or the equivalent to set up a profile. When "old people" were allowed to join, many of the original users dropped the platform. In any case, working-age users fuelled its incredible growth and position as arguably the second-most powerful website in the world behind Google. Due to its public nature, it is wise to act professionally on Facebook. Stories abound of how sophomoric activity and evidence of misbehavior can limit careers. Indeed, Facebook lore includes the story of a fellow who phoned in sick but was tagged in photos that illustrated he was well enough to attend a party—and in a glamorous fairy costume. Keep in mind that no one, certainly not your boss, is interested in updates about your sorcerer's guild, mafia career, or pirate wars. Turn those notices off, or even better, use your mental energy to write poetry or donate time to a community group instead.

Whether or not you "friend" your colleagues depends on several factors:

▷ **The nature of your industry:** Since Facebook has a messaging feature, it can offer security concerns for banks and other institutions that cannot allow unofficial electronic communication. Generally, if your workplace does not allow Facebook, you should refrain from adding colleagues, except for those with whom you also have a personal relationship. Education is another tricky field. While college professors can use Facebook effectively for networking and research purposes, we generally recommend that high school teachers not provide students with any fodder for gossip or practical jokes.

▷ **The culture of your company:** Do senior people in your company use Facebook? If so, keeping up a thoughtful profile enables you to participate in meaningful electronic water cooler talk with higher-ups with whom you wouldn't ordinarily communicate. Investigate whether it is acceptable to take Facebook breaks during the day before doing so.

▷ **Having an alternate profile:** Our colleague Denis Hancock has a substantial presence on Twitter and maintains a LinkedIn profile, but he keeps a very low profile on Facebook. He uses it mostly to share photos of his young daughter, so he not surprisingly limits his Facebook friends to people he would invite to his house. Many people who are uneasy about adding colleagues and clients to Facebook use Linkedin as a diplomatic alternative.

▷ **The makeup of your team:** If you are a supervisor who manages multiple people, it is best to use an all-or-nothing approach to friending subordinates to avoid the appearance of playing favorites. In any case, it is usually better for a supervisor to be passive and wait for subordinates to request the friendship.

Twitter

Building a Twitter following is a great way to build your personal brand, but like blogging, it requires a lot of effort to be successful. You will not remain popular with your followers unless your tweets are frequent and useful. Avoid self-importance. Do not declare yourself a guru. If you are indeed a guru, others will make that assertion. Chris Brogan wisely suggests that no more than one out of twelve social media entries should appear to be self-promotional. Remember to follow Twitter etiquette with respect to attribution, and remember to thank other users who retweet your material. Be interesting and authentic, but remember that Twitter is open—don't post anything you wouldn't want your mother to read.

Mitch Joel, author of *Six Pixels of Separation*, is an expert on personal branding, making regular speaking engagements on the subject—sometimes at events billed as personal branding camps. Among his recommendations is consistent use of the same moniker across all media platforms (for example, when commenting on blog posts or leaving reviews on a site like Amazon). In his case, his actual name works well because Mitch Joel is unusual enough to be remembered, but he suggests that people with more common names find a way to distinguish themselves. He also advises creating a standard visual icon (his is an artsy portrait of part of his face), one that is professional and memorable. He and Chris Brogan agree that you shouldn't use your corporate logo. The most important piece of advice Joel gives is that the image you project must be authentic. That being said, since whatever you say on the Internet stays there, your authentic self can still be your "best self." Cleverness and wit are valuable currencies on the

THE MILLION-FOLLOWER FALLACY

Who are the most influential people within the Twitter community? A group of academics decided to find out.[5] Researchers evaluated three measures of influence: number of followers (referred to as indegree), number of retweets, and number of mentions. The team used a data set of approximately 55 million users (Twitter agreed to white list the IP addresses), almost 2 billion social links, and 1.8 billion tweets, discounting the 8 percent of user accounts that were private and only visible to a selected set.[6]

The study had three principal findings:

1. The number of followers does not, on its own, mean that the user is influential.
2. Influential users can hold significant sway over a large number of topics.
3. Influence is not gained spontaneously or accidentally, but through concerted efforts such as limiting tweets to a single topic.

Since indegree measures popularity, retweets the quality of the content, and mentions the name value of the user, there is little overlap between the top performers in each category. The accounts with the most followers tended to be news organizations like CNN, politicians who effectively use social media like Barack Obama, and celebrities (Wil Wheaton has more than 1.5 million followers). The accounts spawning the most retweets tended to be article aggregators such as Mashable and Guy Kawasaki. Finally, accounts with the most mentions tended to be celebrities, particular those who were popular targets of gossip.

The study determined the top twenty users in each of the categories and found that there were only two common to all three. Ashton Kutcher, who was part of the well-publicized race with CNN to acquire a million followers, is an active user. Sean "Diddy" Combs is also an active user who has struggled a little with the conflict between the geek power of tweet success and a gangsta's street cred (he boasted of having more impact than rival Kanye West, then tried to cover up the statement).[7]

Internet, whereas rants and vicious comments reflect badly on you. It is best to treat your persona in the same way that you present your visual icon: professional and memorable.

Keith Ferrazzi believes that *networking* is the wrong term to describe an authentic personal branding campaign. He says, "You are not 'networking.' You are connecting—sharing your knowledge, resources, time, energy, friends, associates, empathy, and compassion in a continual effort to provide value to others. Real networking is about finding ways to make other people more successful."[8]

Daniel Debow is co-CEO of Rypple, a Canadian firm that builds social software for feedback and coaching. Rypple enables individuals to request immediate feedback from a self-selected group of advisors. The company is continually adding new features, but the essence of its service is illustrated by the following example: after a research analyst delivers a webinar, she sends a request to the people in the room asking them to evaluate her performance. Since the respondents are asked just one question over the Web, the feedback tends to be direct and not couched with extraneous information. It is also anonymous. When Daniel and his co-CEO, David Stein, first explained the concept to a group of analysts, they patiently waded through a flurry of potential-pitfall questions such as "What if someone asks only one person for feedback? How would it be anonymous?" and "What if the question itself would identify the respondent?" It just doesn't happen, they assured the analysts; people don't game the system. Those who are interested in improvement provide and collect genuine data.

According to Debow, people tend to accept feedback in one of two ways: those with a fixed mentality are set in their ways and averse to change, even when it comes to self-improvement, and those with a growth mentality who are actively seeking and psychologically available to self-improvement.[9] Rypple appeals to the latter because it provides a tool for collecting feedback and a dashboard that organizes it and allows the user to track progress over time.

People can improve their personal brands just by participating in Rypple. The youngest generation in the workplace has a reputation for resisting feedback (or at least cringing at feedback that is not glowingly positive). Jean Twenge, author of *Generation Me* and *The Narcissism Epidemic*, says, "When the Net Generation was growing up, everybody got a trophy just for playing, and some schools decided that it would harm students' self-esteem if they corrected mistakes. Many parents also got in on the game of constant praise and were reluctant to see their children as anything less than perfect.[10] By asking for and responding to feedback, Debow declares that Rypple participants announce that "they are open to feedback and are tough enough to take it. They show understanding, maturity, and ambition tempered with humility. All these characteristics are good aspects of a personal brand."[11]

Rypple's Kudo program allows users to publicly recognize their teammates, including granting a digital badge for specific accomplishments (see **wiki-brands.com** for an example). Scarcity is built into the model (users are allowed to bestow only a finite number of badges per month), so the value of the recognition is maintained. As described in Chapter 12, nonmonetary recognition can be extremely powerful, especially among the "grower" population; a self-selected group that is less prone to cynicism.

A potential danger of building a personal brand is that nourishing it often comes at the expense of regular job performance. Indeed, if you don't handle building your personal brand correctly, it can be counter to the interests of your company. Fortunately, the ongoing, anonymous feedback from the team helps the Rypple user identify if his or her pursuit of a powerful brand is viewed as a negative by colleagues.

Personal Branding Success Stories

The individuals profiled here have developed great personal brands by deploying wikibrand tools. It is unlikely that they would have gained as much influence and success under the old communication paradigm.

Robert Scoble

"Technology evangelist" may sound like an unusual term, but it fits Robert Scoble well. The operator of scobleizer.com developed his reputation as one of the most important and influential voices in the industry. His reach is vast: more than 116,000 people follow him on Twitter; he has more than 11,000 fans on his public Facebook fan page (he apologizes that he has "to actually know you" to invite you into his private Facebook site); and his Scobleizer blog is considered one of the tech industry's must-reads. Scoble studied journalism (he discloses in his bio that he is one credit away from his degree) and worked briefly for *Fast Company* magazine, but his voice has had its greatest impact through his self-publishing via social media. And he is active in just about every media there is: his Google bio page directs you to his work on YouTube, Delicious, Digg, Tumblr, Taku, and Pownce. He acts as an aggregator of information, creating lists such as the most influential names in tech and reposting their best thoughts, and writes his own thoughtful and innovative articles about the tech scene.

One of the reasons for his popularity is his accessibility. Not only does he make his e-mail available on his page (with a polite warning that a response may be delayed due to the volume of inbound requests), but his mobile phone and even his calendar are on open display. He regularly invites his followers to meet up with him for dinner, often sending an open invitation encouraging people to find the guy carrying the large Canon camera. His brand image is truly meritocratic: people follow him because he consistently provides them with a combination of original thought and insightful aggregation of the best of technology thought leaders and most compelling technology news.

Guy Kawasaki

Guy Kawasaki is another Twitter star; he has more than 240,000 followers. He posts frequently, often redirecting readers to his Alltop, which is an aggregation site of news feeds from outlets such as CNN, the *New York Times*, and Techcrunch, as well as thought leaders such as Seth Godin, Chris Brogan, and Joe McNally. Alltop's FAQ page differentiates itself from a search engine: "A search engine is good to answer a question like, 'How many people live in China?' However, it has a much harder time answering the question, 'What's happening in China?' That's the kind of question that we answer."

Capitalizing on his Twitter popularity by redirecting his followers to an advertising-supported site has earned Kawasaki a fair number of critics (although, in fairness, anyone with a huge Twitter following will always draw criticism from Twitter users who don't understand why everyone isn't interested in their own musings). Some people also denigrate Kawasaki's delivery style; specifically, he reposts some material four times in eight-hour cycles throughout the day.

Remarkably, his response to this criticism drives more authenticity to his personal brand. He explains that he publishes in this manner so that his notes are less likely to get lost in the information torrent experienced by Twitter users who follow a lot of people. Because his followers are from all over the world, his cycle allows for them all to be reached at a convenient time of day. Twitter is like a stream or, depending on your involvement, a raging river. If you follow of lot of people, you miss many posts unless you are constantly viewing. Further, he carefully explains various methods of adjusting the way people interact with him to avoid the problem (for example, he has another Twitter feed that publishes the same information only once, so a user can swap that for the main feed). If none of his solutions are acceptable for the user, he politely offers them the opportunity to unfollow him altogether and "have a nice life." He means it. Twitter, by its opt-in nature, really leaves no excuse for receiving information you don't want, since you choose exactly the type of content you receive.

CHAPTER 16

THE FUTURE

Brand Participation Comes Alive in the Company

We expect that by 2020 the term *social media* will be considered a quaint idiom or at least have a very different meaning than it has today. Marketing's transition from broadcast to conversation will, however, continue unabated. Emerging technology will enable companies to listen with greater acuity and respond more precisely and quickly to customer demand. The Net Generation, which has become accustomed to customization and as they accumulate more wealth and spending power, will demand nothing less.

Radian6's Amber Naslund thinks her job title of director of community will be obsolete in the future. Community management will not exist as a stand-alone job; those responsibilities will be absorbed back into other positions in sales, marketing, customer service, product management, and public relations.[1]

Nigel Dessau, senior vice president and chief marketing officer at AMD, believes that the concept of social media will not even be discussed by 2015, except to describe a collection of tools. He does believe that communication will continue to be consumed in

> "Where we're going . . . we don't need roads."
>
> —**DOC BROWN**,
> *from the movie*
> Back to the Future

bite-size chunks rather than in bulk. Communication will be less text-dependent and more audible and visual, perhaps more often displayed in three dimensions.[2]

Customary forms of communication through the primary social media platforms will become more streamlined. Typing the same message over multiple platforms will seem as odd as the different programming languages for the microcomputers of the early eighties seem now (remember the anguish of receiving a Commodore version of Frogger for your birthday when you had an Atari 800). Granted, applications like Ping.fm that allow the simultaneous status updates across patterns do exist, but they are clunky. Remember the gray flannel suit and the Hawaiian shirt from Chapter 15? The tone, cadence, and subject matter of a message is not necessarily appropriate across various platforms.

Implications for the Future of Marketing

In early 2010, we surveyed the members of the LOKBP (short for the League of Kickass Business People), which despite its irreverent name is made up of thousands of serious Canadian businesspeople, including many marketing executives and thought leaders.

One of our questions was "What forms of word of mouth will experience the most growth in the next three years?" Respondents were allowed to give three answers. Our results clearly indicate a strong need for a wikibrands strategy, since six of the top seven choices dealt with social media or customer-led marketing:

Social media marketing	37%
Social network marketing	35%
Mobile marketing	34%
User-generated content	31%
Influencer marketing	28%
Brand communities	20%
Customer forums	17%
Branded entertainment	16%
Cause-related marketing	14%
Brand microblogging	14%
Buzz marketing	13%
Corporate/brand blogging	11%

Will Novosedlik, vice president of brand and communications at WIND Mobile, admits that his long marketing career provides him with some bias, but he says that while customer participation in marketing will accelerate, most of the final marketing material will still be created by professionals. Although the quality of customer-created content continues to improve and will be included as part of integrated campaigns, the professionally created thirty-second spot still has some life in it. Novosedlik is confident that "no one will pay $20 to see YouTube videos in the theater."[3]

On the other hand, Jennifer Evans, chief strategist for Sequentia Environics, reminds us that customers used to build relationships directly with their local general store, without any messages from Madison Avenue. The role of the agent as intermediary will diminish, because companies will increasingly collect granular data about their customers' wants through conversation.

James Cherkoff, director of Collaborate Marketing, believes that marketers need to simultaneously embrace old and new media and develop a combined strategy. The time for partisanship and choosing one media-dominant view of the world above another is over. In the next few years, an environment will exist to validate acceptance of the social operations on an enterprise. You won't be classified as the traditional-friendly CMO or the highly socialized CMO; you will simply be effectively practicing your craft through all the mainstream tools and media at play.[4]

Chief marketing officers will need to spend more time and energy on these new spaces—and quickly. A majority are either less or just equally familiar with the use of social media and community building tools than are their customers.[5] The rise of the participation marketplace and the advance of brand communities are rapidly changing the marketing world in the following ways:

1. **Changing role of the CMO:** Chuck Brymer, CEO of DDB Worldwide, has championed the idea of a chief community officer. He advocates changing the CMO's orientation from the Four Ps to the Three Cs (conviction, collaboration, and creativity).[6] Brymer suggests that the future responsibilities of the CMO should include the following:

    Building community around the brand using multiple channels, and ensuring that the organization is living its message

    Knowing the community's wants, needs, and lifestyles, and using those data for marketing efforts

Monitoring, responding, and interacting with the community to build relationships

Facilitating and nurturing an environment that empowers the community to rally behind and feel co-ownership for the brand

In the future, CMOs must externalize marketing processes and create a transparent and seamless flow of communication inside and outside the organization, across employees, customers, partners, prospects, and detractors alike.

2. **Focus on people:** As Cherkoff says, "I've always felt that if you're in marketing, you shouldn't really be focusing on the promotional channels. You should be focusing on the market and what the market is doing—and ninety-nine times out of a hundred the market is made up of people."[7]

   Communities are markets of people. The goal is to create a listening infrastructure that incorporates customer support, social media, word of mouth, co-innovation, co-selling, co-supporting, and co-marketing with customers. It is an imperative that takes time and money.

3. **New customer-focused marketing skills:** Customer-facing functions are now looking for flexible, well-rounded people with strong technical skills, empathy for the customer, and good listening skills. Marketing people must work collaboratively across the organization and with the community, instilling customer centricity throughout the company in the process.

4. **Money and resource allocation:** According to private equity firm Veronis Suhler Stevenson, the top four rising segments of marketing expenditure for the four years after 2010 will look like this:[8]

Word of mouth	27%
Internet/mobile	14%
Branded entertainment	13%
Custom publishing	11%

What do all four have in common? They're all interactive, targeted, customized, and content-driven. The future of marketing will be guided not only by these significant media dollar shifts (broadcast to digital) but also by overall redistribution of effort toward the participation marketplace.

5. **Reinvention of the agency:** Jim Cuene, director of interactive marketing at General Mills, puts it this way:

> Companies are critically dependent on their agencies as a way to run lean internally. But 90 percent of ad agencies are still trying to figure out how to deal with display and social media . . . And a lot of the "social media agencies" are making it up every day, as they go along. No one has this figured out, and big companies aren't really staffed right to figure it out themselves.[9]

It is the most widely agreed-upon comment on the future: eighty-three percent of marketers agree that agencies need to radically reinvent themselves to stay relevant.[10] If agencies are to play a valuable role in using traditional media creativity to deliver engagement and outreach to the community, they will need to change their approach to apply design and creativity to key community touchpoints online and offline in the future.

6. **Partnership building:** By listening to and acting on customer ideas and needs, marketers will play an increasing role as solution providers, including brokering collaborations with outside partners to deliver on community expectations.

   Insight development, product innovation, third-party relationships, and change management skills operating across a network of partners will enable marketers to build brand solutions more effectively in the future.

7. **The rise of video:** All of the computer hardware and smartphone manufacturers, system developers, enterprise software companies, and mobile and Internet service providers are preparing for the next wave of video. The change in Web engagement will be on par with the change from newspaper to TV. As much as we hear the cry of the decline of the TV audience, smart businesses will need to be able to tell and share their stories provocatively through the visual medium more, not less, over the next decade.

8. **The war on privacy:** Two polar opposite directions will exist here. Companies will strive to know as much about you as they can in order to meet and match your wants and needs in the right place at the right time. Some customers will willingly serve up their personal information, buying history, and attitudes in exchange for these customized benefits. But as we have seen with international governments' need to monitor text messages and companies' and social networks' missteps in using employee and user profile information, respectively, many other customers will resist corporate incursions into their life, setting up multiple and

pseudo profiles in communities to balance out the various facets of their lives without telling the full story to outside eyes.

9. **The Influencers are gone; long live the Influencers:** The early roots of the Internet acted as a democratizing force and an equal voice for all. The crowd was supposed to supplant the elite in how the Web worked. Not so fast. With the enhanced database capabilities of companies and software algorithms (like Klout's social influence monitor) that evaluate true influence, companies will enhance microtargeting efforts of Influencers. Leading A-list bloggers have already started to endorse private networks of their influential social circles to manage their traffic flow and avoid being affected by hackers, spammers, bots, and multilevel marketers. Although these people might be different than the journalists, news editors, and celebrities of past eras, digital Influencers will become much more well known, sought after, and powerful than they are currently.

Who Wins—Facebook, Twitter, Google, or Someone Else?

At the time of this writing, Facebook is the leading social platform based on most metrics, including active users and growth rate. Facebook enjoys high switching costs (you have already set up your profile), excellent utility (much easier than sharing vacation photos or organizing events over e-mail), and network effects (your friends are there). However, many previous kings have been toppled—remember Friendster? As recently as 2008, MySpace was the leader, but it fell fast (see the following sidebar for our take on its decline).

In fact, we do not believe the platforms in their current, isolated format will exist; instead, person-to-person communication will happen in real time in a platform-agnostic manner. If an overarching aggregator evolves, it is more likely to be an open source (or at least neutral) creation than it is a corporate site like Google Wave. In *Wired* magazine, Ryan Singel opined:

> Think of being able to buy your own domain name and use simple software such as Posterous to build a profile page in the style of your liking. You'd get to control what unknown people get to see, while the people you befriend see a different, more intimate page. They could be using a free service that's ad-supported, which could be offered by Yahoo, Google, Microsoft, a bevy of start-ups, or web-hosting services like Dreamhost.[11]

WHAT HAPPENED TO MYSPACE?

Any evaluation of social media success stories will usually include Facebook and Twitter, perhaps even an effective corporate blog or a YouTube contest. It seems odd that it was as recently as 2008 when Facebook surpassed MySpace as the most popular site based on unique monthly visitors. In fact, as of this writing, MySpace still holds a lead over Twitter based on the same metric.

The Will Ferrell movie *Talladega Nights: The Ricky Bobby Story* incorporated MySpace in a successful multimedia campaign when Facebook was just beginning to allow "old people" to join. The title character, a goofy but likeable NASCAR driver, "signed up" to the site, quickly attracting more than fifty thousand fans.[12] At the time, friending someone was a new concept, and the marketers hoped that the association would encourage people to see the movie.

Why has MySpace fallen out of favor? While some people think that the site's appearance is showy and not professional enough to suit a business audience, Microsoft research and social media expert danah boyd[13] has a more provocative explanation. In a 2007 essay, boyd argues that socioeconomic class is the determining factor in whether teens choose Facebook or MySpace, with the "serious" students choosing the former. Facebook, which originally required an .edu e-mail address to activate an account, encouraged a bit of snobbery (let's not forget that Mr. Zuckerburg was a Harvard student when the dream began), whereas MySpace reached out to high school students. Here is an explanatory excerpt from boyd's essay:

> Most teens who exclusively use Facebook are familiar with and have an opinion about MySpace. These teens are very aware of MySpace, and they often have a negative opinion about it. They see it as gaudy, immature, and "so middle school." They prefer the "clean" look of Facebook, noting that it is more mature and that MySpace is "so lame." What hegemonic teens call gaudy can also be labeled as "glitzy" or "bling" or "fly" (or what my generation would call "phat") by subaltern teens. Terms like "bling" come out of hip-hop culture where showy, sparkly, brash visual displays are acceptable and valued. The look and feel of MySpace resonates far better with subaltern communities than it does with the upwardly mobile hegemonic teens. This is even clear in the blogosphere, where people talk about how gauche MySpace is while commending Facebook on its aesthetics. I'm sure that a visual analyst would be able to explain how classed aesthetics are, but aesthetics are more than simply the "eye of the beholder"—they are culturally narrated and replicated. That "clean" or "modern" look of Facebook is akin to West Elm or Pottery Barn or any poshy Scandinavian design house (that I admit I'm drawn to), while the more flashy look of MySpace resembles the Las Vegas imagery that attracts millions every year. I suspect that lifestyles have aesthetic values and that these are being reproduced on MySpace and Facebook.[14]

After various well-publicized privacy gaffes in 2010, Facebook came under fire from many angles. Four New York students received funding for their venture Diaspora, which describes itself as a "privacy-aware, personally controlled" social network.[15] The Electronic Privacy Information Center and other groups filed complaints with the Federal Trade Commission alleging that Facebook deceives users about how their data are shared.[16] May 31, 2010, was declared "Quit Facebook Day," although only thirty-six thousand users committed to leave—a fairly anemic accomplishment that doesn't even consider recidivism (how many will go back once Facebook withdrawal sets in). The ringleaders of the movement could still claim some victory, however, as Facebook responded to the uprising with promises to review its privacy policy again.[17]

Facebook finds itself in a tricky situation: it has not effectively monetized its huge traffic. We have both shared a great deal of personal information with Facebook and are surprised at how noncompelling we find our targeted ads. If Facebook continues with an advertising model (and there is serious doubt that a subscription model would fly), it will need to work even more closely with its customers. And as media commentator Scott Hepburn points out, "We're not Facebook's customers: we're its product. Even if we took to the streets with pitchforks and torches, Facebook has no obligation to us. We're not the customers; the advertisers are. We are the product the advertisers buy."[18]

One of the reasons that most social media fans who consider themselves the digerati (Chris Brogan calls them the *nerderati*) choose Facebook (and are now moving to Twitter) is that they tend to discount MySpace. In the same way, educated white-collar workers (and the old people who were late adopters of social media) personally tend to choose Facebook over MySpace; a bias they may take with them when they evaluate marketing strategy. A lot of users still inhabit MySpace and present an opportunity for marketers, especially for specific markets.

Even after Facebook became the leader, many musicians stayed with MySpace because it was better suited to share songs and generate music— not to mention they wanted to avoid the switching costs involved in moving a fan base (many people will not bother to follow). Still, MySpace needs to make improvements to keep artists engaged. Toronto- and Paris-based singer Lenni Jabour explains, "MySpace feels kind of obsolete to me. I barely go there anymore—maybe once or twice per month. The ads and spamming are more than I want to deal with on a regular basis. My network on Facebook and Twitter is far more active, likely because it is more 'personal' and interactive. MySpace feels too remote and spacious."[19]

The Fight to Replace E-Mail

Regardless of which specific platform "wins," business and personal communication will continue to move away from e-mail. Already most people have moved personal activities like planning parties or sharing photos to social networking or Web applications like Flickr or Evite. Businesses will shift to collaborative software suites, microblogging sites like Yammer, and free Web-based document-sharing programs like Google Docs. "Information and knowledge wants [sic] to be free, available to those who want and need it at the time and place of their choosing," said Brian Magierski, co-founder and senior vice president of strategic alliances for Moxie Software. "Next-generation knowledge-sharing and discovery software platforms break the barriers of legacy e-mail and document systems, freeing people to connect to share knowledge whenever and wherever it's appropriate to accomplish shared goals." [20]

A Gartner research study predicts that that by 2014, "social networking services will replace e-mail as the primary communication tool for 20 percent of business users. Companies will either build out their own corporate social networks, or they will allow greater use of existing networks for work. Over time, a sizable majority of users will rely less on e-mail and more on social tools, especially for status updates and tracking down a coworker with the right expertise." [21]

The same report suggests that 50 percent of firms will use microblogging technology, while 5 percent will use a stand-alone product. Jeffrey Mann, research vice president for Gartner, states, "It will be very difficult for microblogging as a stand-alone function to achieve widespread adoption within the enterprise. Twitter's scale is one of the reasons for its popularity. When limited to a single enterprise, that same scale is unachievable, reducing the number of users who will find it valuable. Mainstream enterprises are unlikely to adopt stand-alone, single-purpose microblogging products." [22]

Mobility

Scott Monty, head of social media at Ford, says that location-based services like Yelp, GoWalla, and Fourscore are getting a lot of hype, but the majority of people who have yet to set up a Twitter account "think we are talking another language." He believes that these new platforms have a long way to go before the general public picks them up and before they hit the mainstream. The hyperlocation is still compelling; people want to be involved with their friends and family.[23]

Social media expert Euan Semple agrees. Even though he and his former team at the BBC were actively using blog technology ten years ago, the majority of consumers are still novices with this technology. Although more and more people will be using technology to communicate with companies in a sophisticated manner, many will still be learning social media basics. In fact, successful companies will need to develop slick interfaces that make engagement easy; technophobes may not even realize that a computer is involved.[24]

Location-based services will become more prevalent, particularly as more people carry devices equipped with GPS. Piers Fawkes, founder of PSFK, a leading trends and innovation consultancy, believes "intelligent cities" will spring up. Location-based technology will make for more efficient, sentient, helpful, and communal cities.[25]

It's an exciting thought to our digital urban souls. Here are some examples of location-based services:[26]

▷ Requests for the nearest business or service, such as an ATM or a restaurant
▷ Turn-by-turn navigation to any address
▷ Location of people on a map displayed on a mobile phone
▷ Automatic alerts, such as notification of a sale on gas or warning of a traffic jam
▷ Location-based mobile advertising
▷ Asset recovery combined with active radio frequency to find, for example, stolen assets in containers where GPS won't work

As the technology becomes richer and the functionality more ubiquitous, more marketing dollars will be spent on location-based services. This focus, of course, will overwhelm consumers if they are subject to advertising blasts whenever they pass a business. Savvy firms will offer simple, intuitive tools that allow individuals to opt in to their messages.

In the developing world, innovation will focus on mobile apps, because cell phones are the primary platform people use to access the Internet there. Euan Semple believes that places like Africa will leapfrog Europe and North America with respect to mobile innovation, and firms will look to them to provide more effective trials than the more developed world.[27] In fact, the mobile phone is expected to be the chief method of banking in the developing world, as people will use them to make micropayments to each other.

Augmented Reality

Augmented reality refers to live direct or indirect view of a physical, real-world environment whose elements are enhanced by computer-generated imagery (for example, the first down line that appears on a football broadcast). With more people equipped with smartphones and webcams, opportunities abound for business applications. Dan Fletcher writes in *Time*: "One of the best examples yet is the virtual box simulator from the U.S. Postal Service, which taps into your webcam to let you figure out what size box is needed to ship an item through overlaying a semitransparent 3D model of the box." [28] Within the marketing sphere, augmented reality can allow a real estate agent to show how an apartment will look when it's furnished with a client's possessions or enable a shopper to try on clothes virtually.

Technology Interface

We expect people to interact differently with different technology interfaces; certainly there will be less input via ten fingers on a QWERTY keyboard and more thumbing on portable devices. We've already seen an appendage switch; if you are in your forties or older, you almost certainly press elevator buttons with your index finger. Watch a twentysomething—because of texting and PlayStation-type video games, he or she is more likely to use the thumb. Already, a technology exists that can determine with 90 percent accuracy the age, gender, and culture of a typist based on the speed and cadence of as little as ten keystrokes. [29] There will be more iPod-like dials and three-dimensional dashboards. More auditory and visual clues will be provided and contributed to. Think Tom Cruise's workstation in *Minority Report* but with less need for the use of the hands.

A team of scientists at Carnegie Mellon has interesting technology called Skinput, which uses bioacoustic sensors to pick up the signature sounds of a finger tapping on specific locations on the skin. The "control pad" is projected directly onto the user's skin and can control electronic devices. [30]

In the globalized, technology-driven culture we are headed toward, engaged brands that can orient their companies around the shifts quickly, partner with social networks and garage-based innovators, and immerse themselves in their customers' worlds will find that the future is friendly.

PART 6

THE WIKIBRANDS PRIMER

CHAPTER 17

REFERENCE GUIDE

Wikibrands Extended

Companies are just beginning to tap the power of wikibrands. As technology evolves, success stories accumulate, and long-held marketing tenets fade, forward-thinking companies will harness their customers' passion and ingenuity to redefine the nature of their brands. Successful business strategies will rely less on "managing perceptions" and "controlling the message" of a brand and more on inventing new ways to get people to interact genuinely with their brands. We're talking about real, deep-seated interaction, not just lip service. This evolution can only intensify as our level of digital sophistication and do-it-yourself and collaborative culture grows and exerts significantly more influence in the marketplace and at the boardroom table.

The fight for wikibrands is real. All across the world right now, there is a struggle being played out at all levels in the company between doing what is right for the customer and what is right for the company. These battles cannot be mutually exclusive nor can they be resolved from the corporate office alone. They frequently will be won or lost in the front-line trenches and outside the company perimeter.

"Don't fear failure so much that you refuse to try new things. The saddest summary of a life contains three descriptions: could have, might have, and should have."

—LOUIS E. BOONE,
co-author of
Contemporary Marketing *and*
Contemporary Business

A transformative change needs to happen across all key customer-facing functions—including marketing, customer service, executive, technological, product development, communications, research, operations, human resources, and agency provider—to enable a more open, more authentic, more dialogue-focused, and more customer-value- and customer-advocacy-driven organization. The prism for how a company values and protects its resources—including the role of the brand, bottom-line financial drivers, assertion of proprietary company assets, and long-term planning—needs to also shift to acknowledge an enhanced role of the customer.

In studying some of the world's top wikibrands up close, we offer actionable recommendations for a journey to the world of wikibrands.

Eleven Ways to Develop a Wikibrand

Wikibranding offers an opportunity to break from the pack in an age of informed, connected, collaborative, and demanding customers. Here is a comprehensive prescription for this new evolution in brands.

Overall: Remember "Alignment, Alignment, Alignment"

Wikibranding cannot be a siloed functional exercise; CMOs and brand or customer managers need to provide hands-on leadership in developing alignment vertically and across functions to make their organization more open sourced and customer-centric. Organization-wide implementation requires the following:

▷ **Aligning the goals of the business with its wikibrand efforts:** Create lockstep agreement between your goals and brand efforts and tie executive and company bonuses to key wikibrand measures at the scope and level that General Electric has implemented across its business groups.

▷ **Engaging the CEO/COO as the chief wikibrand evangelist:** Championing the rewards for going wiki while warning of the risks of maintaining brand status quo must come from the top of the organization.

▷ **Getting your organization to live among the tribe:** Rally your company around a customer-orientation perspective and spend time with them as equals, not as mere objects to be studied, as Nike does.

▷ **Building an army of believers:** Establish customer-brand councils of equal functional partners to help hardwire wikibranding into every aspect of your organization.

▷ **Marrying marketing to human resources:** Focus wikibrand practices on customer-facing staff functions to "live the brand," as lululemon does with its employees.

▷ **Influencing the water-cooler grapevine:** Use intranets and internal blogs to create a continuous and seamless conversation and open wikibrand debate across your organization. IBM does this through its network of internal blogs and podcasts.

▷ **Launching a manifesto:** Publish a short and provocative statement that bridges the gap between rhetoric and experience and publicly declares wiki practices and values for internal and external groups—just as Mozilla and lululemon do with their organizations.

Brand Engagement: Open Up Your Brand to the Conversation

Learn from the recent high-profile mistakes of General Motors, Sony, and Wal-Mart. To obtain value from adopting wikibrand practices, companies must embrace both a philosophical and real transformation, including a change of attitude regarding transparency to external users, customers, and Influencers. Wikibrand engagement is harder work than traditional branding. "Being social" versus merely "doing social" involves all of the following:

▷ **Opening up the boardroom:** Engage executive groups answering the question "How can we enrich our customer's life?" This was exhibited by Starbucks's Howard Schultz bemoaning the commoditization of its business and returning to growth by asking his executive team to "think small" again.

▷ **Bringing the customer culture up close:** Getting involved with customers on their own turf helps you to learn their language, sources of influence, and points of brand dissatisfaction or need, and it helps define Influencer traits. Harley-Davidson's executive and front-line personnel brilliantly follow this practice.

▷ **Harnessing the Hawthorne effect:** Asking, "How can we involve you?" and "What value can we bring you?" gets customers involved in your cause and leads to relationships. It also ensures that customers get the knowledge, content, and tools they want without messing up what they already like about your products or company.

▷ **Implementing listening programs:** Ensure and motivate company behavioral change so that all company touchpoints lead to a two-way brand dialogue. Virgin does this by empowering its front-line staff to make day-to-day brand decisions.

▷ **Posing challenges and validating answers:** Provide education and opportunity for customers by reflecting the creativity and input of your audience, as Doritos did with its consumer-generated Super Bowl ads and revenue-generating product launches.

▷ **Building a platform and providing the tools:** Build online communities, both affiliated and owned, where advocates can create, share, and digest ideas with few barriers to participation. Mozilla models this practice through its Firefox ambassador programs around the world.

Brand Orientation: Make Marketing the Product and the Product an Experience

Successful wikibrands demonstrate remarkable consistency between communications and product; often, they're inseparable. These brands tap into a new customer zeitgeist and desire for freedom, customization, and entertainment, and they recognize that purchase decisions are frequently driven by distinct individual and emotional needs. Here are some recommendations for resonating with these norms:

▷ **Making the brand buzz throughout the customer experience 360 degrees:** Turn the ordinary into the remarkable by creating customer-centered brand touchpoints at every stage of customer contact, just as Apple does across its retail, online, communications, product/packaging, and service experience.

▷ **Offering it their way:** Develop avenues for personalization and customization, as Moo cards does by offering personalized and customized designs and formats for people's business stationery.

▷ **Building "heart share":** Create emotional, sensory-laden, and memorable offerings. Doubletree does this simply by distributing ten million chocolate chip cookies to its visitors each year.

▷ **Focusing on a distinctive, brandable customer experience:** Incorporate aesthetics, entertainment, education, and escape into a brand experience, as Stella Artois has through its Belgian beer brand experience around the world.[1]

Brand Tone: Make It Real, Be Open, and Seed an Idea

Traditional marketing has bred a stimulus-response culture: the bigger the stimulus, the bigger the response. Over time, consumers have learned to effectively tune out these approaches. Companies that have adopted wikibrands, on the other hand, are developing genuine customer relationships through the following methods:

▷ **Being *truly* authentic:** Share the good with the bad, be honest, reveal your motives, and be opinionated and provocative. Stonyfield Farms has exhibited this attitude through its blogs.

▷ **Exposing the company to transparency:** Set up guidelines so that all employees can feel comfortable about getting involved in openness, as Intuit has done through its employee-authored corporate blogs and developer forums.

▷ **Humanizing the brand:** Tell stories, communicate in a personal voice, and sell part of a dream, like lululemon has done in developing a $4 million-per-store business by selling yoga and workout gear.

▷ **Thickening the skin:** Expect, welcome, and learn from negative comments, as Dell has done with its Direct2Dell blog, which diffuses previously unanswered dissatisfaction and anger through conversation.

▷ **Cultivating a brand religion:** Seed an idea that transcends the brand and provides an expanded view of what role the brand can play in consumers' lives to encourage them to chip in. Dove did this with its "Campaign for Real Beauty."

Brand Targeting: Chase the Influencers and Evangelists

Opinion leaders, lead users, prosumers, Influencers. Whatever you call them, you need to target this small group effectively and let them carry the weight of delivering brand insights, innovation, and word-of-mouth evangelism. Here are some strategies to try:

▷ **Identifying the front row:** Find the traits, motivations, and activities of Influencers, as Procter & Gamble has done with its teen and mom panels, Tremor and Vocalpoint.

▷ **Building the bridge:** Trigger Influencer involvement using three levels of rewards:

  Intrinsic—cause association, challenge, creativity, curiosity, do-it-yourself appeal, fun, self-reward

  Extrinsic—sense of belonging, early or exclusive access, exposure, fame, recognition, social currency, validation, VIP treatment

  Explicit—products, cash, employment, points, tangible rewards

▷ **Getting intimate:** Develop the tools and skills required to build deep profiles of individual customers, as eBay has done with its PowerSellers.

▷ **Socializing with the core:** Build and support advisory councils of 250 to 1,000 Influencers for each desired target audience segment/product. Timex, Google, and Phillips have established such councils to produce new innovation and guidance on direction.

▷ **Going steady:** Provide Influencers a narrowcast VIP experience, and create an ongoing set of offline and online tactics to incentivize them and incite referral, as Lego has done with its various user groups.

▷ **Going public:** Rally Influencers to advocate for you through a formalized brand ambassador program, as Mabel's Labels has achieved with its Buzzmamas.

▷ **Building a brand cult:** Promote quality evangelists and contributors based on performance, involvement, and the presence of smart rules, guidelines, and customs, as Mozilla does within its various community and developer groups.

Brand Media: It Takes a Community (Not a Campaign) to Raise a Brand

Wikibrands are reducing their dependence on paid media and transitioning to the tools of the Net Generation—social media, podcasts, wikis, blogs, and virtual worlds—that allow consumers to self-identify as interested brand participants in a competition-free environment. You can achieve this through multiple means:

▷ **Outreach programs:** Build linkability, branding, and conversations on existing social networks and with bloggers, as exhibited by the Stormhoek "Free Wines for Bloggers" campaign and as Molson Coors has achieved with its Brew 2.0 effort.

▷ **Private worlds:** Drive traffic to brand areas that provide better opportunity for openness, dialogue, advocacy, and authenticity, such as Wells Fargo's foray into blogs, podcasts, and virtual worlds.

▷ **Spend reallocation:** Dedicate 20 percent of marketing budgets to non-traditional brand advocacy media. Johnson & Johnson has announced this will be part of its budget for upcoming years.[2]

▷ **Love networks:** Build communities around ideas and passions (rather than brands themselves), as Nike has achieved on an international scale with its soccer-, basketball-, sneaker-, boarding-, and jogging-mad customers.

▷ **Hosting a cause:** Feed the enthusiasm of interest-specific and cause-related networks (but do not try to control them), as HGTV has done

with "Rate My Space," and Vancity has achieved with ChangeEvery
thing.ca.
▷ **Piggybacking:** Tie into existing community groups, as Salomon has
done in snow sports and Marvel and Universal Studios have done with
movie fan site owners.

Brand Innovation: Let Them Play with It, Make It Theirs, and Keep It Rolling

Innovation soon becomes a 24/7 job for wikibrand organizations. Consumers demand that there be no "off switch" on the assembly line, and under
the right conditions, they'll gladly add to and fix the product. You can create a dynamic innovation culture with these methods:

▷ **Giving the brand away:** Ask, "How could our users own the product
and make it theirs?" as Jones Soda has pioneered for the last decade
through its customized labels and gift packs.
▷ **Tapping lead users:** Create and develop a sneak-preview, beta-tester
group, such as the ones that TiVo and numerous software, gaming, and
entertainment companies have implemented.
▷ **Customer triple-playing (create, rate, and develop):** Encourage customers to develop new ideas, host an open vote on the best ideas, and
implement the most popular ones, as Threadless expertly does with its
T-shirt community.
▷ **Implementing manufacturing 2.0:** Launch products more frequently
and less perfectly, enabling audiences to improve them. Create an
after-market support forum to get users to help each other through
owned (Microsoft Channel 9) and customer-generated (Hacking Netflix) sites.
▷ **Practicing the adage "The one who listens is the one who produces":** Assign leadership of customer interaction to qualified employees who are positioned to answer questions and empowered to effect
change internally.
▷ **Creating feedback loops:** Incite dialogue inside companies from customer stimulus and communicate back to your audience about how
their ideas have been acted on, as Intuit does in tracking its customer-
based input from start to finish.
▷ **Producing for the long tail:** Target microniches with higher-margin,
limited editions; exclusive signature lines; and customizable products.
Hershey does this with AllChocolate.com.

Brand Openness: Stretch It Beyond Where You Thought It Could Go

Wikibrands need to cede to consumer power and allow maximum opportunity for customers to modify, mash up, and play with the brand:

▷ **Defining wikibrand DNA:** Solidify core elements—brand name, logo, core idea, belief system, and community—but keep an open mind about the other stuff.

▷ **Putting creative briefs on a diet:** Keep them creative and brief, adopting an approach similar to IDEO's method of visual cards for inspiring designers.

▷ **Pushing edges:** Provide unexpected and remarkable impact based on customer need, as illustrated by Virgin aggressively entering new and poorly satisfied markets.

▷ **Leaving part of the brand story untold:** Host customer-generated marketing and user-generated content campaigns to spark Mentos-like enthusiasm for your brand.

▷ **Partnering up:** Expand your brand around the core idea through mutually beneficial partnerships like Nike and iPod have achieved through joint product launches.

The Marketer's Role: Be a Good Host, Not the Person Onstage

To gain relevancy at the executive table and with the customer base, marketers will need to address the talent, capability, training and development, reward, and structural gaps required for wikibranding:

▷ **Wedding customers to brands and brands to customers:** Identifying customer engagement gaps and bulking up staff at critical brand-customer interaction points is paramount to success.

▷ **Restructuring the brand department:** Alter your marketing organization, as Procter & Gamble has, around your customer (not your brand) to enable dialogue and conversation.

  Consider introducing four key wikibrand manager roles—community manager, brand evangelist, customer experience manager, and brand culture leader.

  Build a media-agnostic and centralized brand activation and support group.

▷ **Affecting the trenches and the horizons:** Ensure that the research and innovation department has the tools to effect wiki innovation and tie marketing performance to return on investment.

▷ **Valuing customers' time as money:** Set targets for time spent with customers—a minimum of 20 percent for customer-engaged, head-office staff and 5 percent for the executive team.

▷ **Motoring innovation downstream:** Expand your resources to support accelerated product variety and introductions, targeting microniches and customization.

▷ **Leaving the egos at the brand door:** Build your marketing staff with people who have collaborative, cross-functional skill sets.

Brand Positioning: Know Thyself

Adding to the evolving marketer's role of working with customers, brand positioning is governed by the notion that a brand is what you do, not what you say. Wikibrands are building positioning from the inside out in several ways and building a focus before considering technologies to enable that focus:

▷ **Stirring imaginations:** Bring brand positioning and brand ideas to life internally to provide a powerful sense of identity among community members.

▷ **Infecting the tribe:** Create all-encompassing brand-employee experiences and develop collaborative wikitools to maintain a sense of internal company culture and transparency of key business decisions.

▷ **Breeding internal zealots:** Hire employees who embody the lifestyle of the "brand idea," as lululemon has.

▷ **Anchoring positioning in a cause:** Develop a rallying point that supports positioning, seeks to improve the world, and creates pride among brand employees and stakeholders, as Cisco achieved with its One Million Acts of Green.

Brand Measures: Count the Clapping, Not the Attendance

To survive, brand organizations will need to apply more effective measurement of a dashboard of metrics that link explicitly back to revenue, profit, and lifetime value of the customer. They'll also depend on technology to deliver this assessment in real time:

▷ **Tracking actions, not impressions:** Measure the true value of brands via a customized set of key metrics for brand engagement, brand differentiation, brand participation, and brand influence.

▷ **Measuring the number-one brand driver:** Tie organizational activities to the ultimate question, the Net Promoter Score—"Would you recommend this brand to a friend or colleague?"

▷ **Keeping up with the Joneses:** Build real-time measurement through Web analytics, search engine optimization, social media optimization, and mobile technologies within digital, social media, and community-building initiatives.

▷ **Providing reciprocal benefits:** Reward members of your brand community for providing "beyond the call" personal data, access, and feedback.

▷ **Measuring markets of one:** Track performance at an individual customer level.

Fifty-Question Assessment: Readiness for Brand Community

In interviewing and studying over one hundred wikibrand companies, the following questions have collectively helped them determine their organization's readiness for building a brand community.

BUSINESS OBJECTIVES AND GOALS
1. Why are you starting a community?
2. What are your qualitative and quantitative goals?
3. How will you measure your progress toward these goals, and how often?
4. Is your community capable of supporting more than one set of goals?
5. Who is the primary owner of the community—members, the company, or a hybrid?
6. What functional area will be accountable for the community?
7. What is the expected timeline for seeing community performance improve the business?
8. What corporate initiatives could benefit from supportive communities?
9. How can your community focus complement your business objectives?
10. How exclusive do you want to make the community?
11. What is the depth of interaction expected from your community?
12. What are the top three areas of community-building benefits?
13. What scale of community is expected?

ORGANIZATION CULTURE AND RESOURCES
14. Is your CEO comfortable with opening up the brand to its customers, fans, and stakeholders?

15. Who would be a suitable and available executive champion of community efforts?
16. Do you have a group of employees who would be motivated to spend extra time on the community?
17. What is your desired interaction with the audience, and can you deliver on it? Do you want to truly listen and capitalize on your customers' input?
18. What financial and human resources are required to build an effective community for your brand? Do you have these resources? Can you get them?
19. Do you have access to skilled resources to plan and build the community (strategy, technology, and new media)?
20. Do you have access to skilled resources to manage the community (communications, administration, and research)?
21. What budget and methods do you have to support recruitment of a community?
22. Do you have the budget to support maintenance and expansion of community for at least two years?
23. Does your company have an open culture? Will it be able to deal with inconvenient truths and negative commentary that come up in any type of open community?
24. What legal/regulatory hurdles do you need to overcome?
25. Do you have a lot of news, variety, or initiatives to share?
26. Can you generate enough content to keep the community vibrant?
27. Do your human resources and incentive systems support community?

BRAND COMMUNITY FOCUS, STORY, AND PURPOSE
28. Is your brand interesting/compelling enough to be the focal point of a community?
29. What conversations about your brand are already happening online?
30. Does your brand have a strong point of view and well-differentiated positioning?
31. How well known is your brand?
32. Do you have a simple, concrete idea to convey in recruiting people to your community?
33. Can your brand credibly pull off this idea?
34. Are your potential members naturally collaborative around your brand?
35. Is this a sustainable brand commitment or a short-term idea?
36. Will people feel emotionally connected through your community?
37. Do you have a story that can act as a rallying cry for prospective members?

38. Can your brand provide enough escape, education, entertainment, or profound experience through community to keep members engaged? Is there a bigger idea linked to the brand that can?

39. Can your community, brand, and business change based on member involvement?

MEMBER/CUSTOMER/INFLUENCER VALUES, LIFESTYLE, AND DESIRES

40. Who are you targeting, and what do these customers want?
41. Are people asking for this community now?
42. Is this audience already congregating online? Offline?
43. How could your community make members' lives easier?
44. What are the expected motives and incentives for participation?
45. What can you offer your members?
46. What will initially attract them to your site?
47. What will keep them coming back?
48. What will get them to recruit other people to your audience?
49. What is the digital sophistication level of your audience?
50. How would your community compare to those of your competitors?

Moving Forward

The next steps are yours. We feel like perhaps we've done the easy job in providing you a new paradigm for reinventing your company, no matter how big or small. The tougher part is the sweat and toil, persistence, customization, and alignment for getting it to work and stick. We'll leave that to you.

In moving the discussion from the buzzword, *social media*, to the real driver, *social business*, we hope you walk away understanding the importance and often-ignored role of brand in a connected marketplace and the seven compelling business environmental reasons to drive change, or further change, in your company. We hope you include a full range of company staff and customers in the effort and not make this a departmental-driven campaign but a rallying point for changing a company's overall culture, like ripping off an adhesive bandage, either slowly or in one fell swoop.

We hope you sequentially and thoroughly tackle the challenge by using the FLIRT model presented and learn from the successes and pratfalls from the world's leading wikibrands. We hope you embrace the longevity of this change and the need to incubate wikibrand community building and customer innovation as an ongoing rallying cry that affects the human resources you apply, the internal change required, the stage growth of your communities, and the difference in metrics monitored and analyzed.

Finally, we hope you understand that the world is not static and that change is a mantra of the best wikibranders. What is true today most certainly will be different two, five, and ten years from now. Stay engaged. We can help out in that area by continuing the conversation and exposure to new strategies and tactics from the world's best wikibrands at **wiki-brands.com**. In the meantime, enjoy the wikibrands ride. Carpe diem!

Endnotes

Foreword

1. Don Tapscott, *The Digital Economy* (New York: McGraw-Hill, 1995).
2. Al Ries and Laura Ries, *The 22 Immutable Laws of Branding: How to Build a Product or Service into a World-Class Brand* (New York: HarperCollins, 1998).
3. Don Tapscott and David Ticoll, *The Naked Corporation* (Toronto, ON: Viking Canada, 2003).

Chapter 1

1. Charlene Li, "New Study: Deep Brand Engagement Correlates with Financial Performance," Altimeter.com, July 20, 2009.
2. Technorati, "State of the Blogosphere 2009," Technorati.com.
3. "Global Internet Audience Surpasses 1 Billion Visitors, According to comScore," press release, comScore.com, January 23, 2009.
4. International Telecommunication Union, Corporate Annual Report, 2008, p. 40.
5. Nielsen Company, "Led by Facebook, Twitter, Global Time Spent on Social Media Sites up 82% Year over Year," January 22, 2010.
6. Interbrand, "The 2007 Brand Marketers Report: Interbrand's Annual Survey on Brands and Branding," 2007, p. 8.
7. Paul Thomasch, "Big Turnover in '07," Reuters, March 12, 2007.
8. Mike Linton, "Why Do Chief Marketing Officers Have Such a Short Shelf Life?" Forbes.com, May 15, 2009.
9. "Digital Marketing Driving Transformation in Global Marketing Organizations, Reports CMO Council," CMO Council on the Marketing Outlook study and State of Marketing report, April 19, 2010.
10. A *mashup* is a digital media file containing text, graphics, audio, video, and/or animation that recombines and modifies existing digital works to create a derivative work.
11. GlobeScan Radar 2010 Research Program, "Tracking Global Opinion on Business and Society," December 2005, p. 3.
12. Although many people refer to this cohort as Generation Y (first birth year in 1977) or Millenials (first birth year in 1981), we prefer the "Net Generation" because technology is the defining driver of the generation. See Don Tapscott, *Grown Up Digital: How the Net Generation Is Changing Your World* (New York: McGraw-Hill, 2009) for more details on the rationale.
13. Jack Neff, "Clutter Pollution Solution—Make Them Pay for Bad Ads," *Advertising Age*, AdAge.com, April 8, 2007.

14. Laura Petrecca, "Product Placement, You Can't Escape It," *USA Today*, October 10, 2006.
15. Peter Kim, "Consumers Love to Hate Advertising; Clutter, Interruption, and Irrelevance Spur Ad Avoidance," BeingPeterKim.com, December 9, 2006.
16. Larry Dobrow, "Multi-taskers Represent Multiple Threat: Simultaneous Media Usage Reaches New High," *Media Daily News*, March 24, 2004.
17. John Consoli, "'Millennials' Big for Media Biz," *Mediaweek*, June 21, 2006.
18. "Supermarket Facts: Industry Overview 2006," Food Marketing Institute, fmi .org.
19. "eBay Fact Sheet," eBay, accessed May 25, 2010.
20. Eliot Van Buskirk, "Millions Would Pay for iTunes Cloud-Based Subscription: Study," in *Epicenter*, a blog on Wired.com, July 15, 2010.
21. Amazon.com, accessed May 25, 2010.
22. All stats collected from company websites, May 25, 2010.
23. Robert Putnam, *Bowling Alone: The Collapse & Revival of American Community* (New York: Simon & Schuster, 2000).
24. Scott Davis, "Microsoft Executive Circle," presentation, Prophet.com, March 2006.
25. Microsoft News Center, "Microsoft and Cisco: Collaborating for the Future of Technology," transcript of discussion, New York, August 20, 2007.

Chapter 2

1. The more things change, the more they stay the same.
2. Paul Dunay, "Fire Your Director of Social Media!" *Buzz Marketing for Technology*, pauldunay.com, December 22, 2009.
3. For what is considered the most thorough explanation of why the documents must be forgeries, see Joseph Newcomer, "The Bush 'Guard Memos' Are Forgeries," flounder.com/bush2.htm, September 11, 2004.
4. Jonathan V. Last, "What Blogs Have Wrought: How the Guys Sitting at Their Computers in Pajamas Humiliated the Suits at CBS," *Weekly Standard*, September 27, 2004.
5. Statistics collected from Wikipedia.org on June 15, 2010.
6. Kevin Poulsen and Kim Zettler, "U.S. Intelligence Analyst Arrested in Wikileaks Video Probe," Wired.com, June 8, 2010.
7. Interview with David Bradfield, April 21, 2010.
8. Scott Bedbury and Stephen Fenichell, *A New Brand World: Eight Principles for Achieving Brand Leadership in the Twenty-First Century* (New York: Penguin Books, 2003), p. 169.
9. John Geraci, Mike Dover, and Don Tapscott, "N-Gen Global Research Study," nGenera Insight, 2008.
10. Jay Ehret, "The Experience Economy: 10 Years Later," *The Marketing Spot*, The MarketingSpotBlog.com, August 5, 2009.
11. "The Buzz Report," *Agent Wildfire*, agentwildfire.com, June 2010.

12. Ibid.
13. "New VSS Study Shows Fast Growth in Communications Industry, Subscription TV, and Consumer-Supported Media over 35 Years," *Veronis Suhler Stevenson,* vss.com, April 27, 2010.
14. Ibid.
15. Deloitte, "State of the Media Democracy," December 2009.
16. "The Buzz Report," *Agent Wildfire,* June 2010.
17. Andrew Eisner, "How Addicting Is Social Media?" referencing the Retrevo Gadgetology report, *Retrevo,* blog on Retrevo.com, October 9, 2010.
18. "The Buzz Report," *Agent Wildfire,* June 2010.
19. John Gerzema and Ed Lebar, *The Brand Bubble: The Looming Crisis in Brand Value and How to Avoid It* (San Francisco: Jossey-Bass, 2008); for summary of stats, see SlideShare presentation "52.01.Brand Bubble" by John Gerzema; Robyn Greenspan, "Consumers Becoming Marketing Resistant," ClickZ.com, April 23, 2004.
20. "Capitalizing on Complexity: Insights from the 2010 IBM Global CEO Study," IBM.com, February 2010.
21. Geraci et al., "N-Gen Global Research Study."
22. "Meet the Conversation Catalysts," *Keller Fay,* KellerFay.com, December 4, 2006.
23. Deloitte, "State of the Media Democracy."
24. A *mashup* is a digital media file containing text, graphics, audio, video, and/or animation that recombines and modifies existing digital works to create a derivative work.
25. Jessie Scanlon, "Is Recession the Time to Boost Ad Spending?" *Businessweek,* May 1, 2009.
26. "Bazaarvoice and CMO Club Survey: CMOs Look for Higher Social Media Measurability in 2010," December 8, 2009.
27. Interview with Lois Kelly, April 29, 2010.
28. Marguerite Reardon, "Cisco: Collaboration Is the Future," CNET, December 11, 2007.
29. Frank Piller, "The Consumer Decides: Nike Focuses Competitive Strategy on Customization and Creating Personal Consumer Experiences—Data about the Nike Plus Personalization System," *Mass Customization and Open Innovation News,* February 26, 2007.
30. Jody Schoger, "Livestrong CEO: Social Media Will Change Health Care Forever," *Women with Cancer,* March 12, 2010.
31. Interview with Sean O'Driscoll, April 2, 2010.
32. Links to videos for these campaigns can be found at wiki-brands.com.
33. Mike Hollywood, "2008 Business in Social Media Study," *Cone,* coneinc.com, September 11–12, 2008.
34. Tom Webster, "Twitter Usage in America: 2010," Edison Research study, Edison research.com, April 29, 2010.

35. The Global Social Media Check Up, Burston-Marsteller white paper, February 25, 2010.
36. Interview with James Cherkoff, April 7, 2009.
37. Interview with Jay Baer, April 13, 2010.
38. Ibid.
39. Interview with Ross Kimbarovsky, March 22, 2010.

Chapter 3

1. Bernajean Porter, WOW Technology Conference, Phoenix, AZ, April 28, 2007.
2. The phrase "If I have seen further, it is by standing on the shoulders of giants," is commonly attributed to Sir Isaac Newton in a 1676 letter to fellow scientist and polymath Robert Hooke. As trivia fans, we wish to report that some people consider it a veiled insult directed at Hooke, who was of slight stature and had a pronounced stoop (a dwarf standing on the shoulders of giants).
3. The authors also wish to thank nGenera Insight, a division of Moxie Software. Some ideas and concepts found in this book are based on proprietary research conducted by nGenera and are used with the corporation's permission.
4. We were joined on this journey by more than one hundred research staff members, industry practitioners, and thought leaders. An exhaustive list is provided at wiki-brands.com.
5. This project was conducted under the editorial leadership of Anthony Williams and John Geraci.
6. This project was conducted under the program and editorial leadership of Denis Hancock and Bob Morison, with research support provided by Alex Marshall.

Chapter 4

1. Soren Gordhamer, "The New Social Engagement: A Visit to Zappos," *Mashable*, July 2009.
2. Interview with Brian Fetherstonhaugh, April 20, 2010.
3. We've met Brian's daughter, Alison, who was eighteen at the time of this writing, and can vouch for the fact that he knows what he's talking about. Her story (the Alison diaries) is discussed in Don Tapscott, *Grown Up Digital: How the Net Generation Is Changing Your World* (New York: McGraw-Hill, 2009), p. 186.
4. Fetherstonhaugh, interview.
5. Ibid.
6. Ibid.
7. Ibid.
8. Paul Rogers and Jenny Davis-Piccoud, "Organizing the Frontlines: Turning Decision into Action," Bain & Company survey, Bain.com, June 22, 2006.

9. "Meet the Conversation Catalysts," *Keller Fay*, KellerFay.com, December 4, 2006.

10. Renee Dye, "The Buzz on Buzz," *Harvard Business Review*, HBR.org, October 1, 2001; and "How To Articles: A Business Case for Customer Service Excellence" *i-Sight*, CustomerExpressions.com, referencing a Thomson Lightstone Omnitel report, 2004.

11. Financial and location information accessed from CNBC.com on June 9, 2010.

12. "Lululemon Athletica Q1 Profit Surges, Boosts 2010 Outlook," press release, RTT News, June 10, 2010.

13. "The Lululemon Love Affair," *Digital Journal*, December 26, 2006; and interview with Chip Wilson, June 24, 2010.

14. Interview with Chip Wilson, June 24, 2010.

15. "Smart Steps," BC Government Report, January 2007.

16. Interview with Jackie Huba, April 12, 2007; and Running Room.com stats.

17. Anthony D. Williams and Don Tapscott, *Wikinomics: How Mass Collaboration Changes Everything* (New York: Penguin Group, 2008), p. 130.

18. Interview with Jake McKee, April 7, 2009.

19. Jake McKee, "Success by 1000 Paper Cuts," *Communityguy blog*, April 2, 2009.

20. "MINDSTORMS NXT Rubik's Cube Solver by Hans Andersson," *The Brothers Brick blog*, July 21, 2008.

21. Brendan Koemer, "Geeks in Toyland," *Wired*, February 2006.

22. McKee, interview.

23. Note that we both worked for Procter & Gamble, and referring to any of the company's brands in such a manner could most charitably be described as a career-limiting move!

24. R. Underwood, "Jones Soda's Secret," *Fast Company* 92 (2005): p. 74.

25. Mike Dover, "What Time Did You Make It Back from Liberty City?" *Wiki nomics.com blog*, April 29, 2008.

26. Brooks Barnes, "To Create Buzz, TV Networks Try a Little 'Blogola,'" *The Wall Street Journal*, May 15, 2007.

27. Jennifer Medelsohn, "Honey, Don't Bother Mommy. I'm Too Busy Building My Brand," *The New York Times*, March 12, 2010.

28. Interview with Janet Kestin, April 23, 2007.

29. "Grand Effie Goes to Dove's Real Beauty," Effie Awards press release, Effie.org, June 8, 2006.

30. Interview with Niraj Dawar, January 13, 2010.

31. Mack Collier, "Lead, Follow, or Get Out of the Way," *Marketing Profs*, MPDaily Fix.com, July 5, 2006.

32. Suzanne Vranica and Chad Terhune, "Mixing Diet Coke and Mentos Makes a Gusher of Publicity," *The Wall Street Journal*, June 12, 2006.

33. "Reinventing the Marketing Organization," *Forrester Research*, Forrester.com, July 2006.

Chapter 5

1. Stuart Elliott, "Letting Consumers Control Marketing: Priceless," *The New York Times*, October 9, 2006.
2. Emily Wexler, "Overall Winner—Frito-Lay Canada's Tony Matta: Raising the Stakes," *Strategy Magazine*, StrategyOnline.ca, December 1, 2009.
3. Dave Carroll presentation and follow-up conversation, East Coast Connected, Toronto, May 20, 2010.
4. Ibid.
5. Chris Ayres, "Revenge Is Best Served Cold—On YouTube," *The Times Online*, July 22, 2002.
6. Carroll presentation and follow-up conversation.
7. Interview with Constance Steinkuehler, January 14, 2009.
8. Interview with Simon Pulsifier, May 26, 2010.
9. Keith McArthur, "Absolut-ly Over! Vodka Maker Replaces Iconic Ad Campaign," *The Globe & Mail*, April 27, 2007.
10. Bradley Horowitz, "Creators, Synthesizers and Consumers," *Elatable blog*, February 16, 2006.
11. Julie Bosman, "Chevy Tries a Write-Your-Own-Ad Approach and the Potshots Fly," *The New York Times*, April 4, 2006.
12. Interbrand, "The 2007 Brand Marketers Report: Interbrand's Annual Survey on Brands and Branding," 2007, p. 16; and Interbrand, "The 2009 Brand Marketers Report: Interbrand's Annual Survey on Brands and Branding," 2009, Interbrand.com.
13. "Browser Share for April 2010," NetApplications.com, May 2010.
14. Erica Jostadt, "Introducing the Mozilla State of the Internet Report," *Mozilla blog*, blog.mozilla.com, March 31, 2010.
15. Andrew Gordon, "A Team Effort," *PR Week USA*, January 23, 2006.
16. Interview with Asa Dotzler, April 22, 2007.
17. Mozilla.com, December 15, 2004.
18. "The Fox Tales Launches: Firefox Crop Circles, a Prom Queen, and More Zany Stories!" PRLeap.com, August 14, 2006.
19. Dotzler, interview.
20. "Saving Starbucks' Soul," *BusinessWeek*, businessweek.com, June 27, 2007.
21. Interview with Joe Pine, May 24, 2010.
22. "Q&A with Howard Schultz," *BusinessWeek*, businessweek.com, September 9, 2002.
23. Interview with Mary Graham, April 9, 2007.
24. Ibid.
25. Denis Hancock, "Starbucks: Tracking a Wikinomics-Enabled Marketing Success Story," *Wikinomics blog*, November 13, 2008.
26. Interview with Denis Hancock, May 31, 2010.
27. Ryan Singel, "Sony Draws Ire with PSP Graffiti," *Wired*, Wired.com, December 5, 2005.
28. Laura Patterson, "How Marketing Can Go Beyond the 'Make It Pretty' Syndrome," MarketingProfs.com, May 13, 2008.

29. Peter Kim, "Reinventing the Marketing Organization," *Forrester Research*, Forrester.com, August 9, 2006.
30. Interview with William Azaroff, May 28, 2010.
31. Andrew Wahl, "The Best Workplaces in Canada?" *Canadian Business*, Cana dianbusiness.com, April 10, 2006.
32. Azaroff, interview.
33. "The Buzz Report," *Agent Wildfire*, agentwildfire.com, June 2010.
34. Marcel Lebrun, "The Yellow Brick Road to Social Media Maturity," presentation, Radian6, February 26, 2010.

Chapter 6

1. Jenny Ambrozek and Joseph Cothrel, "Online Communities in Business: Past Progress, Future Directions" (VC2004 Report presented at the 7th International Conference on Virtual Communities, The Hague, Netherlands, June 15, 2004).
2. Interview with Adam Garone, May 13, 2010.
3. Ibid.
4. Ibid.
5. Ibid.
6. Ibid.
7. Interview with Alan Moore, April 8, 2009.
8. Stephen Baker, "Beware Social Media Snake Oil," *BusinessWeek*, December 3, 2009.
9. Twellow search statistics.
10. "Employee Engagement Survey," IABC, August 3, 2010.
11. "Social Media in Business—The Next Revolution," Growth Lab Consulting, March 2010.
12. Simon Sinek, StartwithWhy.com.
13. Interview with Sami Viitamäki, March 26, 2009.
14. Interview with Joe Cothrel, April 2010.
15. "Five Social Software Predications for 2010 and Beyond," Gartner study, Gartner .com, February 2010.
16. Interview with Jamie Pappas and Polly Pearson, March 29, 2010.
17. Ibid.
18. EMC Case Study, Jive Software.
19. EMC website, emc.com; Pappas and Pearson, interview.
20. Interview with Kira Wampler, March 25, 2010.
21. Ibid.
22. Ambrozek and Cothrel, "Online Communities in Business."
23. Lee Odden, "Big Brand Social Media Interview: Wells Fargo, Home Depot, UPS & Graco," *TopRank Online Marketing blog*, toprankblog.com, October 22, 2008.
24. Natalie Zmuda, "Tropicana's Sales Plunge 20% Post Re-Branding," *AdAge*, adage.com, April 2, 2009.

25. Adapted from Chip Heath and Dan Heath, *Made to Stick: Why Some Ideas Survive and Others Die* (New York: Random House, 2007), pp. 14–18.
26. For a complete list of these strong brand community ideas, peruse our list of case studies at wiki-brands.com.
27. Interview with Gary Koeling, September 2008.
28. Stephen R. Covey, "Work Life Balance: A Different Cut," Forbes.com, March 21, 2007.
29. Interview with Diane Hessan, April 3, 2009.
30. Seth Godin, *Tribes: We Need You to Lead Us* (New York: Portfolio, 2008), in Acknowledgments section referencing a Hugh MacLeod cartoon.

Chapter 7

1. James Cherkoff and Johnnie Moore, "Co-Creation Rules," ChangeThis.com, December 2006.
2. "T-10, Yay 2000–2002," *Threadless blog post*, May 13, 2010.
3. Laurie Burkitt, "Need to Build a Community? Learn from Threadless," Forbes.com, January 6, 2010.
4. Will Novosedlik, "Drinking from the Fountain of Youth," *Strategy Magazine*, strategyonline.ca, April 1, 2010.
5. "The Buzz Report," *Agent Wildfire*, agentwildfire.com, May 2010.
6. Interview with Sami Viitamäki, March 26, 2009.
7. Clay Shirky, "How Social Media Can Make History," video, TED.com, June 2009.
8. Emanuel Rosen, *The Anatomy of Buzz: How to Create Word-of-Mouth Marketing* (New York: Doubleday Business, 2000), pp. 31–51.
9. Kiva.org, "Facts and History."
10. Facebook.com, "Statistics."
11. Data collected from Wikipedia.org, June 9, 2010.
12. Ibid.
13. Ben Parr, "YouTube Surpasses Two Billion Views Daily," mashable.com, May 17, 2010.
14. Alexa.com statistics, June 2010.
15. Wayne Friedman, "Online Ads Surpass TV Ads in Recall, Likability," MediaPost.com, April 22, 2010.
16. Interview with Rod Brooks, November 2009.
17. Gary Vaynerchuk, *Crush It! Why NOW Is the Time to Cash In on Your Passion* (New York: HarperCollins, 2009).
18. In 2007, Molson encountered controversy when it launched a Facebook contest that asked customers to upload party photos. Critics accused the contest of promoting underage drinking.
19. Interview with Ferg Devins, April 2009.
20. Colin Shaw, *The DNA of Customer Experience: How Emotions Drive Value* (Hampshire, United Kingdom: Palgrave Macmillan, 2007), p. 8.
21. Word of Mouth Marketing Association, Ethics Code, WOMMA.org.

22. A *meme* is an idea or element of social behavior passed on through generations in a culture, especially by imitation.
23. cbc.ca/green and wiki-brands.com.
24. Rick Spence, "Surprise Marketing Tactics Endear," *Financial Post*, March 3, 2008.
25. A flash mob is a large group of people that assembles suddenly in a public place, performs an unusual and pointless act for a brief time, then quickly disperses. The term *flash mob* is generally applied only to gatherings organized via telecommunications, social media, or viral e-mails.
26. Lois Kelly, *Beyond Buzz: The Next Generation of Word-of-Mouth Marketing* (New York: AMACOM, 2007), pp. 107–128.
27. Rob Walker, "Pizza with a Plan," *The New York Times Magazine*, September 11, 2009.
28. Judy Kneiszel, "Ones to Watch: Naked Pizza," *QSR Magazine*, June 2010.
29. Jason Kincaid, "A Sign of Things to Come: Naked Pizza Erects Twitter Billboard," *TechCrunch*, April 24, 2009.
30. Interview with Robbie Vitrano, May 16, 2010.
31. "The Learning Pyramid," National Training Laboratories, NTL.org, 2005.
32. Priyanka Joshi, "Facebook Trumps Photo-Sharing Sites," Rediff, business .rediff.com, July 12, 2010.
33. "Visual Networking Index Report, 2009–2014," Cisco.com, June 2010.
34. Christian Briggs, "Blendtec: A Viral Case Study," SociaLens.com, April 2009.
35. Agent Wildfire Influencer survey research, *Agent Wildfire*, agentwildfire.com, May 2008.
36. Robert Ciadini, *Influence: The Psychology of Persuasion* (New York: Harper Collins, 1998).
37. Sam Decker, "Social Commerce 101: Leverage Word-of-Mouth to Boost Sales," ClickZ.com, February 9, 2010.
38. Erik Qualman, "Statistics Show Social Media Is Bigger than You Think," *Socialnomics blog*, Socialnomics.net, August 11, 2009.
39. Jyri Engeström, "Why Some Social Network Services Work and Others Don't —or the Case for Object-Centered Sociality," Zengestrom.com, April 12, 2005.
40. Iain McDonald, "Social Object Theory: The Secret Ingredient for Powering Social Influence in Marketing Campaigns," *Razorfish Digital Outlook*, Razor fish.com, 2009.
41. "Doritos Viralocity Winner Announced," Techvibes.com, April 12, 2010.
42. Eric Karjaluoto, *Speak Human: Outmarket the Big Guys by Getting Personal* (Vancouver, BC: smashLAB, 2009), p. 154.

Chapter 8

1. Interview with Jake McKee, April 7, 2009.
2. A *petabyte* (derived from the SI prefix *peta-*) is a unit of information equal to one quadrillion (short-scale) bytes, or one thousand terabytes. Google processes about twenty-four petabytes of data per day.

3. Facebook.com, "Statistics," February 2010.
4. Dan Pink, *Drive: The Surprising Truth of What Motivates Us* (New York: River-head Books, 2009); and "Dan Pink on the Surprising Science of Motivation," TED.com, August 2009.
5. "2010 Razorfish Outlook Report," Razorfish, Razorfishoutlook.razorfish.com, January 2010.
6. "CMOs Need Greater Engagement Internally and Through Social Networks for Their Brands to Thrive: Hill & Knowlton and CMO Club Study," PR Newswire, PRNewswire.com, November 16, 2009.
7. Jeffrey Hayzlett, "How Video and Social Media Helped Kodak Get Its Mojo Back," *Streaming Media East 2010, Larry Kless's weblog*, May 2010.
8. Clive Thompson, "Is the Tipping Point Toast?" *Fast Company*, February 1, 2008.
9. Bill Heil and Mikolaj Piskorski, "New Twitter Research: Men Follow Men and Nobody Tweets," *Harvard Business Study*, HBR.org, June 1, 2009.
10. Charles Arthur, "What Is the 1% Rule?" *The Guardian*, guardian.co.uk, July 20, 2006.
11. Dave White "State of the Blogosphere: The How of Blogging," Technorati, October 13, 2009.
12. Rand Fishkin, "Top 100 Digg Users Control 56% of Digg's HomePage Content," *SEOmoz blog*, seomoz.org, July 2006.
13. Augie Ray and Josh Bernoff, "Forrester Announces Peer Influence Analysis: An Analytical Framework to Inform Social Media Marketing Strategy," *Forrester Consumer Technographics*, Forrester, Forrester.com, April 20, 2010.
14. Interview with Tricia Mumby, May 2010.
15. Ibid.
16. "The Influencers: Influence Study," *Agent Wildfire*, agentwildfire.com, 2008.
17. Ibid.
18. Keller Fay/OMD Study results, KellerFay.com, June 25, 2008.
19. Facebook.com, "Statistics"; and "State of the Twittersphere—Q4-2008," Hubspot.com, December 22, 2008.
20. Interview with Scott Monty, June 3, 2010.
21. Andy Sernovitz, *Word of Mouth Marketing: How Smart Companies Get People Talking*, Revised Edition (New York: Kaplan Press, 2009).
22. Charlene Li, "Forrester's New Social Technographics Report," *Forrester blog*, forrester.typepad.com, April 21, 2007.
23. Heidi Cohen, "Building Online Communities by the Numbers," ClickZ.com, February 21, 2009.

Chapter 9

1. "Study: 54% of Companies Ban Facebook, Twitter at Work," referencing Robert Half Technology study, Computerworld.com, October 6, 2009.
2. James Glick, "Infographic—Is Your Country Embracing Social Media?" referencing Lightspeed research, TheNextWeb.com, December 14, 2009; and Internet World Stats, "World Stats," internetworldstats.com.

3. Bill Brenner, "Seven Deadly Sins of Social Networking Security," *CSO*, cso online.com, June 30, 2009.9

4. Brent Coker, "Workplace Leisure Internet Browsing," University of Melbourne, media.marcom.unimelb.edu.au, April 2, 2009.

5. Casey Hibbard, "How IBM Uses Social Media to Spur Employee Motivation," *Social Media Examiner*, February 2, 2010.

6. Todd Watson, "Smarter Social Media" (presentation, *South by Southwest*, Austin, Texas, March 16, 2010).

7. Ibid.

8. Joan M. DiMicco et al., "Research on the Use of Social Software in the Workplace" (position paper presented at the CSCW 2008 conference workshop "Social Networking in Organizations," November 8–12, 2008, San Diego, California).

9. Hibbard, "How IBM Uses Social Media."

10. Jolie O'Dell, "Many World Cup Players Banned from Social Media," *Mashable blog*, June 12, 2010.

11. The full privacy statement can be found on the Facebook site. Many commenters have pointed out that it is a longer document than the Declaration of Independence.

12. Interview with Jason Falls, June 2010.

13. "The Buzz Report," *Agent Wildfire*, agentwildfire.com, June 2010.

14. "Social Media Tips: Sharing Lessons Learned to Make Your Business Grow," Kodak.com.

15. Lee Odden, "Joseph Jaffe Interview," *TopRank Online Marketing blog*, toprank blog.com, April 13, 2008.

16. Matt Dickman, "Social Media and B-to-B Marketing," Marketing Profs, March 10, 2007.

17. Innocent Drinks corporate website, innocentdrinks.co.uk.

18. Intel Social Media Guidelines, "Moderation Guidelines," Intel.com.

19. Interview with Rob Kozinets, April 2009.

20. "2010 Corporate Counsel New Media Engagement Survey," ALM Legal Intelligence study, 2010.

21. Peter Zack, "Facebook Not the Place to Store Your Photos," Enticingthelight .com, July 26, 2010.

22. Facebook, "Terms," Facebook.com, early 2010.

23. Roger Clarke, "Information Wants to Be Free," Australian National University, rogerclarke.com, February 24, 2000.

24. Creative Commons website, creativecommons.org.

25. Charlene Li, "Kudos to Chevy Tahoe: It Takes Guts to Brand in Social Computing," *Groundswell blog*, forrester.typepad.com/groundswell, April 6, 2006.

26. Seth Godin, "The Reason Social Media Is so Difficult for Most Organizations," *Seth Godin's blog*, sethgodin.typepad.com, December 10, 2009.

27. No, it's not *octopi*. *Octopuses* is the correct plural, since the word's root is Latinized Greek.

28. Albert M. Muniz, Jr., and Thomas O'Guinn, "Brand Community," *Journal of Consumer Research* 27 (2001): p. 427.

29. A hashtag represented by the # symbol organizes discussions in Twitter and makes it easier to search for other conversations. For example, a tweet about the iPhone launch might be #iPhone. The Follow Fridays ritual means that on that day, Twitter users encourage others to follow people they find interesting. *Retweet* refers to posting a copy of someone else's message and giving them attribution. "Tweet up" refers to in-person meetings between Twitter users. "Fail whale" refers to the animated picture of a whale that appears when the Twitter network is overwhelmed.

Chapter 10

1. Dov Siedman, *How: Why How We Do Anything Means Everything . . . in Business (and in Life)* (Hoboken, NJ: John Wiley and Sons, 2007).
2. "The Worst Predictions of 2006," *BusinessWeek*, December 29, 2006.
3. Jon Swartz, "More Marketers Use Social Networking to Reach Customers," *USA Today*, August 28, 2009.
4. Interview with Richard Binhammer, April 13, 2010.
5. "2009 Engagement Report: Ranking the Top 100 Global Brands," EngagementDB, engagementdb.com, June 2009.
6. Binhammer, interview; and "2009 Engagement Report," EngagementDB.
7. Manish Mehta, "Isn't the Value of Social Media What Business Is All About?" *The Huffington Post*, December 8, 2009.
8. Binhammer, interview.
9. Postrank.com, "Engagement."
10. Jeremiah Owyang, "Slides: Four Social Media Trends for Business in 2010," *Web Strategy blog*, January 22, 2010.
11. Steve Rubel, "The Next Great Media Company Won't Have a Web Site," Steve Rubel.com, September 30, 2009.
12. "Digital Brand Experience Report," Razorfish, Razorfish.com, 2009.
13. Interview with James Cherkoff, April 7, 2009.
14. S. L. Brown, A. Tilton, and D. M. Woodside, "The Case for On-Line Communities," *The McKinsey Quarterly* (January 2002): p. 11.
15. Cherkoff, interview.
16. Pear Analytics, "Twitter Study—August 2009," pearanalytics.com.
17. Brown et al., "The Case for On-Line Communities." For a comprehensive listing of community features and word-of-mouth building sales conversions and better customer experience, visit Bazaarvoice.com/research/stats.
18. "2009 Tribalization of Business Study" (Deloitte/Beeline Labs paper, June 2009).
19. "2009 Edelman goodpurpose™ Study," Edelman/Strategy One, October 21, 2009.
20. Keller Fay/OMD study results, KellerFay.com, June 25, 2008.
21. Interview with Piers Fawkes, May 14, 2010.
22. Interview with Alan Moore, April 8, 2009.

23. Mark Walsh, "Survey: Most CMOs to Boost Social Media Budgets in 2010 (and It Had Better Pay Off)," *MediaPost News*, December 9, 2009.

Chapter 11

1. Seth Godin, *Tribes: We Need You to Lead Us* (New York: Portfolio, 2008).
2. Nielsen Company, "Global Faces and Networked Places: A Nielsen Report on Social Networking's New Global Footprint," blog.nielsen.com, March 2009.
3. Albert M. Muniz, Jr., and Thomas O'Guinn, "Brand Community," *Journal of Consumer Research* 27, no. 4 (March 2001), pp. 412–432.
4. "2008 Tribalization of Business Study" Deloitte, Beeline Labs, and Society for New Communications Research, tribalizationofbusiness.com/2008-study.
5. "Deloitte Study: Enterprise Value of Online Communities Yet to Be Realized," Deloitte.com, July 2008.
6. "What Companies Gain from Listening: The Effect of Community Membership on Members" Communispace.com, May 2006.
7. University of Southern California—Annenberg School, "The 2007 Digital Future Report," digitalcenter.org.
8. Emily Riley, "Social Networking Sites: Defining Advertising Opportunities in a Competitive Landscape" (Jupiter Research, March 2007).
9. David Daniels, "Retail Marketing: Driving Sales Through Consumer-Created Content" (Jupiter Research, August 2006).
10. Interview with Sean O'Driscoll, April 2, 2010.
11. Interview with Suzanne Siemens and Madeleine Shaw, November 10, 2009.
12. Interview with Don Tapscott, May 29, 2010.
13. Keith Ferrazzi with Tahl Raz, *Never Eat Alone: And Other Secrets to Success, One Relationship at a Time* (New York: Currency Doubleday, 2005), p. 180.
14. Roger Smith corporate website, About Us section, rogersmith.com.
15. 1000awesomethings.com, About section.
16. Ibid.
17. Powers won the men's half-pipe event at the 2002 Salt Lake City Games.
18. Interview with Chris Matthews, April 5, 2010.
19. For more information on sabermatics, Bill James (the leader of the movement), and its impact on business strategy, read Michael Lewis, *Moneyball: The Art of Winning an Unfair Game* (New York: W. W. Norton, 2003).
20. Fred Bierman, "Bucks Fans Respond to Bogut's Incentive," *The New York Times*, December 13, 2009.
21. Chris Sheridan, "Squad 6: A Night with Bogut's Crazies," ESPN.com, March 29, 2010.
22. Henry Jenkins, *Convergence Culture: Where Old and New Media Collide* (New York: New York University Press, 2006), p. 95.
23. Chris Brogan and Julien Smith, *Trust Agents: Using the Web to Build Influence, Improve Reputation, and Earn Trust* (Hoboken, NJ: John Wiley and Sons, 2009).

24. Screen-grab on the Wikibrands website (wiki-brands.com).
25. Interview with Victor Samra, April 8, 2010.
26. Ibid.
27. Interview with LaSandra Brill, April 9, 2010.
28. Ibid.
29. Ibid.
30. Jere Hester, "Dope Twitters Away a Job Offer," NBCDFW.com, March 23, 2009.
31. *ASR* stands for aggregation service router.
32. LaSandra Brill, "Building a Community with Social Media and Web 2.0," Cisco PowerPoint presentation, July 2008, slideshare.net/lasandra5.
33. Interview with Adam Wallace, April 16, 2010.
34. Ibid.
35. Samra, interview.
36. Matthews, interview.
37. Ibid.
38. Wallace, interview.
39. Jim Hopkinson, "Interview with Adam Wallace and Brian Simpson" (*The Hopkinson Report*, January 5, 2010).
40. Samra, interview.

Chapter 12

1. Interview with Mike McDerment, March 5, 2008.
2. Visit wiki-brands.com for some of our more fabulous purchases.
3. Data collected from Twitter, May 26, 2010.
4. Interview with Sean O'Driscoll, April 2, 2010.
5. Ibid.
6. Tony Hsieh, e-mail to Zappos employees, July 22, 2009.
7. "Historian Admits Leaving Devastating Anonymous Reviews Savaging Rival's Books on Amazon," *The Daily Mail*, dailymail.co.uk, updated April 24, 2010.
8. Interview with Don Mitchell, March 7, 2010.
9. Helen Coster, "The Secret Life of an Online Book Reviewer," *Forbes*, December 1, 2006.
10. Mitchell, interview.
11. Coster, "Secret Life."
12. Interview with Tracy Benson, March 31, 2010.
13. Ibid.
14. "Best Buy and Zurich Win Direct Marketing Award," *Business and Leadership*, October 21, 2009.
15. Paul Gi, "Rewarding Superusers—A Great Example from Best Buy," *Lithosphere blog*, lithosphere.lithium.com, December 24, 2009.
16. Interview with Krista Thomas, April 19, 2010.
17. O'Driscoll, interview.
18. Interview with Scott Wilder, April 7, 2009.

19. Interview with Christine Morrison, March 24, 2010.
20. Wilder, interview.
21. Morrison, interview.
22. Wilder, interview.
23. Ibid.
24. Ibid.
25. Interview with Howard, a retired certified public accountant, May 6, 2010.
26. Interview with Marilyn Pratt, April 9, 2010.
27. Ibid.
28. Ibid.
29. Ibid.
30. Interview with Steve Molis, April 7, 2010.
31. Ibid.
32. Ibid.
33. Interview with Matt Brown, April 7, 2010.
34. Howard, interview.

Chapter 13

1. Sarah Blue, "How to Be a Great Community Manager," *TechVibes blog*, June 12, 2009.
2. Daniel Terdimen, "Newsmaker: The Community Spirit of Yahoo's Fake," CNET.com, March 23, 2007.
3. Lee Odden, "Joseph Jaffe Interview," *TopRank Online Marketing blog*, toprank blog.com, April 13, 2008.
4. Interview with Kasi Bruno, May 7, 2010.
5. "2008 Tribalization of Business Study," Deloitte, Beeline Labs, and Society for New Communications Research, tribalizationofbusiness.com/2008-study.
6. Interview with Amber Naslund, April 26, 2010.
7. Ibid.
8. Susan Fournier and Lara Lee, "Getting Brand Communities Right," *Harvard Business Review*, April 2009.
9. Naslund, interview.
10. Interview with Euan Semple, June 10, 2010.
11. Bill Johnston, "The State of Online Community," Forum One Networks, forum onenetworks.com, July 2008.
12. Interview with Mathew Ingram, May 6, 2010.
13. Naslund, interview.
14. Interview with Jennifer Evans, May 18, 2010.
15. Interview with Scott Monty, June 3, 2010.
16. Ibid.
17. Juliana Crispo, "Four Personality Traits of a Successful Social Media Community Manager," Technorati, June 1, 2010.
18. Ranking current as of June 4, 2010.

19. Interview with Steve Ressler, May 7, 2010.
20. Ingram, interview.
21. Ibid.
22. Interview with Will Novosedlik, May 7, 2010.

Chapter 14

1. Interview with Scott Monty, June 3, 2010.
2. Interview with Amber Naslund, April 26, 2010.
3. Jim Lenskold, "New Survey Results: Challenges Remain for ROI Measurements, but Discipline Pays Off," MarketingProfs.com, April 3, 2007.
4. Interview with Sean O'Driscoll, April 2, 2010.
5. Jeremiah Owyang and John Lovett, "Social Marketing Analytics: A New Framework for Measuring Results in Social Media" (executive summary, Altimeter Group, April 22, 2010, p. 13).
6. Connie Guglielmo, "Dell Rings Up $6.5 Million in Sales Using Twitter (Update 2)," Bloomberg.com, December 8, 2009.
7. Chris Bucholtz, "Putting ROI Numbers on Communities," *Inside CRM blog*, March 2, 2009.
8. Jim Sterne and David Meerman Scott, *Social Media Metrics: How to Measure and Optimize Your Marketing Investment* (Hoboken, NJ: John Wiley & Sons, 2010), p. 48.
9. Interview with Marcel Lebrun, April 19, 2010.
10. Brendan Murphy, "The True Value of Social Media: How Social Media Is Forcing Us to Redefine Our Marketing KPIs," *22Squared*, June 2010.
11. Andreas Eisingerich, Gunjan Bhardwaj, and Yoshio Miyamoto, "Behold the Extreme Consumers," *Harvard Business Review*, April 2010.
12. Ibid.
13. The Turing test is a proposal for a test of a machine's ability to demonstrate intelligence. It proceeds as follows: a human judge engages in a natural language conversation with one human and one machine that tries to appear human. All participants are placed in isolated locations. If the judge cannot reliably tell the machine from the person, the machine is said to have passed the test.
14. Sterne and Meerman Scott, *Social Media Metrics*, p. 35.
15. Interview with Edward Terpening, March 31, 2010.
16. Interview with Krista Thomas, April 19, 2010.
17. Interview with Euan Semple, June 10, 2010.
18. Lisa Belkin, "Moms and Motrin," *The New York Times Magazine*, November 17, 2008.
19. Ibid.
20. Interview with Jennifer Evans, May 18, 2010.
21. Owyang and Lovett, "Social Marketing Analytics," p. 13.

22. Ray Schultz and Richard H. Levey, "Reichheld's New Metric: The Net Promoter Score," *Chiefmarketer*, February 22, 2006.
23. Lebrun, interview.

Chapter 15
1. Interview with Dan Schawbel, June 16, 2010.
2. Mary Madden and Aaron Smith, "Reputation and Social Media," Pew Research Center, pewinternet.org, May 26, 2010.
3. Ibid.
4. Jessi Hempel, "How LinkedIn Will Fire Up Your Career," *Fortune*, March 25, 2010.
5. Meeyoung Cha, Hamed Haddadi, Fabricio Benevenuto, and Krishna P. Gummadi, "Measuring User Influence in Twitter: The Million Follower Fallacy" (proceedings of the International AAAI Conference on Weblogs and Social Media [ICWSM], Washington, DC, May 23–26, 2010).
6. For more details on this impressive study, visit twitter.mpi-sws.org.
7. Milo Yiannopoulos, "P Diddy Gets Busted Boasting About His Twitter Followers . . . Then Tries to Cover It Up?" Telegraph.co.uk, March 16, 2009.
8. Pete Kistler, "10 Pearls of Wisdom from Keith Ferrazzi, Networking Ninja," *Personal Branding blog*, May 26, 2010.
9. Interview with Daniel Debow, March 23, 2010.
10. Interview with Jean Twenge, March 31, 2010.
11. Debow, interview.

Chapter 16
1. Interview with Amber Naslund, April 26, 2010.
2. Interview with Nigel Dessau, April 19, 2010.
3. Interview with Will Novosedlik, May 7, 2010.
4. Interview with James Cherkoff, April 7, 2009.
5. "Com.motion Poll," Veritascanada.com survey, November 30, 2007, and December 10, 2008.
6. Chuck Brymer, "Swarm Marketing: Building Influential Brands with Conviction, Collaboration and Creativity," DDB Yellow Paper Series, DDB.com, April 13, 2008.
7. Cherkoff, interview.
8. "The VSS Forecast," *Veronis Suhler Stevenson*, vss.com, August 5, 2008.
9. "Interview with Jim Cuene," *TopRank Online Marketing blog*, toprankblog.com, May 14, 2008.
10. "The Buzz Report," *Agent Wildfire*, agentwildfire.com, May 2009.
11. Ryan Singel, "Facebook's Gone Rogue; It's Time for an Open Alternative," *Wired*, May 7, 2010.

12. Elizabeth Holmes, "On MySpace, Millions of Users Make 'Friends' with Ads," *The Wall Street Journal*, August 7, 2006.

13. The lowercasing of her name is deliberate; see danah.org/name.html for the explanation.

14. danah boyd, "Viewing American Class Divisions Through Facebook and MySpace," *Apophenia Blog Essay*, June 24, 2007.

15. "Facebook Alternative Diaspora Fully Funded," *BBC News*, updated June 3, 2010.

16. Michael Hiltzik, "Is Your Privacy Secure Online? There's No Way to Know," *The Los Angeles Times*, June 6, 2010.

17. Tom Spring, "Quit Facebook Day Was a Success Even as It Flops," *PC World*, June 1, 2010.

18. Scott Hepburn, "We Are Facebook's Product, Not Its Customers," *Media Emerging blog*, mediaemerging.com, March 2010.

19. Interview with Lenni Jabour, April 20, 2010.

20. Interview with Brian Magierski, June 10, 2010.

21. Anthony Ha, "Analyst: E-mail Will Lose Ground to Social Networks," *Venture Beat blog*, venturebeat.com, February 3, 2010.

22. "Five Social Software Predications for 2010 and Beyond," Gartner study, Gartner.com, February 2, 2010.

23. Interview with Scott Monty, June 3, 2010.

24. Interview with Euan Semple, June 10, 2010.

25. Interview with Piers Fawkes, May 14, 2010.

26. Stefan Steiniger et al., "Foundations of Location-Based Services" (University of Zurich overview paper, 2006).

27. Semple, interview.

28. Dan Fletcher, "10 Tech Trends for 2010," *Time*, November 22, 2009.

29. Jeremy Armstrong, "Internet Perverts Could Be Snared by Special Tracking Keyboard," Mirror.co.uk, March 26, 2010.

30. "'Skinput': Human Skin as Touchpad," *The Futurist*, July–August 2010.

Chapter 17

1. For more information on customer experience, refer to B. Joseph Pine II and James H. Gilmore, *The Experience Economy: Work Is Theater & Every Business a Stage* (Boston, MA: Harvard Business School Publishing, 1999).

2. "Johnson & Johnson Puts Account in Review," MarketingVox.com, April 2007.

Index

Note: Page numbers followed by *f* refer to figures.

About the Authors

Sean Moffitt is the president of Agent Wildfire Strategy & Communications Inc., a leading social influence, word-of-mouth, and customer engagement firm. He is also an internationally respected and connected Web professional and sought-after speaker, lecturing at corporations, associations, and universities throughout the world on cultural trends and the reinvention of marketing and business. With one foot in traditional business and the other in new digital worlds, he has led the efforts behind established brands such as Molson, Guinness, and Procter & Gamble, and he now partners with many Fortune 500s and start-ups as an evangelist for Web-enabled customer engagement and collaboration in business. Visit agentwildfire.com and his blog Buzz Canuck for his musings on all things Web, marketing, and new culture, or contact him at smoffitt@agentwildfire.com.

Mike Dover is the managing partner of Socialstruct Advisory Group. As vice president of research operations for New Paradigm (later nGenera Insight), he oversaw the research programs underlying *Wikinomics: How Mass Collaboration Changes Everything* by Don Tapscott and Anthony D. Williams, as well as *Grown Up Digital: How The Net Generation Is Changing the World* by Don Tapscott. He also provided editorial support for more than a dozen other books, including *Authenticity: What Customers Really Want* by Joe Pine and James Gilmore and *DIY U: Edupunks, Edupreneurs, and the Coming Transformation of Higher Education* by Anya Kamenetz. He can be reached at mike@socialstruct .com.

A full and ongoing suite of news, case studies, links, updates, events, community, and social extensions continues at **wiki-brands.com**. We'd genuinely love it if you'd visit, join, engage, and share your thoughts here.